HELP, IT'S BROKEN!

HELP, IT'S BROKEN!
A FIX-IT BIBLE FOR THE REPAIR-IMPAIRED

ARIANNE COHEN

filipacchi publishing   Woman's Day

To my mother,
who can't fix anything, but gets an A for effort.

CONTENTS

WELCOME

You are holding the best, most informative, sassiest home repair book ever printed. Your luck is amazing—congratulations and welcome to a whirlwind tour of home repair.

"But why," you might ask, "do I need a sassy little home repair book?"

Because there will come a day—tomorrow, next week, next month—when you wake up in the morning and something is broken. You will have a flood, water coming in through your ceiling, no heat, or, oh yes, a geysering toilet. And you will panic. It's fate, I promise. Since you know that a home repair disaster is in your future, why not go easy on yourself and have a good reference book around to help you?

"Fair enough," you say. "But why do I need *this* little book?"

Because while most repair books teach you how to fix things, this book teaches you how to both fix things yourself and how to get other people to fix things for you. In other words, our goal is not nec-essarily to teach you how to use a wrench (though that may well happen), but to make sure that you use your smarts to get someone who knows what they're doing to use the wrench, hopefully for free. We're very realistic around here.

This book understands that staring blankly doesn't help: I've tested that strategy. I also know that thick books with repair jargon—"joists," "joints," "flush"—don't help. But if you understand how things work, you will know how to fix them. With this in mind,

each section explains the basics of how things actually operate before explaining how to fix them in a few simple steps.

If you enjoy coming home to light and heat, if you want a living space that does not involve sparking appliances, smoking vents, or exploding toilets, if you appreciate living in an antipanic, antiexplosion, antileak kind of place, this is the book for you!

HOW TO USE THIS BOOK

This book can be used in a variety of ways: you can depend on it in times of catastrophe, read it cover-to-cover as a primer for your new digs, or keep it as consistent, educational bathroom reading—in any case, it's a quick and informative book that can save you thousands of dollars and a lot of hassle.

I suggest first reading this book from beginning to end in order to gain a better understanding of your dwelling. In particular, the beginning of each section provides great general information, which can later be relied upon in need-to-know-now situations.

Chapters 2 through 7 are particularly handy for emergencies, teaching you how to fix things. These pages equip you for dealing with hundreds of specific break scenarios, with an emphasis on interior repairs, perfect for apartment-dwellers. For example, when ten gallons of dark brown water erupts from your toilet while you are home alone, you need to know what to do (see page 129).

Chapters 8 through 10 show you how to locate a good professional or enlist a friend's help on the cheap, teaching you who to call when.

Chapters 1 and 8 are mandatory reads: Chapter 1 summarizes the must-know repair information, while Chapter 8 teaches you how to keep your home safe from intruders, fires, and other hazards that you probably hadn't thought of.

Many people ignore the back pages of books. Here that would be a mistake, because the last pages contain a friendly calendar of semiannual things to check on, a list of useful home repair resources, and a wonderful index for finding specific repairs.

ARE YOU PREPARED? A QUIZ

Answer the following questions according to how you would react in the following home repair situations:

1 If home repair were judo, what color would your belt be?
   a Black (as in ___ & Decker).
   b Blue.
   c Yellow.
   d Belts are so last year.

2 You are watching a friend fix his sink. He says, "Hon, I need an auger." You:
   a Hand him a cold lager from the fridge.
   b Stare blankly.
   c File sexual harassment charges.
   d Hand him an auger.

3 If someone offered you a wrench, you would:
   a Correct him; you asked for the ranch.
   b Correct her; you asked for a screwdriver.
   c Correct him; you asked for a screwdriver, light on the OJ.

4 Your overly attractive repairman's pants hang noticeably low. You:
   a Take a seat and make popcorn.
   b Offer to help him pull them up.
   c Are appalled and leave the room.
   d Are too concentrated about following his repair steps to notice.

5 "Sawzall" is:
   a Plural for "I saw you," as in "I sawz ya'll at the shore last week."
   b The newest WWF superstar. His wife, Sawbabe, competes as well.
   c A power saw that saws through anything.
   d A misspelling of the word "seawall," as the computer dictionary seems to think.

6 "Jack Plane" is:
   a The daily nonstop flight from La Guardia to Jacksonville.
   b The name of your high school prom date, you think.
   c The Air Force's super-secret stealth jet that can elude radar, drop bombs, shoot missiles, swim and fly into outer space, all with an electric engine—invented by a friendly guy named Jack.
   d A tool used for smoothing wood.

7 You plug your cellular phone charger into an outlet, and all the lights go out. You:
   a Cry. Dark is scary.
   b Call 911.
   c Go replace the fuse.
   d Pull your second cell phone out of your zebra-print purse.

SCORING

1 a = 5, b = 3, c = 2, d = 1
2 a = 1, b = 1, c = 3, d = 5
3 a = 1, b = 5, c = 0
4 a = 2, b = 2, c = 2, d = 5
5 a = 3, b = 3, c = 5, d = 2
6 a = 1, b = 0 (unless you really did go to the prom
   with Jack Plane, in which case b = 5), c = 0 , d = 5
7 a = 1, b = 0, c = 5, d = 2

PERSONAL ASSESSMENT

30–35 POINTS
You are a home repair goddess. This book will rub
your ego 'til it shines, like the gleaming surface of
your brand-new gold-plated claw hammer.

25–34 POINTS
You are completely average. Though you don't
really know what you're doing, your common sense
and our helpful instructions will pull you through.
Please start with Chapter 1, Help, Where Do I Start?
The Must-Read Chapter.

10–24 POINTS
You don't know an auger from a postage stamp.
Most days you deny that a home repair crisis exists
yet are hostile toward the offending appliance.
When you do acknowledge the situation, you try
to fix it and usually make the situation worse. Thus
far, you have been pretty lucky and haven't blown
up your block. Before your luck runs out, you need
some home repair aid. This book can help.

9 POINTS OR FEWER
You are a safety risk to yourself and those around
you. This book may save your life, and/or the lives
of hundreds of your friends and acquaintances.
Please put on some kind of protective headgear
and turn directly to Chapter 1, Help, Where Do I
Start? The Must-Read Chapter.

CHAPTER 1

HELP, WHERE DO I START? THE MUST-READ CHAPTER

THE ART OF LABELING

Say you have a water leak and you're not sure when it started or where it's coming from. What you do know is that at this rate, your wall will be rotted through before the repairperson arrives. Wouldn't it be dandy if you knew exactly where the main water shutoff was, and could simply go turn it in the direction the label indicates? Or, better yet, if you could find the water shutoff for only that floor of the house?

To prevent home-break disasters, your main strategy is to be meticulous *before* something breaks, and label *everything*. The labels are not only for you: they are for your house sitter, your visiting friend, or your spacey partner who needs a clue.

TAG: YOU'RE IT!

Tagging should not take very long. With twenty minutes of walking around your house, you can potentially save yourself thousands of dollars of damage, while making your house much more user-friendly.

YOU NEED

- × Thin, all-purpose string
- × Little plastic labels
- × Pen or permanent marker
- × Someone who knows what he or she is doing

    String labels are preferable to sticker labels. Sticker labels can melt in heat, such as on hot water pipes, and make a real mess.

WHAT TO LABEL

Rules of Pen: If it has a knob or handle, it needs a label. If it measures something—temperature, pressure, voltage—it needs a label. If you have no idea what it does, it needs a label.

THINGS TO LABEL

- × Main gas line and shutoff, and any other gas lines
- × Main water shutoff
- × Hot water pipes, hot water heater, and shutoff
- × Circuit box or fuse box, including which circuits/fuses control which rooms (these may be easier to label alongside the control panel with a permanent marker)
- × Furnace controls, particularly the on-off switch
- × Washing machine intake and outtake hoses—you can't change them if you don't know which is which
- × Any other knobs, pipes, or controls that you see but can't identify

THE BIG THREE SHUTOFFS

Like the NBA Final Four, the Big Three shutoffs can make you a lot of money—if you know the right information. They are the *main water shutoff*, the *main electric switch*, and the *gas line shutoff*. You need to know where they are and how to turn them off quickly.

For example, if you find a major puddle in your room and don't know where it's coming from, you don't need to understand the problem; you simply need to stop the leak by shutting off the main water valve and call for help. The same applies to electrical or gas troubles. Walk around your living space and find all three. Here is a Big Three rundown:

MAIN WATER SHUTOFF Usually located near where your main water supply enters your home (which is usually near an outside wall, often in the basement). The main water shutoff shuts off the water supply to your residence. Be forewarned that once you turn this lever, flushing won't work. You need to turn it off if
a *You have a pipe or water leak*
b *You are performing a plumbing-oriented repair*
c *Your residence will be empty for an extended period of time*

MAIN ELECTRIC SWITCH Located on your main fuse or circuit box (often as an oversized handle or switch).

The main electric switch turns off electricity to your living space. Turn it off
a *During bad storms or natural disasters*
b *During a water leak, especially one near electrical outlets or equipment*
c *When performing electrical repairs, especially if you are not sure how to shut off electricity to the area you're working on*

GAS SHUTOFF Blocks the fuel source to your living space. It is a lever located on the gas meter and needs to be turned 90 degrees to "Off." Smaller gas shutoffs are located on various gas pipes. Turn it off
a *If you have a fuel leak*
b *If you are performing repairs on a gas-using appliance (such as a stove)*
c *During a natural disaster*

For shutoffs, indicate with an arrow which way is on and which way is off. Write the name on one side of the label, and what it does on the other:

Main shutoffs are pivotal to know for emergencies, while localized shutoffs are helpful for small breaks and repairs, so you can still use the toilet while you fix the sink. Looking at the various pipes, hoses, knobs, and valves in your living space should give you a good idea of what to label.

Keep in mind that control panels and shutoffs are often spread across multiple floors in houses and apartment buildings. Just because you found some shutoffs in the basement doesn't mean that you found everything. For example, a three-story house might include

× Main gas and water shutoffs in the basement
× A main circuit box in the basement
× Water shutoffs for the third floor in the attic
× A circuit box on the second floor
× A laundry room electrical and water shutoff on the first floor

Know where everything is: if you live in an apartment or sublet, ask your landlord which shutoffs are where, because in an emergency, the shutoff for the water pouring into your room might be locked inside your neighbor's apartment, or vice versa.

DANGEROUS BREAKS

Uh-oh, something's wrong: there is smoke, water, or gas in your living space and you don't know what to do. Flailing about shrieking, "Heeelp, it's broken!" won't help, and neither will calling your dog, crying, or staring at the gathering catastrophe. If you live somewhere, you need to know how to quickly identify and respond to a potentially dangerous situation.

FIVE SIGNS THAT SOMETHING IS VERY, VERY WRONG

× Flooding or streaming water, especially near electrical outlets or appliances
× Smoke in your living space or the smell of burning, particularly from an electrical source
× Gas leaks, the smell of gas, or damage to an exterior gas meter
× An activated carbon monoxide alarm
× A circuit that trips repeatedly or flickering lights that you can't stop

In all five of these scenarios, you need to leave immediately. In the case of smoke, gas, or carbon monoxide, go outside and call a professional from a cell phone. If you are short on cash flow, you should have a "rainy day" fund of a few hundred dollars, for use when it's raining water (or carbon monoxide) inside your living space.

WHO YA GONNA CALL . . .

When in doubt, *call the fire department*. Each of the above scenarios has the potential to involve fire or to become life threatening, which is the domain of the fire department. Fire personnel will usually come immediately without flashing lights, and often vacuum up the mess for you, free of charge. This is particularly true of salaried suburban departments that don't have too much to do—it's either helping you or playing on the pole. It is perfectly legitimate to call and say, "Hi, I just accidentally hit my gas meter with my car, and I want to make sure I don't have a gas leak. Can you help me?"

Yes, you'll feel like a dufus for not stepping on your brake earlier, but it's better than the feeling of self-implosion. Fire personnel are trained to deal with these situations. If they are busy or not able to help you, they will say so, and tell you who to call.

WHO ELSE TO CALL, AND WHAT TO DO IN THE MEANTIME

SMOKE Leave the residence and call 911 or the fire department, always. It doesn't matter if the smoke is from an electrical outlet, from an appliance, or from the large fire in your living room. If the smoke is coming from a contained electrical source, turn off the power supply to that part of the house with your circuit or fuse box, or if you're not sure how to do that, turn off your main electricity shutoff (see page 18). Even if you have stopped the smoke, it's a good idea to call the fire department nonemergency number to have someone come identify and remove the hazard.

WATER If it's near anything electrical, call the fire department and turn off your main electricity shutoff. If not, call your plumber. If you know where the water is coming from, turn off the water supply to that area of the house. If not, turn off your main

water shutoff (see page 18). Crying while you do this is okay.

GAS Natural gas is potentially the most dangerous household substance. It can result in sudden flash explosions and fires. If you smell gas, *leave* and call the fire department. Damage to a gas line either inside your house or to the outside gas lines also warrants leaving and calling. If you feel that it is safe, turn off the main gas supply to the house before you leave, but do not risk your safety. (If you're one of those people who thinks that gas smells good, ignore that feeling.)

CARBON MONOXIDE If your carbon monoxide alarm goes off, *get out of your living space immediately* and call 911. Carbon monoxide is an invisible, odorless, deadly gas that can kill in minutes, so you could feel fine in an extremely dangerous situation. If you don't have a carbon monoxide detector, go purchase a few for your living space and place them on your walls between knee and eye level, away from draft-causing doors and windows.

TRIPPING CIRCUIT BREAKERS, FAILING FUSES, AND FLICKERING LIGHTS

If you repeatedly lose power in an area of the house for no apparent reason and can't pinpoint the problem to one appliance, call the electrician—bad wiring can be a fire hazard. If power is flickering in one area and the problem is not a dying bulb or an outside storm, flip off the circuit breaker or remove the fuse for that area of the house, unplug everything with a plug, and call your electrician—you probably have a problem behind your walls that needs professional help. If you lose power to your entire house, it is probably an outside utility problem, so call the electrical company. Expect a complex, labyrinthine telephone voice system that doesn't involve humans ("If you hate us, please press two.").

ANIMALS Any wild animals in your living space warrant a local animal control call. Chipmunks, bats, and rats count. Animal control will either come over or tell you what to do. Some areas do not have twenty-four-hour animal control departments, in which case you will end up calling the local police nonemergency number, which this author has done multiple times. Feel free to beg a police officer to come help you with an animal in the middle of the night if a bat has you too freaked out to wait until morning. If you have other pets in the house, lock them in a different room. They may tip you off in the first place by acting unusually strange.

HOW TO REPAIR: FIXING IT YOURSELF

You have decided to learn to fix things yourself. Congratulations! Self-sufficiency is always empowering, not to mention convenient—you'll feel like a superhero for a day and show off your new repair to unimpressed friends for months.

WHAT YOU NEED TO FIX IT YOURSELF

×   A helpful home repair guide, such as this one. Mark up the margins with useful notes, diagrams, and reminders—this is your repair book.
×   Your toolbox (see page 22). *Every* needed tool and product for a repair should be within reaching distance before you start. Open complicated caps ahead of time.
×   Gloves, overalls, sneakers, and a tarp.
    –   *Gloves*: They will protect your skin from chemicals, and breaking finger-nails is never fun.
    –   *Overalls*: Not just a fashion statement, overalls are the repair outfit of choice for a reason: they're great. They are durable, have lots of pockets, and will last forever. While overalls are by no means a requirement for home repair, comfortable clothing on which you won't mind smearing oil and rust is key.
    –   *Sneakers with good, gripping soles*: Falls are easy due to liquids and tools lying on the floor, not to mention good dancing music in the background.
    –   *Tarp*: Laying a tarp means an easy cleanup.
×   Time. Leave yourself at least double the time recommended in a home repair guide, and triple the time it would take a professional.
×   A friend, or someone who knows what he or she is doing. Friends make things fun, and will calm you

if you are worried about messing up.
×   Some music. Turn up the jams. I recommend the classics:
    –   *Good, good, good, good, foundaaations . . .*
    –   *Hey Mr. Pipe Repairmaaan, fix a pipe for meeee . . .*
    –   *In the tooolbox, the meeetal toolbox, the haammer sleeps toniiiight . . .*
    –   *And IIIIIIIIIIIIII, know how to fix yoooouuuuuuuu . .*
    –   *Summer fixin', having a blast. Summer fixin' . . .*

BEFORE YOU BEGIN, A BIG REPAIR HINT

Most repairs consist of taking things apart, fixing or replacing the defective parts, and putting them back together again. So any time you disassemble something, take the time to lay out the pieces *in the order your removed them, facing the correct direction*. This will save you hours of frustration when you're oh-so-close to being done.

You can also jump on the Digital Age bandwagon and take pictures to remind yourself how the pieces go together. Pictures are equally useful for taking to the home repair store to show what you need.

@#%$*@%&!!

Sometimes self fix-it projects don't go so well. We understand this. Many of my fondest child-hood memories are of watching my mother struggle with various chores of homeownership, such as teetering off a ladder while trying to get a dead bird out of the gutter or trying to install a new doorknob without the proper tools and the wrong size knob. Sometimes such activity requires the use of colorful language. Consider it part of the atmosphere.

SETTING UP FOR HOME REPAIR

When performing a repair with the slightest safety hazard, such as an electrical fix or a perilous tree trimming, you should have either someone or a phone nearby. If you have no friends or phones, a metal or plastic *whistle* can attract assistance with an SOS signal (three short, three long, three short). That, or shriek, "Fire!" Research shows that people respond to calls of fire more than to calls of "Help!" In an effort to avoid your learning about home repair dangers via trial and error, here are some safety tips:

PRODUCTS AND CHEMICALS

Any time you are working with products or chemicals, you need to

× Keep chemicals far away from domestic animals. For example, pets seem to think that deadly antifreeze is a pet treat.
× While repairing, keep the lids *closed.* Have only one product open at a time, as vapors can chemically interact with each other. While using the product, keep the opening partially covered.
× Open all windows. Vapors from home repair products can be noxious, so air circulation is a plus. Some chemicals recommend a dust mask on the label. If you have any lung-related health concerns, such as asthma, don't be shy of the Mask Martian look.
× Avoid skin contact. Regardless of the product or chemical, sloshing chemicals on your epidermis is a poor idea. Wear gloves, as well as long sleeves, when appropriate.
× Dispose of leftover liquids as recommended on the bottle's instructions. In other words, do not dump random chemicals down your drains—you can do severe plumbing damage with a corrosive, as well as pollute the local water supply. When in doubt, call your local hardware store and ask.
× Clean all tools that come in contact with the chemical or product, such as paintbrushes, as recommended on the bottle. Water won't always work.

MESSY REPAIRS

Anytime you are performing a repair that involves a muddle of liquids, dusts, or other contaminants, you need to do the following:

× Place a large tarp or drop cloth underneath the

general repair area. Put old carpet or plywood sheets on the floor if you are worried about floor damage.
× Close the air vents to the room. Cover vents with heavy plastic and masking tape to keep dust and fumes localized (you can reuse the plastic for the next job).
× Open nearby windows, unless it's a day where excessive weather poses more threat than the repair.
× Close doors to other rooms, to prevent contaminating your entire living space.
× Keep your hands clean—wear gloves and wash frequently, particularly with plumbing.
× If appropriate, wear a face mask (the kind doctors wear, not the kind that make you look like Richard Nixon).
× Expect odors, dirt, rust, dust, sludgy substances, and general messiness—it's gonna be gross.

INTO THE TOOLBOX

Tools are a pivotal part of home repair. Hands are great, but when up against metal and wood, they just don't cut it. Weekend warriors often feel paralyzed not because a repair is complicated, but because they don't have the proper tools. Fittingly, this section is all about tools, explaining every tool mentioned in the book, as well as a few gizmos you might run into in the future. Tools are cheaper than you might think—plastic putty knives cost under a dollar—so don't let money be a deterrent.

THE TWELVE ABSOLUTE ESSENTIALS

The main weakness of most beginner repair guides is that they proclaim to be basic, and then list seventy-six "must-have" tools. No self-respecting first-time repairperson is going to purchase seventy-six tools on a first trip to the hardware store.

In an effort to simplify your life, here is the real must-have toolbox:

YOUR TOOLBOX

1   HAMMER

Hammers nails, with a claw to pull them out. Own one heavy hammer and one lightweight hammer.

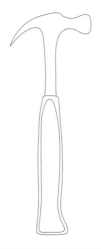

2 PUTTY KNIFE

Used for applying putty or pasty substances and scraping off anything. Extremely useful, comes in plastic or metal varieties.

3   MULTIBIT SCREWDRIVER

Look for one with eight to ten exchangeable bits. Some bits will be flathead (the tip is a straight line) and some Phillips head (the tip is a cross). Tightens and loosens a variety of screws.

4   ADJUSTABLE WRENCH

Tightens and loosens a variety of nuts and bolts.

5   SLIP-JOINT PLIERS

All-purpose big pliers that grip and turn everything from faucet parts to stuck jar lids. Adjustable jaw opening.

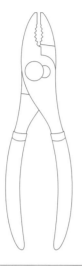

6   LONG-NOSE (NEEDLE-NOSE) PLIERS

Thin pliers for gripping, bending, or retrieving small parts.

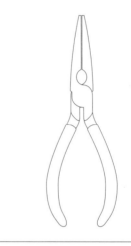

7   AWL

Sometimes called a scratch awl. Your main use will be to make a prehole indentation by tapping the awl into the surface with a hammer. Also very useful around the house when you need "something very sharp."

8   UTILITY KNIFE

Cuts anything. Retractable blades are safest. Purchase extra blades.

9 TAPE MEASURE

Measures everything from furniture to children.

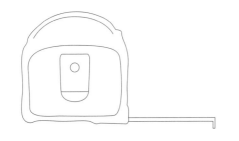

10 COMBINATION SQUARE

A carpenter's level, ruler, and protractor in one. A centered bubble (the "level" part) shows whether your surface is flat, while making straight lines, 90-degree, and 45-degree angles easy to draw. You'll use it constantly, especially for picture hanging.

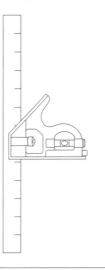

11 PIPE WRENCH

A larger wrench with a C-shape mouth that wraps around a variety of standard-size pipes to loosen or tighten pipe attachments.

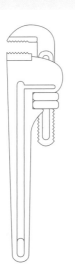

12 TOILET PLUNGER

Enough said.

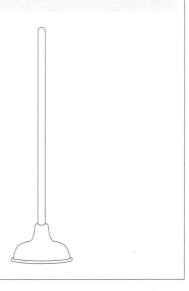

TIP

Most tool names are takeoffs on other tool names, so once you learn the basic list, you'll know what most tools do based on their names alone. For example, once you know what a Phillips screwdriver looks like, you'll also know what a Phillips screw head looks like.

Many of the Absolute Essentials are handy in day-to-day life—utility knives cut everything from metal to denim, while long-nose pliers are great for extracting jewelry from sink drains. Your toolbox won't go unused.

THE RECOMMENDED TOOLBOX

With the following additional tools around, you'll be able to do most basic repairs:

POWER DRILL Though known for drilling small holes in wood, masonry (aka, stonelike substances), metal, and plaster, drills can also sand, buff, and screw, depending on what attachment you put on the end. If you want to install something that requires a hole, get one. Corded drills are more powerful, while cordless drills are portable. You'll be amazed how much you use them.

NUT DRIVER Used to loosen six-sided bolts or nuts, which will fit perfectly inside the hollow tip. Sometimes a wrench just won't fit, so nut drivers are useful.

HEX KEYS Also called Allen wrenches. Some screws are topped by a six-sided indentation. To loosen or tighten the screw, you need a hex key to stick inside the indentation and turn.

DRAIN AUGER OR CLOSET AUGER Clears plugged sink and toilet drains. Drain augers are narrower, for small-diameter pipes, while closet augers are ideal for toilets and wider drain pipes. Will save you from embarrassing moments, such as having to introduce your toilet mess to a plumber.

C-CLAMP Usually used in woodworking to hold pieces of wood together before they are glued or secured. However, can be very useful when gluing anything that you don't want to hold while drying.

STUD FINDER A handheld electronic gadget that lights up or sounds a tone when held next to a vertical wall stud. You can also locate studs with your knuckles (see Finding Studs, page 53); stud finders are cheap, easy, and accurate.

VOLT OHM METER Tells you whether outlets and electrical appliances are working or not. Incredibly useful. (See page 84.)

NAIL SET The perfectionist's friend. After hammering, presses nails neatly and evenly into surfaces. If you don't care, don't get one.

MULTIPURPOSE WIRE TOOL Cuts all sorts of wires in all sorts of ways. Great for replacing plugs and shortening cords.

RUBBER JAR OPENER While not a "tool," per se, the thin pieces of rubber used to open jam and pickle jars are also useful in getting a grip on a nut or doorknob that won't loosen. Keep one in your kitchen, but use it for everything.

PICTURE HANGING WIRE Hangs everything, fixes eyeglasses, and holds loose pieces—such as lamp shades and grilles—in place.

Though the above tools are a solid start, you will quickly expand into the far greater array of tools and variations in handles, shapes, blades, widths, and angles. There is truly a tool for everything, though in most cases a combination of basic tools will work.

TOOL SHOPPING TIPS

× Own the Absolute Essentials (page 22).
× Purchase additional tools as needed.
× Always look for tools with rubber-grip handles, which will help you grip while preventing accidental electrocution.
× Tools have a big price range. If you think you're going to use a tool only once, get it cheap. Higher quality tools are recommended when possible—they'll last forever (you can buy them secondhand).
× Versatile and adjustable is always the way to go. For example, a pair of slip-joint pliers with an adjustable jaw and both smooth and gritted surfaces will keep you covered in the plier department for the foreseeable future, as opposed to five pairs of specialized pliers.

× Buy a toolbox that is significantly larger than you think you'll need. The Absolute Essentials will fit into a smaller box, but your toolbox will triple in size quickly.

TIP

Yard sales are a great place to buy a complete set of tools. Men have a tendency to spend their whole lives collecting too many tools and upgrading regularly, while their wives have a tendency to sell them.

TOOLBOX VERSUS TOOL LAND

If you are planning to do a lot of work in one area, such as when building a motor, store your tools on pegboards around your work area. You will also need a workbench, which is much cheaper to build than to buy. However, if you just laughed out loud at the thought of building a motor, a toolbox is a better idea so you can transport your tools to your repair areas.

TIP

Try to get your toolbox as a birthday or holiday gift. Family members love giving functional gifts. Try subtlety: "Mom, I need a toolbox. Here is a complete list of the tools it should have in it. I would like a pale blue box."

POWER TOOLS

Power tools allow you to perform repairs faster and easier, moving through any material with great speed. However, you can also cut/drill/saw/chop a hole in your hand/leg/arm/foot with great speed. Power tools are also pricey and heavy and require more maintenance, know-how, and storage space.

For any basic repair, you should be fine without power tools, but purchase them when you feel they'll be useful. Always ask the hardware store employee for instructions, even if there are instructions in the box, and make sure you have an appropriate child-free, pet-free, moisture-free storage space waiting at home.

One rule: a very bright woman once said, "I make a habit of never holding anything if I don't know what

it is." There is a reason we call her "bright." Never hold anything powerful if you don't know what it is.

GOING HARDCORE: HOW TO USE A POWER DRILL

Power drills are arguably the most useful power tool around, and there are a bunch of repairs in this book that use them. Each drill comes with a set of different-sized "drill bits," which are the metal pieces that rotate on the end of the drill to make a hole. Most of your drilling will be to install items (such as peepholes or shelves); the instructions will tell you what size bit to use. The standard bit is called a twist bit, a spiraling steel bit that comes in various sizes and makes holes in many materials. The drill bit package will say what materials the bits can drill through—drywall, brick or stone, plaster, etc.—so choose accordingly.

People are often surprised by the mess that a tiny drill hole can make. Sawdust will fly everywhere. Always lay newspaper before you begin and move or cover any valuables or equipment. Safety goggles are, as always, a requirement.

To drill a hole, home repair experts will frequently attach the proper-size drill bit, eyeball where they want a hole, and drill the hole. However, drilling in a straight line is harder than it looks, and nothing is worse then a diagonal hole in the wrong place. Here are a few baby steps you can take to ensure that your drilling experience goes as planned:

1 Before you begin, use a pencil dot to clearly mark where you want your hole.
2 The initial indentation is often where new drillers accidentally drill at an angle. To prevent this, take an awl and hold its tip against your dot. With a hammer in your other hand, hammer the awl into the dot, creating an indentation of ¼ inch to ½ inch.
3 Drill your hole with a bit that is smaller than the needed size. So, if you are installing a ½-inch peephole, place a ¼-inch bit on the end of your drill. Put on your safety goggles, hold the drill steady with 2 hands, place the bit into the indentation. Gently lean into the drill, and drill straight through the indentation.
4 Now, take your ½-inch bit and drill cleanly into the hole you already made, enlarging it. Perfect.

If you need to drill a hole into but not through a surface,

you can buy a little rubber ring that you place around the drill bit to tell you where to stop drilling. However, a well-placed piece of masking tape or a painted-on blob of White-Out directly on the bit will also work.

Power drills can also be used for buffing, sanding, or inserting screws, depending on the attachments you use. Always follow directions carefully, and don't be afraid to bring your drill into the hardware store—or your office, if you work with handy types—and ask how to do what you need to do.

RENTING: THAT OTHER OPTION

If you need a tool that is either too pricey for your budget or that you'll never use again (example: a sawzall), consider renting. Most tool-rental yards are affordable, rent by the day, and should be listed in your local phone book.

SAFE REPAIR SUPPLIES

It is convenient to have certain safety supplies on hand. For example, say you are painting a room without a lot of ventilation, and after a few minutes of rolling paint onto the wall, the fumes start getting to your head. It would be much easier to reach into your toolbox and grab your respirator than it would be to stop painting, change your clothes, go outside, hike to the hardware store, purchase a respirator, and come back. Own the following:

- × Safety goggles (for spewing repairs)
- × Respirator (for fumy repairs)
- × Rubber gloves (for wet repairs)
- × Leather gloves (for dry repairs)
- × Dust mask (for dusty repairs)
- × Earplugs or protectors (for loud repairs)

If you're thrifty, you can get all of them for under $20. Once you have them in the house, you will employ them for other uses: the safety goggles for your niece's science project, the rubber gloves to bathe your pet, the earplugs to block out the raucous 2 AM party next door . . .

THE FASTENERS: NAILS, SCREWS, BOLTS, NUTS, AND HOOKS

Like most home repair accoutrements, fasteners come in a dizzying array of sizes and shapes for different materials and purposes: there are screws with tops designed for easy installation but near impossible removal, special nails meant for use on boats, and washers meant to look pretty. As a general rule, fasteners are either already attached to whatever you're fixing or will be included in an installation kit, so you will rarely have to buy without an example in hand. Purchasing a "kitchen drawer" kit of assorted fasteners is a good idea—they are very affordable, and very handy.

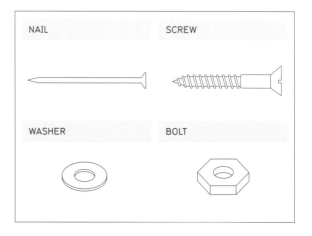

NAILS Nails are used to attach two materials together, usually wood. You are probably familiar with their other use, as makeshift wall hooks. Nails can be measured in inches, but more often are measured in "penny" size, which is a combination of length and diameter (thickness). One-inch nails are "2 penny" or 2d, 2-inch nails are 6d, 3-inch nails are 10d, 4-inch nails are 20d, 5-inch nails are 40d, and 6-inch nails are 60d. Yes, it's confusing, but go with it.

SCREWS Screws are essentially thick nails with "threads," the spirals that go down their shafts for good gripping. Screws are stronger than nails when attaching two materials. The length of the screw is measured in inches, while the diameter (thickness) of the screw is measured in gauge. Bigger gauges = thicker screws. For future reference, screws bigger than ¾ inch and 6 gauge usually need a predrilled hole before the screw can be inserted. Smaller screws can be inserted directly into the material. Sometimes the shape of the top, or "head," is also described as oval, round, flat, etc. For example, a 3-inch 16-gauge flathead screw is an enormous, fat screw with a flat top.

BOLTS Bolts are essentially big screws with no sharp point—the shaft ends are flat. They are held in place with nuts, metal rings that screw up and down the shaft spirals. You can loosen and tighten the nut with a wrench, thereby inserting and removing the bolt as you please. Bolts hold things together temporarily, as opposed to screws, which are permanent and can be inserted directly into surfaces. Bolts are measured in diameter (thickness), length (inches), and the number of spirals ("pitch," which is the number of spirals per inch).

NUTS Nuts are the metal rings that screw up and down the shaft of a bolt. The most common example in your life is probably your toilet seat: look under the caps behind the closed toilet lid. A bolt is inserted downward through the back of the seat and sticks out on the bottom of the toilet, where a nut is screwed on.

WASHERS A miscellaneous category, washers are the thin metal rings usually used between a screw or bolt top and the surface it is tightened into. Washers are protectors: they protect the bolt or screw top from damaging the surface by digging into it. They also help distribute the pressure of the screw or bolt.

HOOKS, ETC There are a wide variety of hook and hanging devices that you probably know best from your attempts to hang various decorations and plants around your living space. An "eye" is a closed circular hook (think "little metal hole"); cup hooks are the biggish hooks screwed directly into a surface, often used for hanging plants or cups.

THINGS THAT STICK: TAPE AND ADHESIVES

You probably suspect that Super Glue and duct tape should not be used for everything. This is accurate. But you probably don't know what you should be using instead, and you therefore continue to choose between the gray tape and the glue that makes your fingers stick together. Here's a rundown of the most useful adhesives.

TAPES YOU SHOULD KNOW ABOUT

1 DUCT TAPE

WHAT IT DOES Fascinatingly, duct tape is meant to attach air ducts to each other. The public has found that duct tape (or "duck" tape) is a moderately strong tape great for attaching anything to anything, and is relatively moisture-and cold-proof. Duct tape comes in a variety of colors to match the object you're taping.

WHY YOU NEED IT Duct tape is great for temporarily holding anything together, and is very durable due to its plastic coating. However, it leaves behind thick tape marks, is not attractive, and is *not* very heat resistant.

2 FLUE TAPE

WHAT IT DOES Duct tape's forgotten metallic cousin, flue tape had a stronger adhesive and is much more heat resistant than duct tape.

WHY YOU NEED IT Flue tape can be safely used on hot areas or appliances and is quite strong.

3 ELECTRICAL TAPE

WHAT IT DOES The black tape that people use when they don't have any duct tape. Intended for binding insulated electrical cords, but most often used to hold together broken black objects.

WHY YOU NEED IT Electrical tape is waterproof and heat proof, but thin and not very strong. It's slightly stretchy, ensuring a tight seal despite movement.

4 CARPET TAPE

WHAT IT DOES The most underappreciated tape. Double-sided tape made of cloth or plastic, meant to hold any kind of carpet to the floor.

WHY YOU NEED IT Carpet tape is great for all the floor coverings that you trip over daily. Put the tape on the floor, lay down the carpet, then jump on the carpet until secure. Purchase a waterproof version for doormat or balcony use.

TAPES YOU SHOULD KNOW ABOUT

5 MASKING TAPE

WHAT IT DOES A weak tape that doesn't damage anything, but can leave behind adhesive. Its beige color is unfortunate. In home repair, it's useful for covering window and door frames that you don't want to paint, though paint tape is better.

WHY YOU NEED IT Masking tape is generally used because it's slightly larger than Scotch tape. Replace it every couple of years, because old masking tape gets gooey and hard to remove.

6 PAINT TAPE

WHAT IT DOES A 1-to-3-inch-wide tape in bright colors used for protecting trim, frames, and other areas that you don't want to paint.

WHY YOU NEED IT Paint tape won't damage surfaces and doesn't leave behind residue. It's perfect for painting.

7 METAL FOIL TAPE

WHAT IT DOES This is the ideal outdoor tape, for emergency fixes of falling gutters, damaged siding, or metal screen doors.

WHY YOU NEED IT Metal foil tape is weather-and-water-proof, and only really useful outdoors. Its bright metallic appearance makes it hard to blend in.

8 PLASTIC TAPE

WHAT IT DOES The see-through tape you use to seal up postage boxes. It also works well on plastic parts and toys.

WHY YOU NEED IT Plastic tape is thick and relatively weak, but a cheap and necessary part of moving.

9 FOAM MOUNTING TAPE

WHAT IT DOES The tape you've never heard of. An extremely strong foamy two-sided tape used for hanging things.

WHY YOU NEED IT Foam mounting tape is great for hanging light things on masonry surfaces, such as a lightweight painting on a brick wall. Beware that the strong tape can damage paint.

10 WALL-REPAIR TAPE

WHAT IT DOES A strong, usually clear fiberglass tape that adheres to plaster, drywall, and joint compound. Can be painted over.

WHY YOU NEED IT Incredibly useful, wall-repair tape can stop drywall or plaster wall damage in its tracks, saving you from a major wall repair. See Cracking Up: Splits in the Wall (page 42)

11 CLOTH TAPE

WHAT IT DOES It's cloth with a sticky side. Many people use cloth tape to repair things that really need stronger tape.

WHY YOU NEED IT Cloth tape is ideal for fixing books and scrapbooks. It's quite weak, but has the advantage of coming in many colors so that you can camouflage.

12 ANTISLIP TAPE

WHAT IT DOES The black, sandpaper-esque tape used to keep you from falling.

WHY YOU NEED IT It's a good policy to stick some antislip tape on the floor of your tub, leaving a clear area for your bottom during baths. It's also good for steps, particularly outdoor slippery ones.

GLUES

Glue lingo is unnecessarily complicated and tends to show up on package instructions without explication. Here's some help:

"SETTING" means the time the glue takes to get hard.
"CURING" means the time the glue takes to dry and reach its full glue potential.
"TOXIC" means don't eat it.

So, if you were to accidentally glue your fingers together with Super Glue, the setting time would be quite fast, maybe twenty seconds. The curing time would be forty-five minutes, meaning that the inner sections of the glue would take hold, and freeing your fingers might require professional help. Most glues set in ten to fifteen minutes, but take twelve to twenty-four hours to cure. This is why after you glue something, you're supposed to *leave it alone* for a day.

Keep in mind that glues are a safety hazard for children and pets—yes, dogs will eat Super Glue—and should be stored safely and high. Because brand names change, the chart on the next page classifies glue by internal ingredients.

UH-OH, I DIDN'T MEAN TO GLUE THAT

Glue accidents happen. All the glues listed here, with the exception of resin glues and white glue, are removable with acetone, which is usually what your nail polish remover is made of. You can go buy polish remover at the drugstore, or buy a bottle of acetone at the hardware store. Be careful, though, because acetone can also damage the surface of surrounding objects and fabrics. Resin glues are removable with water if still wet. Water will always dissolve white glue.

ALL ABOUT SANDPAPER

Sanding comes up a lot in life, it is necessary for painting and shaving down anything that you miscut.

Sandpaper consists of pieces of thick paper with abrasive particles attached to them. It is categorized according to the size of the grits, from around 20 to 600 grit, and labeled "very fine," "fine," "medium," and "coarse." But this is confusing, because what does "medium" really mean? Here's a quick chart.

GRIT	DESCRIPTION
50–80	Very coarse, often used by professionals for initial wood sanding or with mechanical sanders.
80–100	Rough, used for sanding wood or plaster.
100–150	Relatively rough, often used for the final sanding of wood, or for smoothing out old, thick paint.
150–200	The most common, used for dry paints or smoothing undercoats.
200–45	Gentle grits used for carefully sanding new paint or delicate objects.
450–600	Used for sanding while still wet, such as a piece of furniture you just painted.

HOW TO SAND

You will probably sand only bare wood, painted surfaces, or plaster. You always want to sand in the direction of the wood grain, steadily moving the sandpaper back and forth. Going against the grain can seriously damage the wood. The exception is paint: if brushstrokes are visible, sand in the direction of the brushstrokes.

Sandpaper has the same life as your nail file, and you want to replace it when it has a whitish coating of wood between grits and no longer works as well. Sanding blocks helpfully attach two to four different grits onto one cheap block, and are recommended. If you have a sanding attachment for your power drill, you can use that for a faster job, but you may need to follow up with a high-grit paper to remove any minor scratches.

GLUES YOU SHOULD KNOW ABOUT

WHAT YOU WANT TO GLUE	MAIN GLUE INGREDIENT	YOU KNOW IT AS	TIPS
FURNITURE MADE OF METAL, WOOD, OR GLASS	Acrylic	Most brands say "acrylic glue" in the corner.	Good for outdoor furniture.
SMALL CHINA, GLASS, PLASTIC, OR WOOD OBJECTS	Cellulose	The tiny tubes of "liquid cement"	If you spill some, you might not be able to get it off. Try nail polish remover.
LOOSE COUNTERS, SHOES, RUBBER, GLASS	Contact cement	Contact cement	Ideal for all the things Super Glue didn't work on. Waterproof.
THIN CRACKS IN PLASTIC, METAL, OR RUBBER	Cyanoacrylate	Super Glue, Krazy Glue	Doesn't work on "porous" materials that seem to absorb the glue. Water-resistant, but not waterproof.
TWO DIFFERENT MATERIALS, SUCH AS GLASS TO WOOD OR METAL TO RUBBER	Epoxy	Says "epoxy" in the title.	Heavy-duty. Usually comes in two parts that you have to mix together.
METAL TO METAL	Liquid solder	Says "solder" in the title.	Heavy-duty. Don't touch it directly.
MY POPSICLE STICK HOUSE	White glue	Good ole Elmer's	Smell brings back kindergarten memories. Works on paper, wood, and isn't toxic. Washable.
WOODEN FURNITURE AND CABINETS	Resin	Carpenter's glue, plastic resin glue	Any glue with "resin" in the title is good on wood.

GREAT PRODUCTS YOU SHOULD KNOW ABOUT

There are a few incredible products out there that are well-kept secrets of the home repair world. I'm doing my part to spread the word:

GOO GONE The brand name for a superb cleaning liquid that removes anything gummy. Bumper stickers are no longer permanent, and neither is the gum stain on your floor. Among other substances, Goo Gone can remove tape residue, old tape, makeup, candle wax, tar, crayon, fresh paint (if still wet), tree sap, oil, grease, blood, ink, and asphalt. This is strong stuff, so always test a bit on a hidden corner of the surface you want to clean, to make sure it won't cause any damage.

MINERAL SPIRITS An artists' staple for thinning oil paints and cleaning brushes, mineral spirits can also be useful in getting rid of oil-based stains and sticky residue, such as bumper stickers or old tape. It is less strong than Goo Gone, and therefore less potentially damaging and good for a first attempt. I suggest the "odorless" variety, unless you want your living space to smell like a chemical plant.

CONTACT CLEANER A simple spray removes corrosion on electrical contacts, making it the easiest way to clean up electrical parts. Ideal for plugs that don't seem to be working or for charging connections that no longer seem to conduct electricity.

LIGHT HOUSEHOLD OIL A mind-boggling array of lubricants exists for different parts that move at different speeds. Use light household oil for most anything: grinding parts, sticking locks, anything. It is petroleum-based, so if a label says no petroleum, don't use this; be cautious with plumbing repairs, because you don't want the oil to enter your water supply.

WD-40 The grandpa of lubricants, it stops squeaks and loosens just about anything metal. WD-40 is like the olive oil of repair: you can't really go wrong. If you have a nut that you can't loosen or rusting patio furniture, spray some on.

COMPRESSED AIR Most known for its computer keyboard–cleaning abilities, compressed air cleans small spaces without further embedding the dirt and dust particles.

ANTISTATIC SPRAY Antistatic spray will solve the problem of the carpet or curtain that repeatedly shocks you. Static is common in dry air, particularly in heavily carpeted or upholstered environments. Spray away, just not on your skin.

STUMBLES AND TUMBLES: THE LADDER

The bulk of home repair injuries involve one sneaky, manipulative piece of equipment: the ladder (cue scary music). Yes, she may look helpful and friendly, a simple contraption of wood and metal. But the ladder is a sliding menace to your health and bone structure.

Most people throw out the instructions to their ladders, or never had them in the first place. If you had them, you would know that the instructions clearly say: "Do not use on nonflat ground surfaces, or place against nonflat objects." What does this mean? Do not lean your ladder against a tree, propping it up in the grass. No matter how steady you feel and how sturdy the grass feels, you will feel very differently when the ladder flips you onto the sturdy grass from 15 feet up.

Of course, not all things that need to be fixed are conveniently located above a flat surface. If you must get to that tree branch, lock the ladder into place and have someone built like a linebacker steady it from below. Ladder flips are inevitably surprising, so even if you feel stable, you're probably not. Be careful.

LADDER INSTRUCTIONS AS LIFE THEORY

My friend Matt thinks that ladder instructions can be used as a Life Philosophy. Most ladder top steps are branded with the directions:

a Stay centered.
b Don't reach too far.
c Wear shoes with grip soles.

Apply liberally to all aspects of your being. . . .

YOUR FIX-IT NOTEBOOK

Your stuff is going to break. And it will most likely happen when you are late for work and your cat just vomited on your shoes, or when you are expecting a party of fifty in twenty minutes. You'll think, "Well, I guess it could be worse." Then you'll remember, "No, really, it couldn't."

You have probably already experienced most home breakdowns. You were intimately familiar with the showerhead that dripped constantly in high school and the stove that only cooked when it felt like it; you've lived with clogged drains and leaky faucets; you have seen water damage marks on ceilings, and have blown a fuse or two in your time. The problem is, you probably weren't paying very much attention when these items were fixed. The break happened, someone fixed it, and you paid. You probably remember the bill amount. These are the highlights in your memory.

You should have a fix-it notebook to prepare yourself to deal with broken objects, particularly breaks you have seen before. Home repair is rather repetitive. Faulty heating systems, leaky pipes, defective toilets, and fuses that blow monthly are all breaks that you will encounter again and again. In order to catch onto the break and repair trends in your own life, you need to start paying attention and writing things down.

The value of a Fix-It Notebook stashed inside your toolbox is clearly demonstrated by the following story.

MARY AND BOB WITH THE BROKEN SHOWERHEAD:
A LOVE STORY (SORT OF)

Once upon a time, Mary had a burgeoning crush on Bob, and Bob had a broken showerhead. Mary kept him company while he replaced the showerhead, staring in awe, and faking deep interest in home repair by taking scrupulous notes. A few years later, long after Mary had moved through many other boyfriends (one relationship was quickly annulled after elopement in Vegas), tragedy struck: Mary's showerhead mysteriously stopped flowing properly. She became worried about repair costs. Then she became frazzled at the thought of hiring a plumber. Then genius struck: "Why don't I use the notes I took from when I loved Bob?" Mary found her notebook, opened up her notes, looked at the showerhead, and quickly figured out a general understanding of how the showerhead works. With this knowledge, Mary removed the showerhead, unclogged the obvious mineral deposits with a toothpick and vinegar, and reattached the showerhead perfectly. Mary was thrilled with herself, all thanks to her long-lost fondness for Bob. She was so excited that she reconnected with Bob, rekindled their love, and is now embarking on her second marriage (though her family still thinks it's her first).

Based on this story, you can sort of see the purpose and beauty of your Fix-It Notebook. Yes, buying a notebook sounds silly, but your Fix-It Notebook is where you will take notes on all the home repairs you see, and it will save you in the future. After a few years, you will find that your notebook holds the solutions to around 75 percent of the breaks you see, and you will simply flip to a page and know what to do. This strategy is far superior to relying on others to help you for the rest of your life. All you need is some home repair lust, a pen, and a notebook.

HOOKED ON OPTONICS

In order to have something to write in your Fix-It Notebook, you need to watch people fix things. This is the biggest secret hidden in this book: *People learn how to fix things by watching other people fix things.*

When something breaks, most women hire someone else to fix it, escort him or her to the location of the break, return to whatever they were doing, and then write a check. The reason women are often unskilled at home repair has nothing to do with a lack of talent or ability, and everything to do with the fact that they don't *watch.* If you paid attention from time to time, the money saved on home repair costs over a decade could:

a Send you to graduate school for a couple of years
b Send you to Borneo for a couple of years
c Send your mother to Morocco for a couple of years
d Pay for the cell phone bills from Borneo for a
   couple of years

Home repair is not all that complex, particularly if you have seen the repair three times. This said, when someone is fixing something—whether it's the landlord fixing your toilet or a neighbor renovating a room—take a minute to sit down and watch, and if nothing else, prevent yourself from getting ripped off next time. Most repair folk will enjoy the company, and with a professional, it's a one-on-one tutorial at no additional cost.

THE SUPER SEVEN-AND-A-HALF QUESTIONS TO ASK A REPAIRPERSON

1 Could you please explain to me what you are doing? I'm really interested.

2 What does this product/tool do?

3 Do you use this order of steps for a reason?

4 What are the safety risks of this repair?

5 Can I help you with anything?

6 If I were to perform this repair myself, do you have any recommendations?

7 Where did you get that replacement part?

7½ How did you know which one to choose?

"PUT THE WHATCHAMACALLIT INTO THE DOOHICKEY"

Your Fix-It Notebook is just that, your notebook, so write whatever makes the most sense to you. Color code, jot down what the repairperson says, draw pictures, anything. The intention here is not for you to re-create a professional home repair guide, but for you to write down what you need to know, in your own language. Here is the second big secret of this section: *You don't need to know what it's called.*

You barely even need to know what it does. You just need to know what to do. So draw pictures of parts and tools needed, and use any words or pictures that will inform you. I also recommend putting stars next to pivotal or difficult steps and places where you might need help, such as lifting or moving an object.

On the next page is an example of a page in a Fix-It Notebook for fixing a toilet that leaks water onto the bathroom floor. This is a rather complex repair to replace the toilet's wax seal, which has deteriorated to cause a leak.

This is a great example of a complex repair that seems quite straightforward after you have watched someone else do it. A plumber could easily charge you a couple hundred dollars for this repair, but you already know from watching that once the water supply is disconnected, it's a relatively disaster-proof repair, as long as you remember to plug up the sewer drain and you don't drop the toilet. You can now do this repair for free for the rest of your life.

REPAIR INFO THAT SHOULD BE IN YOUR FIX-IT NOTEBOOK

× List of tools
× List of products
× Numbering of the steps (important!)
× Notes on any safety concerns
× Lots of notes to yourself on the purpose of each step
× Whatever else will help *you*

MY TOILET SEAL REPLACEMENT

I NEED

× rubber gloves
× lots of rags
× new toilet seal
× that putty stuff
× wrench
× scraper (plastic, Neal says could use plastic knife)

STEPS

1 Turn off H2O flow to toilet (green handle behind toilet).

2 Open tank lid (#), flush, hold down lever til tank empties. Soak up rest with rags in tank.

3 *Pull apart water line from shutoff valve (so no water possible).

4 Take off bolt covers at bottom of toilet; loosen nuts with wrench (careful don't crack toilet!).

5 *Put on gloves. Put hands inside rim; rock whole toilet to loosen a bit.

6 *Lift toilet, put on side (heavy! Get help). Rmbr that tank attached, so whole thing. (Lift from inside bowl to prevent cracking.)

7 On bottom of toilet, scrape off old seal. Put on new seal in same place.

8 Put some putty on floor bolts (helps stay straight)

9 Take rags out of floor hole, rock toilet back up. Sit on lid to help settle.

10 Retighten nuts (not too tight, might crack).

11 Reconnect supply line to water, turn on water, test.
  - Neal says always careful not to crack porcelain—really easy to do.
  - Neal says can replace supply line at end if looks old.

GENERAL INFO THAT SHOULD BE IN YOUR FIX-IT NOTEBOOK

× A diagram of your circuit or fuse box, with good labels
× Drawings of all main gas and water shutoffs, with notes on their locations and what they control
× Directions and pictures of all repairs you have witnessed
× Quick summaries of all previous breaks, who fixed it, their phone number, how much it cost, and whether you were satisfied—tape the actual bill into your notebook
× Notes on anything the former owners of your residence had to say, including what their biggest problems were (note that former owners might not be completely forthcoming on the scope of their hassles)
× Directions for all maintenance maneuvers that you need to do regularly, such as annually replacing the dryer hose or changing that unreachable outside lightbulb
× Notes to yourself on finicky appliances and persnickety equipment in your residence

OTHER STUFF THAT SHOULD BE IN YOUR FIX-IT NOTEBOOK

× **Repair bills** taped in so you can compare parts and labor costs, and intelligently point out that you are being scammed, such as, "Excuse me, I had Mendez Plumbers perform a similar repair four years ago, and they only charged half of what you're billing me. Could you please explain the discrepancy?"
× **The receipts and instructions** for all your home repair purchases, which often include company phone numbers. As you acquire a collection, your documentation will probably expand into an accordion folder next to the toolbox.

If something breaks and you don't have any information, you are helpless and at the whim of a professional repairperson, so write it down.

DON'T LOSE YOUR FIX-IT NOTEBOOK

The major strength of a Fix-It Notebook is that you don't have to remember *anything*, except for where you put your Fix-It Notebook. (I recommend inside your toolbox.)

PREPARATION IS LIKE VALIUM

Congratulations, you are now prepared! Instead of panic, you can turn a knob, make a phone call, and continue on with your day. Three cheers for do-it-yourself home repair.

LORDS OF THE LAND: APARTMENTS AND LANDLORDS

Landlords are a miscellaneous but very necessary topic that needs to be in the front of the book. The relationship between tenant and landlord has always been tenuous. The word "eviction" is very old, dating back to the Dark Ages; the phrase "I hate my landlord," even older.

The main benefit of renting is that in addition to getting a living space that you couldn't afford to buy, you also get a person who fixes things. Landlords fix things because they have a vested interest in the space: they either own it and want the property to increase in value, or they are paid by the owner to look after the space. *While it may seem free, you are actually paying for home repair every month as a significant portion of your rent.* This said, your first responsibility toward mutual happiness is to pay that rent, preferably on time.

Landlording is a business. And like all businesses, greasing the wheel—read: tips and holiday checks—will help your cause. The landlord gets paid whether he or she does your repairs or not, and has little incentive to respond promptly to all repair requests. So, unless your break threatens the value of the property, the landlord may or may not react to your requests. That means that the broken air conditioner, the leaky sink, and the increasingly frequent cockroach appearances may well be ignored by the landlord, depending on his temperament.

Some landlords are wonderful, nice people who will treat you with respect and fix everything instantly. Others may be nice but have full-time jobs, families, and other tenants that limit their ability to help you. And some are just evil. In general, landlords are satisfactory, but not overly impressive in the quality of their work. Some cut corners to save money or are not worried about the aesthetics of their repairs. Generous holiday tipping can ensure good performance.

Locales have varying laws regarding tenants and landlords, though all require landlords to provide residences that are adequately safe from fire, infestations, intruders, and weather. Call up your local town hall for a brochure listing tenants' rights. If your landlord ignores repeated requests to fix your broken front-door lock, start creating a "paper trail" by writing a series of friendly-but-serious dated letters, saying that he is legally obligated to fix the front-door lock. If he still doesn't respond, you can take copies of the letters with you down to town hall.

DON'T BE A SUCKER

Landlords and homeowners are often happy to rent damaged property, and you don't want to be the sucker stuck with a damaged home and disputed repair bills. If you can't identify messy wires from a masonry problem, bring along a friend when apartment or house hunting. If you get the chance, ask former tenants how their landlords have treated them.

Dependence on a landlord for all home repair is never a good idea, as you will learn when your toilet explodes during your landlord's vacation and you end up footing an exorbitant plumbing bill, so keep reading.

CHAPTER 2

HELP FOR WALLS, CEILINGS, DOORS, WINDOWS, AND FLOORS

Look at the box you're in: the walls, the ceiling, the floors, the way the door swings back and forth, the type of windows that you have. Think about all the boxes you've been in before, and all the boxes you'll be in the future. Most people spend much of their lives staring at walls, with no idea what they're looking at, let alone how the ceiling and floor work or how to fix them. When kids bounce off the walls, what are they really bouncing off of? Here we'll talk about your six sides: walls, a ceiling, and a floor, and the exits, doors, and windows.

WALLS

WOODEN WALLS

If you hacked at your walls with a sledgehammer, you would find a big rectangle skeleton of wood: vertical pieces of 2 x 4-inch wood ("studs") nailed every 16 inches to horizontal top and bottom pieces of wood ("plates"). A strong horizontal piece of wood is above each window or door opening. This is the wall skeleton.

The smooth wall surface—which you're familiar with from hanging posters or making shadow puppets—is made of either plaster or drywall laid over the skeleton. For plaster walls, thin strips of wood or a thin sheet of metal grating ("lath") is placed over the skeleton. Gobs of cement-like plaster can be smoothed out over the lath, creating a classy, well-insulated, and vaguely expensive wall. The other option is drywall, which is flat gypsum boards covered with a layer of paper. (Gypsum is made of the same stuff as plaster of Paris.) The boards are around ½ inch thick and are nailed or screwed onto the wall skeleton. The thicker the layers of drywall or plaster, the better the sound and heat insulation. The decorations you see, such as paint or wallpaper, are applied over the plaster or drywall.

TIP

Little-known fact 2 x 4 boards are not actually 2 x 4 inches—they are 1.5 x 3.5 inches. And 2 x 6-inch boards are really 1.5 x 5.5 inches, and 2 x 3-inch boards are 1.5 x 2.5 inches, and on and on. Blame this one on men.

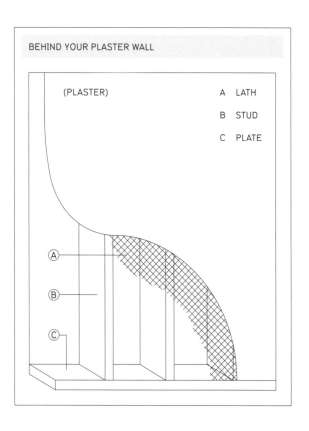

BEHIND YOUR PLASTER WALL

(PLASTER)

A   LATH

B   STUD

C   PLATE

SHE'S A BRICK ... HOUSE

Some walls are made of brick or concrete blocks. This option is particularly popular in college dormitories—remember the ugly gray cement towers? They were completely flame resistant. Exterior walls are made of two stacks of brick, with a space in between, usually filled with insulation. Inside walls are usually made of stacks of concrete blocks. A plaster wall can be applied over the interior wall, so that no bricks or blocks are visible inside the home. The bricks are attached to each other with mortar, a mix of cement, lime, sand, and water.

TILE WALLS

Tile walls, like the ones in your shower, are nothing more than ceramic tiles glued to any wall surface with adhesive. Tile is as known for its echoing capabilities as it is for its waterproofness, so keep it far away from rooms in which you prefer sounds not to be broadcast.

WHY DO I HAVE WALLS?: FOUR REASONS

1 Walls hide the so-called guts of a home: the plumbing, ventilation, and electrical systems and such visual monstrosities as elevator shafts.
2 Walls also insulate from temperature. It would be quite expensive to heat a room with a ten story ceiling, but much more feasible to maintain warm air in forty 18 x 12 x 8-foot rooms.
3 Walls insulate from sound. If a baby started crying in the corner of a ten-story room, the sound would fill the space. But people in a penthouse apartment wouldn't even know there's a baby in their building.
4 Some walls hold up the building. There are two kinds of walls: weight-bearing and non-weight-bearing. Weight-bearing walls are part of the structure of your home, holding up the ceilings, roof, and floors. Non-weight-bearing walls are purely cosmetic, dividing a space into prettier, smaller spaces. If you want to move things around, non-weight-bearing walls can be knocked down without damaging the building; they are often identifiable by their hollow structure, producing a "hollow" sound when you knock with your knuckles. Weight-bearing walls are identifiable as the more solid walls that are almost always exterior walls, or walls in the same position on each floor—go upstairs or downstairs and look at the wall placement.

PARTITIONS: THE FAKE WALL SOLUTION

Anyone who has crammed more people than are meant to fit in a living space has probably thought, "Wow, if only there was another room here." Creating another room is as simple as popping up another wall. Look up "partition" or "wall" in the phone book, and a number of companies will gladly offer their services, to the tune of $200 to $2,000. The better option is to find a carpenter college student who will be happy to build a wall for around $150. If you're not in a college town, a flyer at the supermarket or posting on an Internet board should locate an affordable local handyperson. Before you build,

double-check with your landlord or local building codes. There are minimum room-size, hallway-size, window-count, and ventilation provisions as well as fire codes to consider.

The new partition will probably be a wooden skeleton that's attached to your existing ceiling, floor, and wall. If you're low on cash and know that the situation is temporary, feel free to explain this to the builder, and request the flimsiest wall that's safe—a few pieces of wood and some drywall—while reminding him that these are not expensive materials. Keep in mind that visual privacy is not the same as sound privacy: you can hear everything through drywall.

THE GREAT WALL HAS A HOLE

Once a wall is damaged, it's easy to identify its material. As a general rule, plaster bulges and cracks, while drywall will form a hole similar to damaged cardboard. For example, if you slam a chair leg into a plaster wall, the plaster will chip and crumble, while the leg will go right through the drywall, leaving a peeling hole.

HOW TO REPAIR WALLS

Whether you damaged your wall moving or got angry and kicked it, wall damage happens. Luckily, minor wall dents and tiny holes look much worse than they are, and are pretty easy to fix.

Wall repairs usually loosen small particles of dust and drywall into the air, so set up newspaper or a tarp below the area you are repairing and open a window. Move any equipment that might be sensitive to dust into another room. Goggles are suggested, particularly for contact wearers, and surgical masks are useful for those with asthma and lung problems. Spackling compound, drywall compound, and plaster all take eight to twenty-four hours to dry, so a fan pointed at the area will help.

Wall repairs are sensitive to water and high humidity, so don't bother patching a hole if the Hurricane of the Decade is passing through or you haven't yet found your water leak source. You'll probably want to paint over the patch when you're done, so see Painting Over a Hole (page 50).

CRACKING UP: SPLITS IN THE WALL

Let's face it: you're lazy and you're not emotionally attached to your wall. The cheapest, most noncosmetic way to fix a crack in any type of wall is to go to the store and buy "wall repair tape." Clean around the crack with a damp rag and let the area dry. If necessary, sand the area with 150- to 200-grit sandpaper and brush away the particles. Cut a piece of tape a half inch longer than the crack at either end and stick it over the crack. As long as you don't bump that part of the wall again, the crack won't extend. Put a bookshelf in front of it.

DENTS OR SMALL HOLES IN DRYWALL

For bigger boo-boos, your personal feelings about the wall don't matter: you need to purchase "spackling compound" to fill in the dent. Its texture is somewhere in between putty and cement. You could also purchase "drywall compound," which is lighter and easier to manage, but not as strong. While you're at it, purchase pieces of medium- and fine-grit sandpaper or a sanding block, which conveniently includes both. Drywall sandpaper, which looks like screening and collects the drywall dust, is also available.

TIP

If you hung so much stuff that your wall resembles an old corkboard, place a bit of spackling into each hole with your finger, level it off, and let the area dry for a day. Come back and gently sand, leaving behind a smooth wall. For super slackers, toothpaste has been known to plug nail holes well enough to fool landlords.

AWOL: MEDIUM HOLES IN DRYWALL

Your landlord will not be amused by the 3-inch hole that the surprisingly sharp corner of your stereo left in your bedroom wall. Nor will he hesitate to keep a hunk of your deposit in exchange. To fix holes that are less than 5 inches in diameter, you need to place a "wall repair patch" over the hole before repeating the above steps for dents and small holes. You are going to place the patch over the hole, and then smear spackling compound over it, giving the compound something to adhere to.

I SEE YOOUUU: LARGE HOLES IN DRYWALL

Can you stick your fist through the hole? If so, you have a "large" hole, with a diameter of more than 5 inches. You need to patch the hole with a piece of drywall and attach it to the vertical wall boards (studs) on either side of the hole. First you will cut the drywall into an even rectangle that goes halfway over the studs on either side of the hole. Then you will nail or screw a new piece of drywall into the studs.

BREAKDOWN PALACE: CRACKS AND SMALL HOLES IN PLASTER

Repairing cracks and small holes in plaster is simple if the metal or wooden strips behind the plaster (the lath) are undamaged. You should be able to determine this by looking right through the hole with a flashlight. If you see wooden strips or metal grating intact, you're good to go. To fix the crack or hole, you are going to make new plaster and smear it in to fill the hole, before sanding it down to smooth out the wall.

HOLES IN WALLPAPER

If you live in one of those '70s homes that doesn't quite qualify as "retro," you know all about wallpaper. A tear or huge stain does not mean that the whole wall of paper needs to be replaced. If you have a piece of the original wallpaper, you're in luck; if the original disappeared circa 1972, take a digital picture of the wall and go to the wallpaper store to try to match it. Be aware that sometimes it is difficult to match perfectly, even if you find the same paper: direct sunlight and aging can fade wallpaper, and different batches of wallpaper can differ slightly.

You are going to hold the new wallpaper on top of the damaged wallpaper, and cut around the damaged area. This will both cut a patch that exactly matches the damaged area, while removing the damaged section.

FILLING IN SMALL DRYWALL DENTS AND HOLES

YOU NEED

- × Putty knife
- × Spackling compound
- × Pieces of medium- and fine-grit sandpaper or drywall sandpaper

STEPS

1 If there are paint chips remaining in the hole or dent, gently scrape them off with a putty knife. In older residences, you will see previous wall colors. Be careful not to further damage the wall with violent scraping.

2 Prepare the spackling as its directions explain, apply it first to the edges of the dent with your putty knife, and then move inward. Your goal here is to make the dented area the same level as the surrounding area.

3 Run the edge of the putty knife, which is preferably wider than the dent, over the entire spackled area, flattening it out evenly and scraping off any extra spackling compound.

4 Let the spackling dry for at least 8 hours. Come back tomorrow.

5 Sometimes a second coat of compound is needed, because the compound sinks into the hole when it dries, leaving a dent. Apply a second coat if needed, and return again in another 8 or more hours.

6 Sand the area smooth enough to be painted, first with medium sandpaper, then with fine sandpaper. You can buy individual pieces of both kinds of sandpaper.

7 If both the wall and the spackling are the same white, you don't need to paint. If you are a perfectionist, paint over the former dent with the same color as the rest of the wall; if you're lazy, move some furniture or a picture in front of the repair. The details here depend on what kind of paint is on the wall and how good you want your wall to look.

PATCHING MEDIUM HOLES IN DRYWALL

YOU NEED

- × Utility knife (yes, sharp kitchen knives have been used)
- × Wall repair patch
- × Ruler or measuring tape
- × Spackling compound
- × Tray, for mixing the spackling compound
- × Putty knife, preferably wider than the hole
- × Sanding block

STEPS

1 While you are at the store purchasing spackling compound and a sanding block, also request a wall repair patch.

2 Back at the ranch, use a utility knife to cut off any particularly rough edges of the hole. Be extremely conservative in your cutting.

3 Cut the wall repair patch to a rectangular shape that extends 1 inch past the hole on either side.

4 Use the compound like glue, placing it on the wall around the hole so the patch has something to adhere to. Often the patch is made out of not-sticky fiberglass mesh or paper tape.

5 Place the repair patch over the hole, sticky side facing the hole.

6 Repeat Steps 2 through 7 in Dents or Small Holes in Drywall (page 45), being careful to blend the edges of the patch into the flat wall surface with the spackling compound.

YOU NEED

- × Flashlight
- × Ruler or carpenter's level
- × Pencil
- × Utility knife
- × Drywall
- × Power drill and drywall screws, at least 1.5 inches long (preferred) or hammer and drywall nails, at least 1.5 inches long

- × Safety glasses
- × Spackling compound
- × Tray, for mixing the spackling compound
- × Putty knife
- × Sanding block

STEPS

1 When you're at the hardware store buying your spackling compound and sanding block, also get a piece of drywall that is the same thickness as the drywall in your wall (measure its width through your hole). You know that wall studs are between 16 and 24 inches apart, so be safe and get a big ole piece that's at least 24 inches long. Many stores sell only enormous pieces of drywall, so bring a sizable automobile, or see if they'll cut it for you at the store.

2 Also buy some drywall screws. Usually drywall screws are recommended over drywall nails, because the screws can't slide out of the studs.

3 Look inside the hole using a flashlight, and find the nearest stud (the vertical beam of wood behind the wall). If it's easier, just stick your hand into the hole and feel along either side of the hole. Make sure there are no wires in sight.

4 Using a ruler or carpenter's level, draw a pencil rectangle around the hole, extending the hole in the direction of both studs. The studs are 3½ inches wide, so you want your rectangle to overlap the stud by a little over 1 inch. With a utility knife, cut out the rectangle around the hole. You will have a big rectangular hole overlapping two studs.

5 Measure 2 sides of the rectangle, and draw a rectangle of the same size on your piece of drywall from the store. Using your utility knife, cut a new piece of drywall that matches the size of the hole. Remember: measure twice, cut once.

6 Fit the new rectangle into the hole.

7 Put on your safety glasses and use your power drill to insert drywall screws into the studs on either side of the rectangle. You should use at least 3 screws per stud. If you don't have drywall screws, use a hammer and drywall nails to gently nail the patch of drywall to the wall studs.

8 Now your hole is patched. There is probably a small space along the 4 edges of the rectangle, which you will need to fill in with spackling compound, by repeating Steps 2 through 7 in Dents or Small Holes in Drywall (page 45). Smear small amounts of spackling compound into the openings and run the edge of your putty knife over the grooves to flatten the compound and scrape off excess. Sand it smooth after it dries.

FILLING IN CRACKS AND SMALL HOLES IN PLASTER

YOU NEED

- × Utility knife
- × Hammer and chisel (for holes surrounded by damaged plaster), if needed
- × Damp rag
- × Plaster mixture
- × Mixing tray or small bucket, for mixing plaster
- × Putty knife, for smaller holes, or trowel, for holes more than 5 inches in diameter

- × Plastic comb or fork (for holes requiring 2 layers of plaster), if needed
- × 150-grit or coarser sandpaper

STEPS

1 Go to the hardware store and purchase a small container of plaster. There are many kinds of plaster, but if you explain what you are doing, an employee will show you what you need. Larger holes require a thicker plaster mixture, so mention the size of the hole to the employee. For a hole more than a few inches in diameter, you also need to buy a "trowel," a flat metal surface with a handle attached, which you use to apply the plaster.

2 Use a utility knife to cut away any sharp edges of plaster. It is okay if you slightly increase the size of the hole. If there is obviously damaged plaster around the hole, as is the case with a water leak, put on your safety glasses and use a hammer and chisel to chip off the damaged plaster, being careful to not damage the underlying lath. (Yes, you can get away with using a hammer and a flathead screwdriver.) With a damp rag, wipe off the crack and surrounding area.

3 Mix the plaster according to the directions on the box. Plaster is like wet cement, and you have around 10 minutes to play with it before it starts hardening. Fans extenuate the process.

4 With a putty knife wider than the crack or hole, or a trowel, smear the plaster onto the hole, extending past the edges of the hole. Run the edge of your putty knife or trowel over the patch to wipe off excess plaster so that the surface is flat.

5 Larger holes will require a second layer of plaster to securely support the area. If this is the case, use a plastic comb or fork to create diagonal scratches on the first layer of wet plaster. This will help the second layer stick to the first layer.

6 Let the area dry completely for 24 hours.

7 If you are applying a second layer, repeat Step 4 with a very thin layer of plaster, dampening the area with a wet rag or spray bottle before you begin applying the top coat.

8 Return a day later, and gently sand the area. You're done and you can either paint over the area or cover it with wallpaper. If your walls are white and you don't mind the look, just leave it or hang a picture.

REPAIRING A HOLE IN WALLPAPER

YOU NEED

× Piece of matching wallpaper
× Masking tape
× Utility knife
× Ruler or straightedge (optional)
× Sponge
× Hair dryer (optional)
× Wallpaper adhesive (unless the wallpaper comes with an adhesive back)

STEPS

1 Hold up a piece of matching wallpaper that is larger than the damaged area and matches the design of that section.

2 Tape it over the damaged section with masking tape, aligning the design exactly.

3 Using a utility knife, cut a rectangle around the damaged area through both the new and old wallpapers. For super-straight cutting, cut along a metal straightedge for support. Optional.

4 The new wallpaper will fall right off. Apply a wet sponge to the damaged wallpaper to remove it.

5 There should now be a hole in the wallpaper where the damage used to be. Let the area air dry, or use a hair dryer.

6 Apply wallpaper adhesive to the back of the patch and place the paper on the hole so that it matches the design exactly.

7 With a barely damp sponge, press on the area to smooth out the patch and wipe off excess adhesive.

8 Let the wall dry for at least 24 hours. The patch will be invisible to all but the most discerning eyes, which usually tend to be attached to small children who stare at walls.

BANGING BIKES

Bikes are a major cause of wall damage. Many people try to store bikes indoors (on the stairwell, in a hallway, on one side of the kitchen, in the bedroom). In addition to being awkward, bikes nick walls, leave skid marks, and fall through walls. Not to mention your roommate who rode the bike directly through a sliding screen door. To prevent this, you have four options:

× Get a good lock and leave the bike outside. (This isn't feasible in many urban areas.)
× Walk down your street and look for potential places to store it—does your neighbor have a big garage or backyard space? Is there space under the outdoor stairwell of the building next door? Be friendly and see if you can make a deal.
× Install spikes perpendicular to a wall, and hang the bike near an entrance. All you need is landlord approval and spikes, nails, and a hammer—any bike or hardware store can help you do this. See Finding Studs (page 53) to make sure you're nailing the spikes into the studs.
× Hang the bike from the ceiling. It's easy to make a pulley system with thick rope and visible ceiling beams, or anything else that's sturdy and high. Bike stores can help you devise your system.

PAINTING

The therapeutic benefits of painting are highly underrated. This is the first time since kindergarten that spreading color is your prime responsibility. Unlike most therapy, it's even productive.

Painting happens for one of three reasons: you fixed a hole and now have a big white patch on your wall; the paint in your room is old and peeling; or you don't like your current decorative motif—puce is *so* out. For all three scenarios, painting is a straightforward process. Professional painters are usually hired out of fear, or because of time constraints—multiple rooms can take weeks if you paint on weekends and wait a full day for each coat to dry. However, if you have the time, painting is definitely a do-it-yourself project.

PREPPING TO PAINT

Paint is going to drip everywhere—on you, your floor, your clothes, and your furniture. Wear old clothes and gloves, unless you really want to be washing your hands all night. Throw tarps or old thick sheets over anything you don't want painted, and set up newspaper across the floor. Leave windows open and fans on to help disperse paint fumes, and wear a surgical mask if you're concerned about fumes. Paints are flammable, so keep cigarettes far away, even while the paint is drying.

You want to unscrew and remove switch cover plates with a screwdriver, so that you can paint right up to the edge of the switch with a small brush. Once the paint has dried, replace the cover plate, and it will look great. Do the same for ceiling light fixtures, outlets, and phone jacks.

If you're not tall, you need to set up a stepladder. Place it strategically so that you can reach the largest possible area without moving. Short people may also want to use extension-handled rollers.

AT THE PAINT STORE: SO MANY CHOICES, WHICH DO I CHOOSE?

The most popular interior paints are latex based.

Latex paints are fast drying, low odor, and easy to clean up due to their water base. They also usually hide brushstrokes when dry, making them a favorite for walls. Oil-based paints are an option, but take around five hours to dry and often show brush marks, requiring a skilled paint job—not the free-wielding brushstrokes you will probably slap on your wall. Either oil-based or latex paints are fine on trim. The cheapest paint is cement paint, which you have seen in unfinished areas such as garages or outdoor basketball courts. Cement paint is sold in a powder and is mixed with water.

There are three categories of latex paint: flat, satin, and gloss.

FLAT paints have more pigment, and therefore absorb light, hiding imperfections of the wall and/or paint job, but can easily scuff. Unless the label says "washable," flat paints are not terribly washable beyond gentle sponging. Also called matte paint, flat paints are common on ceilings.

SATIN paints are the middle ground between flat and gloss, leaving a slight sheen on surfaces. Satin paints can handle light scrubbing and are popular in high-use rooms.

GLOSS PAINTS offer more protection and are ideal for places where humidity might build up, such as bathrooms and kitchens. Gloss paint gives surfaces a shiny look that hides fingerprints and scuffs but exposes wall imperfections by reflecting light. Gloss paints can be safely scrubbed. In general, people choose semigloss paint, which is a happy medium.

There are a few other paint options available:

ONE-COAT LATEX PAINT Also called high-opacity paint, this alternative saves you time by requiring only one coat. However, it is the equivalent of two-in-one shampoo and conditioner: it works, but there is a reason that most people use separate hair products. Two layers of regular paint are recommended.

ANTIMOLD LATEX PAINT Just like its name suggests, this paint is laced to prevent mold and fungus growth. These paints are recommended for bathroom walls and other humid areas, such as basements, or your new steam room annex.

PLASTER LATEX PAINT A paint aimed at recently plastered walls, which can absorb paint. Recommended if painting a wall for the first time.

TINTED CEILING PAINT This newish paint has a pink tint when wet, so that you can make sure you haven't missed a spot. The tint disappears when the paint dries.

LOW-VOC PAINTS VOCs are "volatile organic compounds," which are harmful to the environment and can aggravate asthma or other lung troubles. Paint manufacturers include VOC-level labeling on their products. If this is a concern for you, purchase a paint with a lower VOC level.

If you are choosing a light color to paint on a dark wall, many recommend that you use a "primer" to seal in the darker wall paint, particularly if there is a dramatic color difference. The primer prevents any color from leaking through. You must use it if you are painting over oil paint with latex paint. Primer is usually white, and you paint it on before the first coat of paint—just ask at the store, and they'll give you what you need. Note that primer is cheaper than paint, and you can often get away with one coat of paint after primer, so consider it a money saver.

PAINT VOCABULARY

Paint is often referred to as "finish," because from a builder's perspective, it's the final step on a wall or piece of furniture. "Finish" can also refer to the variety of clear liquid top coats, including glaze paint (a clear or tinted decorative paint top coat), varnish (the protective layer of wood surfaces), lacquer (a hard coating used on floors and cabinets), stains (a color that soaks into wood), finishing oil (an oil that leaves a gentle sheen on wood), and wax polish (the slippery floor top coat of dance studios).

HOW MUCH PAINT DO I NEED?

Before you go to the store, *measure the surfaces* you want to paint. One gallon of latex- or oil-based paint covers approximately 400 square feet. Remember to double the amount for *two* coats.

 TIP

For future measuring approximations, measure the length of your wingspan, the length from fingertip to elbow, and the length between your first finger and thumb when fully spread. Memorize. That way you will always be able to spread your arms a couple of times and know how much paint a room needs.

CHOOSE AND USE: THE ROLLER OR THE BRUSH?

For painting a full wall, you want either a brush or a paint roller. If you prefer paintbrushes, know that

some would consider you masochistic. This author finds rollers to be much easier than brushes, because they allow you to quickly roll on reams of latex paint in any direction, preferably in a zigzag motion. (Oil painting is also faster with a roller, but you need smooth, straight roller strokes.) Purchase a 10- to 12-inch roller and a paint tray, which come in a surprisingly cheap set. There are a variety of "sleeves" (the material covering the roller) to choose from. Sleeves that are thick and textured, such as sheepskin, will give a textured look to your wall. A flat sleeve produces the basic flat-paint-on-a-wall look, which is probably what you're after. The different sleeve textures are called piles, and flat is recommended for smooth walls, while thick piles are preferred for imperfect or textured walls. Purchase accordingly. Paint trays are deep on one side, where the paint pools, and then slope up to an indented tray. Load up the roller by dipping it into the paint and rolling up to the indented part, squeezing out the excess.

If you choose to paint with brushes, buy one that's at least 8 inches wide. It's worth it to spend the extra money on a nice brush, because a cheap brush will leave paint bristles all over your wall. Whether you're using rollers or brushes, you need to also buy a small brush, 2 to 3 inches wide, for the edges of walls and receptacles. An angled 1- to 2-inch brush helps with corners.

Painting with a brush is exactly like painting your nails. Vertical brushstrokes usually work best, the same way you start from the cuticle and work upward. When dipping the brush into the paint, you only need to soak a third of the brush in the paint, and then hold the brush against the side of the can to let excess paint drip off, also just like nail polish.

OTHER PAINT SUPPLIES

PAINT LID OPENER While you're at the store, make sure you'll be able to open the lid at home. A flathead screwdriver will work.

PAINT STIRRER Any wooden stick will serve as a paint stirrer, but if you don't have one, they're free at most paint stores.

PAINT TAPE Paint tape is like masking tape that's slightly thicker, an interesting color like blue or

YOU NEED

- × Rags
- × Paint tape
- × Drop cloth or newspaper to protect floor
- × Can of paint
- × Paint can opener or a flathead screwdriver

- × Paint stirrer
- × Paintbrush or paint roller, paint tray, and tray liner
- × Stepladder (maybe) oil-based paint.

STEPS

1 Wipe down the entire area to be painted with a wet rag, cleaning off all the dust and grime that has accumulated over the years. Either a spray bottle or a bucket will work. Let the whole room dry before you begin painting.

2 Place paint tape over the edges of the area to be painted, including any trim, windowsills, or other surfaces that you do not want to paint. Paint tape is pricey, but it works. Masking tape is cheaper, and is safe on wood surfaces if you remove it within a day. Spread out newspapers or a drop cloth on the floor to protect beneath where you'll be painting.

3 If you're a newcomer, begin by carefully painting the perimeter of the painting area with a small brush, creating a 3-inch frame around the entire ceiling or wall.

4 For a wall, start in the top corner that corresponds to your dominant hand, and begin painting/rolling boxes of approximately 2 square feet (zigzag with rollers; vertical strokes with brushes). Paint one full horizontal row of boxes before beginning the next row. With oil paint, follow the same strategy, except make the boxes in vertical rows—brushstrokes are less likely to show this way. For a ceiling, using a brush or roller (probably a roller), begin at one side, and paint toward the opposite side of the room in boxes of about 2 square feet, filling in each row before you begin the next, until you reach the other side.

5 When you have completed the first coat, let it dry for 4 hours for latex paint, 16 hours for Cement paint needs at least 24 hours to dry

Drying time may be affected by the level of humidity in the air. Note that paint that feels dry to the touch and paint that is dry are not the same thing. Between coats, simply put the paint lid on securely and wrap your dirty brushes in plastic bags.

6 With latex paint, you will almost always need to repeat the process and add a second coat. Oil paint often does not need a second coat, but look at your work and use your judgment. Repeat Step 4 if necessary.

purple, and quadruple the price. It comes in widths ranging from ½ inch to 4 inches, and you use the tape to protect trim, windowsills, door frames, et cetera, by placing the tape on before painting and peeling it off when you're done. Paint tape is preferable to masking tape because it peels off easily, without damaging underlying paint or leaving behind adhesive residue.

PAINT TRAY LINER A liner that fits into your paint tray for easy cleanup. When you're finished painting, let the paint dry on the liner, then peel it off and throw it out.

TURPENTINE OR MINERAL SPIRITS If you are using oil paint, you'll need to soak your brushes in either of these products when you are finished painting.

STEPLADDER If you're painting a high area and don't have a stepladder, now is a great time to buy one. You probably do not need a full-size ladder.

PAINTING THE TOWN: WALL AND CEILING PAINTING

Pop open the paint can, which requires either a paint lid opener or a well-placed flathead screwdriver. Use a paint stirrer or thin piece of wood to stir the paint before you begin. Make sure you've already removed any receptacles, switch covers, or light fixtures.

PAINTING OVER A HOLE

To paint over recently dried plaster or spackling/drywall compound, you need to know the color of the rest of the wall. Once you have the same color, simply paint the area with a paintbrush, carefully overlapping a thin layer with the already painted area. Let the first layer dry completely and see how it looks before determining if you need another layer.

One problem consistently arises: wall paint fades over time, and even if you have paint from the same can, the area over the patch might look darker than the rest of the wall. If this is the case, you're going to have to strategically move some furniture to block the discrepancy, or repaint the whole wall. I vote for the furniture option. If you know the paint has faded beforehand, you can hope that a paint store color mixer can approximate a slightly faded color.

DAMAGE CONTROL: CLEANING UP

Paints are highly toxic and cannot be dumped down a drain like your bartending disasters. Most people avoid disposal by sticking the cans in a basement or garage for future patching. These extra cans will prove invaluable when you accidentally scrape the wall at eye level and happen to have that color on hand, or when you want to call the manufacturer to ask a question.

Ask your local township about disposal options. If you want to clean your latex brushes, wipe off as much paint as possible on newspaper before rinsing them in water and mild soap if needed. Oil brushes will need to be soaked in mineral spirits or turpentine, sold at any paint store.

Paint cans can be hard to close. Try tapping lightly with a hammer. It is suggested that you store paint cans upside down, so that a layer of dried paint doesn't form on top, much like the skin that forms on top of cold soup. Remember that paint is flammable, so keep it far far away from your furnace, gas lines, or resident smokers.

WHILE WE'RE ON THE SUBJECT OF PAINT

It is a good idea to know basic information about the paint of each room. This can be infinitely helpful when you accidentally chip some off and need an ounce of the same color to fix it. ("Um, it's blue—kind of like sky color" won't help you at the paint store.) Ask the landlord or former owner for the following information for each room:

× The brand of paint
× The ceiling color
× The molding (aka trim) color
× The wall color
× Where the paint was purchased
× When the painting took place

The paint color will most likely be both a name *and* a number, such as Neon Magenta 349b. You need both. Knowing when the painting took place is also important, because it will tell you both if the paint is still manufactured and when it needs to be repainted.

WALL WASHIN'

You know all the dust particles you see floating in the air when the sun is shining? Many of them adhere to your walls. Thousands and thousands of tiny pieces of dust. You can tell if your wall is dirty by taking a damp paper towel and wiping a small area of the wall. If the wall brightens or the towel is disgusting, you have some work to do.

A variety of wall-cleaning products exists, and the trick is to find which one won't damage the wall paint, wallpaper, or finish. As a general rule, gloss paint (shiny paint that reflects light) handles washing much better than flat paint (dull paint that absorbs light). First, try cleaning with plain old water. If that's not enough and you have the original paint can, call up the manufacturer and ask which products can be used to clean the wall. Buy said product and follow the both leave behind fragments—so try a nylon rag.

If you have no idea what kind of paint is on your wall, go to the paint store, explain your quandary, and the people who work there will take a guess at a safe product. Even if the cleaner label swears that it's safe on all surfaces, always do a safety check by cleaning a 3-inch space in a low hidden corner of the wall, following the full instructions and allowing a few hours for drying. If the wall covering remains intact, clean away.

HOMEMADE WALL CLEANER

- × 2 parts ammonia
- × 1 part baking soda
- × 1 part white vinegar
- × 30 parts warm water

WHY ARE MY WALLS GROWING MOLD?

Periodically, the media picks up on scary reports of *deadly, fast-growing, people-eating mold!* These stories are characterized by major lawsuits and a family matriarch saying, *"I just didn't know,"* while

sadly pointing at a home that got completely eaten by mold. You should know that this is really rare. Mold is usually a little dot on your wall.
Mold-and-mildew-stained walls are most often found in bathrooms, basements, or areas near a water leak. In addition to being ugly, bad mold can be a health hazard: the toxic spores are easily released into the air. Mold and mildew thrive in dark, wet areas, so your immediate strategy is to relieve the dark wetness with bright dryness.

If you see mold or mildew on your wall or ceiling—characterized by gray, brownish, or black, often circular spots—you need to immediately figure out the cause of the mold. It could be a minor problem, such as a shower that should be used with an open window, or humid weather that warrants a dehumidifier. The mold could also be the first sign of an internal problem, such as a water leak, meaning that the mold originated somewhere in the guts of the house and grew right through the wall.

Mold in your shower stall and on your shower curtain can be easily addressed with the myriad antimold sprays at the drugstore and by remembering to open the shower curtain and a window when you're not in there. Regular walls are more complicated, because you want to effectively kill the very hardy mold spores without damaging the wallpaper, paint, or finish below. You might get lucky and be able to simply wipe the mold off the wall with a sponge, in which case throw out the sponge and watch for regrowth.

Otherwise, take a small bucket and mix 1 part bleach with 10 parts water. Use a bathroom sponge to coat the molded area with the solution. Let it sit for 4 hours, and then scrape the mold off into the trash, along with the sponge. Before you begin, test this process on a small corner of the wall to make sure that there is no damage.

If neither of these options work—bleach should kill the vast majority of mold spores—you have a problem. Inform your landlord and/or contact your department of health, which will have information.

KILLING CHIP: FIXING A BROKEN TILE

As we learned earlier, tile walls are usually drywall

YOU NEED

- Screwdriver
- Putty knife
- Chisel (or screwdriver, or any other tool that can chip off caulking)
- Tile adhesive
- New tile
- Grout
- Small paintbrush (the same width as space between tiles—optional)
- Masking tape (optional)

STEPS

1 Go to the hardware store and explain that you need tile adhesive and grout, and they will hand you 2 small tubes of both. Your grout should be the same color as the grout currently in the wall, which is probably white.

2 Go home and scrape out the old grout around all 4 sides of the broken tile. You want to take whatever small, sharpish tool that you have—a screwdriver will often work—and chip away the surrounding grout.

3 Pick up your putty knife and, starting at the new space along the bottom edge of the tile, scrape the tile out of the wall. It doesn't matter if you break the tile further; it's already going to tile heaven.

4 Once the tile is out, use the chisel to scrape out the remaining grout and adhesive behind the tile. Wipe off any flecks of grout or chisel until the surface is smooth.

5 Open the adhesive and smear it all over the back of the tile.

6 Press the tile into its new home and hold it there for a minute, while wiping away any adhesive that may have squished out. Let the adhesive dry for a few hours.

7 Return with your grout. Open up the grout and squeeze a thin bead around the tile, filling in the 4 sides. With a damp finger, press along the grout, smoothing it into the space. Some people prefer to paint in grout with a small paintbrush—if your grout came in a can, you must.

8 Wipe off any escaped grout. *Neither the adhesive nor grout is dry, even if it feels dry.* Let the area dry for 24 hours before getting it wet. On a vertical wall, it may help to attach the new tile to the surrounding wall or tile with masking tape, just to ensure that it doesn't slide off while drying.

with tiles attached by adhesive. Replacing a tile is as easy as scraping off the broken tile, gluing in a new one, and adding a line of grout around all four sides of the tile. Of course, it helps if you happen to have an extra tile around, which is why longtime homeowners know to keep extra tiles, paint, and every other decorative accoutrement in their basement. If you don't have a replacement tile, follow Steps 1 through 3 below, bringing the remains of the tile to the store to try to match it.

TIP

Some hardware stores sell a dual adhesive and grout product. This means that you can use the same product as both your adhesive and your grout.

HANGING PICTURES AND SHELVES

This is a rather miscellaneous topic that comes up a lot in most people's lives. We all know the woman who moves to a new residence, then leaves her pictures leaning against their future wall homes for months on end. She does this because

1 She doesn't own a hammer or drill
2 She doesn't own a hook
3 She's afraid she'll ruin her wall
4 She's waiting for someone to come hang them for her.

She should pull it together and hang her pictures.

First, you need to determine what kind of wall you're looking at. Drywall or plaster walls are usually obvious: if the wall is not visibly cement or brick, and the wall isn't an exterior wall on a brick house, chances are that the wall skeleton is made of beams of wood.

TIP

Though the eyeballing method is completely valid for making pictures straight, a carpenter's level or combination square (the tool that tells you whether a surface is straight with a little bubble) can be extremely helpful.

HANGING PICTURES ON WOOD WALLS

Before you go at your wall with nails and a hammer in an effort to make your room pretty, you need to locate your wall studs (the vertical planks of wood behind your walls). They are usually located 16 to 24 inches apart and will support your hangings without damaging your drywall or plaster wall surface.

FINDING STUDS (NO, NOT THE BEEFCAKE VARIETY)

× Gently knock along the wall in approximately 2-inch intervals with a cloth-covered hammer or your knuckles. You can also move the buzzing battery end of an electric razor along the wall, though this will drive your neighbors nuts.
× When you hear a "solid" knocking sound—as opposed to a "hollow" sound—you have reached the edge of a stud. (Or the buzzing tone of the razor changes dramatically.)
× Mark this point with a pencil dot.
× Keep knocking along for a few inches. When you return to a hollow sound or a different razor tone, you have passed the end of the stud. Mark the end of the stud with a pencil dot.
× You have now outlined the stud. Place a dot exactly in the middle of the stud, between your two dots.
× Hammer your nails or hooks into the centered pencil dot, or install a screw with a screwdriver or power drill.

You could also buy a "stud finder," a funky little device that beeps or lights up when held over a stud. Stud finders are, however, not free, and your knuckle is. But knuckles aren't always idiot proof.

If you don't have said nails or hooks, go to your local framing store, tell them the size of your picture, and they will sell you one or two little hooks for both your wall and the back of your picture.

HANGING PICTURES ON NONWOOD WALLS

If your walls are made of cement or brick (which the repair folk call "masonry" walls), you can hang the picture anywhere. A hint of this is hearing an evenly solid sound when knocking along the wall. Stick your head out the window. Is your building made of brick? Then some of its walls are, too.

For a masonry wall (any kind of stone or brick), you need to drill an approximately 2-inch hole with a power drill and a masonry bit, and then place an "anchor" in the hole, which is a very thin test tube–shaped piece of metal or plastic that prevents the hole from collapsing. Then you screw in your screw. It is much easier to drill through mortar—the material in the spaces between bricks or blocks—and highly recommended.

1 Mark where you would like to place your screws, preferably in mortar between bricks. To make sure the screws are even, eyeball or use a carpenter's level.
2 Put on safety goggles and drill a hole into each mark with a power drill.
3 Place an anchor in each hole. If it won't fit, gently tap the anchor into place with a hammer.
4 Screw your screw (or hook) into the anchor with a screwdriver.
5 Hang your picture onto the screw.

NOTE

If you have multiple masonry walls, it's a good idea to own a power drill, because you'll use it.

TIP

If you have a bare brick, cement, or other "rocky" wall and are hanging something lightweight, such as a framed poster, skip the drilling and go buy some foam mounting tape. It's a thick layer of foam with super-strong adhesive on both sides. Just cut the tape to fit whatever poster or picture you want to hang, stick two strips of the tape on the wall, and press your picture against the strips. Be warned that the tape is strong enough to damage wall paint and/or the back of your picture, but no one's ever going to see the back anyway.

ATTACHING WIRE TO HANG A PICTURE

YOU NEED

× Picture hanging wire
× Double-sided hook

STEPS

1 Put a few inches of the wire through one screw eye. Wrap the end of the wire tightly around the bottom of the screw eye itself a few times, and then double back to wrap the remaining end around the rest of the wire.

2 Run the wire across the frame to the other screw eye and repeat on the other side, so that the wire is as taut as you can make it—slack will appear when you hang it. If there is a hook attached to the center of the frame, make sure to run the wire through the hook.

3 If there is not a hook attached to the frame, take your double hook and hook one side to the middle of the wire. Lift up the frame and hang the other side of the hook on the wall.

FOR VERY HEAVY PICTURES, YOU MIGHT WANT TO USE TWO DOUBLE-SIDED HOOKS:

1 Thread the wire through both screw eyes, creating a circle with the wire.

2 Where the 2 ends of the wire come together, pretend you are starting to tie your shoes, and complete the first step, passing the right end over the left end, and pulling to tighten the circle.

3 Wrap the wire ends around the already taut wire on each side, securing the now-tight circle.

4 Take your 2 hooks. Place them a few inches apart in the center of the frame, an inch above the wire circle.

5 Lift the bottom wire and hook it on one hook. Lift the top wire and hook it on the other hook. Both wires should be fully taut.

6 Lift the painting, and hang it on 2 nails in your wall.

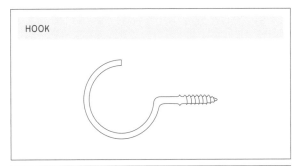

HOOK

PICTURE HANGER

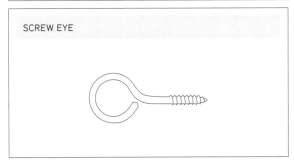

SCREW EYE

THE BACK OF THE PICTURE

Uh-oh, you have no way to attach your picture frame to the wonderful wall hook you just installed. Go to a hardware store or local framer and explain the problem. They will give you a piece of wire and a little double-sided hook, one side for the wire and one side for the wall. Look at the back of the frame. On either side, there should be a little circle of metal called a screw eye, a piece of metal with a round hole on one end, almost like the eye on a sewing needle. (In Repair Speak, "eye" means "little hole.") You will use the screw eyes to secure the wire, so that it extends across the back with a hook in the middle.

If you happen to have a metal frame with no visible screw eyes or other way to attach wire, you can buy little screw eyes with metal teeth to hammer into the back of most frames, or small 1 x 1-inch metal or plastic eyes that glue to the back of the frame. Both are available at the local framer's.

A TIME FOR REFLECTION: MIRRORS

A well-placed mirror can open up a small room, creating the illusion of more space and lighting. If you have a blank space on your wall, consider a horizontal mirror placed at eye level, slanted downward.

A variety of wall decorations creatively incorporate mirrors, such as pieces that make the mirror look like a window. Well-framed mirrors are often very heavy, so follow the two-hook instructions above for those. To slant your mirror at an angle, place the wire high and loose on the back of the frame, or use two sets of wires, one high and loose and one low and tight. Here are some common problems and fixes for both decorative mirrors and the more mundane bathroom type:

DIRTY MIRROR Fingerprints, dust, and toothbrush spray are the hazards of being a mirror. A variety of mirror-cleaning products are sold at drugstores. Spray the cleaner on a rag, and then wipe the mirror in little circles, beginning at a high corner and working down, not leaving behind any streak marks.

GREASY MIRROR You can get grease off a mirror with a solution of 1 part ammonia, 1 part white vinegar, and 10 parts water. Place the solution on the mirror with a rag, let it sit for a minute, then remove it. Be careful, the solution can damage the frame.

FLAKING MIRROR If you have a small patch of glass on your mirror, it means that the silver on the back of the mirror is flaking off. If the damage is minor, flip the mirror over and brush a thin coating of silver paint over the empty spot using a small paintbrush. Only you will know the mirror is damaged.

SCRATCHY MIRROR There is a wonderful product called jeweler's rouge, which you can buy from the jeweler. Ask the jeweler how he suggests that you use it, though rubbing the scratch with a rag and the rouge should make the scratch disappear by filling the scratch with a reflective material. Be sure to wipe all the rouge off the mirror when you are finished.

WHEN IN DOUBT, SHELVE IT

The hunt for cheap furniture is over: shelving is the cheapest and most space-economical means of storage. Indulge your inner pack rat and shelve the many more toiletry products than you remember purchasing, alongside the many desk supplies that don't fit in your desk.

The easiest models to install are adjustable systems consisting of just three pieces: a wooden shelf and two "brackets," the vertical metal pieces sticking out of the wall that support the shelves. Although at first these may seem utilitarian, don't underestimate the decorating beauty that can happen with an attractive shelving or a scarf thrown over a shelf.

WHERE TO FIND ADJUSTABLE SHELVING UNITS

Discount stores sell boxed versions of adjustable shelves, and you can always find a set at a garage sale. However, anyone with a wood workshop is often more than happy to cut a few pieces of wood for you, creating simple shelves that meet your specifications on the cheap. Based on your needs, you can have shelves cut from a variety of woods—plywood, pine, oak, anything—or more exotic materials, such as glass or fiberglass. You could even design your own system of shelves against an adjustable "upright," which is a vertical metal strip of bracket holes that you attach to the wall, allowing you to easily move shelves around. Metal brackets and uprights are cheap and available at any hardware store.

INSTALLING ADJUSTABLE SHELVES ON WOOD WALLS

Adjustable shelf brackets are attached directly to the wall studs (vertical pieces of wood behind the wall), thereby putting the shelf weight directly on the house structure. The screws attaching the shelves to the wall will break if they are too weak, so use the screws that came with the brackets. When in doubt, use the next screw size up, or ask at the hardware store when you're buying your brackets.

If you want to install a longer shelf or a shelf to carry ample weight, install as many brackets as you need at 16-inch intervals.

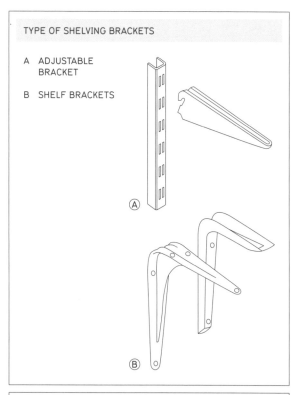

TYPE OF SHELVING BRACKETS

A ADJUSTABLE BRACKET

B SHELF BRACKETS

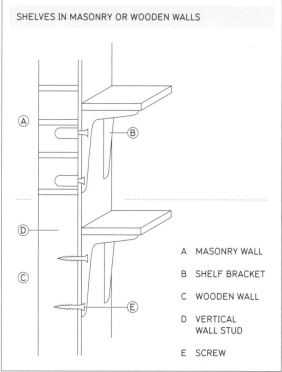

SHELVES IN MASONRY OR WOODEN WALLS

A MASONRY WALL

B SHELF BRACKET

C WOODEN WALL

D VERTICAL WALL STUD

E SCREW

INSTALLING AN ADJUSTABLE SHELF
INTO A WOODEN WALL

YOU NEED

- × Yardstick or
  tape measure
- × Pencil
- × Carpenter's level
- × Metal brackets
- × Safety Goggles
- × Power or hand drill
- × Screws
- × Screwdriver

STEPS

1 Locate the studs behind the wall. If you don't happen to own a stud finder, knock along the wall until you hit a solid "thud," as opposed to a hollow sound (see Finding Studs, page 53). Studs are usually 16 inches apart, so once you find one, you can measure to find the next. Mark the beginning and end of each stud with a pencil, and then put a dot in the center of the stud.

2 Use a carpenter's level to draw a straight horizontal line where you want the shelf to go. If you don't have a level, use a tape measure to make sure your shelf line is parallel to the floor.

3 Hold each bracket up underneath your shelf line, and draw a pencil dot on the wall through each bracket screw hole.

4 Wearing your safety goggles and using your power or hand drill, drill a hole into each dot, using the drill bit and hole depth size suggested in the shelf instructions.

5 With a screwdriver, rotate the screws through the brackets and into the holes.

6 Put the shelf on top of the brackets.

INSTALLING AN ADJUSTABLE SHELF
INTO A MASONRY WALL

YOU NEED

- × Carpenter's level (if you have one)
- × Pencil
- × Metal brackets
- × Safety goggles
- × Power drill or hand drill
- × Anchors (should match screw size—ask at the hardware store)
- × Screws
- × Screwdriver, flathead or Phillips, as needed

STEPS

1 Use a carpenter's level to draw a horizontal pencil line where you want to hang the shelf.

2 Hold up the brackets and mark the wall where you want to install the bracket screws with pencil dots through the screw holes.

3 Wearing your safety goggles and using a power or hand drill, drill holes into the pencil dots, using the bit size suggested in the shelf instructions.

4 Put your anchors into the holes, which might require a bit of hammer tapping.

5 Place the screws through the bracket, and screw them into the anchor with a screw driver.

6 Place the shelf on top of the brackets.

7 If you are placing a lot of weight on a shelf, simply place another bracket in the center of the shelf.

INSTALLING ADJUSTABLE SHELVES ON BRICK OR CEMENT WALLS

Adjustable shelf brackets can be installed anywhere along a solid wall, though I suggest drilling into the mortar between bricks, if that is an option. After drilling a hole in the wall, you will place "anchors" (little metal or plastic test tubes that prevent the hole from collapsing) into the hole, and then screw the screws into the anchors. I use plastic anchors that vary in size depending on the screw size and the weight of the shelves.

INSTALLING SHELVING SYSTEMS

You've made it! You get to install a whole *system* of something!

Shelving systems rely on uprights, which are vertical metal wall strips with lots of bracket holes, so you can easily adjust, remove, or add shelves. I suggest purchasing long uprights, for future shelving acquisitions. The priority in this installation is to make sure that the uprights are parallel to each other and perpendicular to the floor.

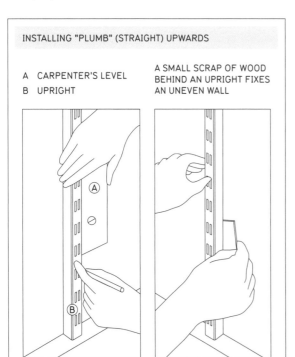

INSTALLING "PLUMB" (STRAIGHT) UPWARDS

A   CARPENTER'S LEVEL
B   UPRIGHT

A SMALL SCRAP OF WOOD
BEHIND AN UPRIGHT FIXES
AN UNEVEN WALL

YOU NEED

- × Yardstick or firm tape measure
- × Pencil
- × Safety goggles
- × Power drill or hand drill
- × Uprights
- × Screws

STEPS

1 Draw a dot on the wall where you want to place the highest screw on the upright. (If you're working on a wall with studs, locate the studs [see page 53]).

2 Wearing your safety goggles and using a power or hand drill, drill a hole on the dot, using the bit size suggested in the shelving instructions.

3 Place the screw through its proper hole in the upright, and screw it into the wall with a screwdriver. If you're working on a brick or cement wall, place an anchor in the hole before you insert the screw.

4 With the top screw loosely tightened, the upright should naturally swing to a vertical position. Check to make sure the upright is exactly vertical with your carpenter's level. Mark the location of the bottom screw.

5 Shift the upright out of the way, and repeat Steps 2 and 3, inserting the bottom screw.

6 Repeat Steps 1 through 5 for the second upright, except only loosely fasten both screws.

7 Put one bracket on each upright. Most slide right into the uprights.

- × Screwdriver (flathead or Phillips, as needed)
- × Anchors (for brick or cement walls)
- × Metal brackets
- × Carpenter's level (if you have one)
- × One marble (optional)

8 Place a shelf across the brackets, and determine whether the shelf is straight, either by eyeballing or by using a carpenter's level. Place a marble on the shelf. If it doesn't roll, the shelf is straight, so you can tighten the upright screws and place brackets and shelves as you wish. If the shelf is not straight, adjust the uprights accordingly.

DOORS

Doors and locks. Almost everyone has the door that closes well only in certain seasons, or the squeamish lock that requires a bizarre set of turning rituals to open. If you were slammed on a daily basis, you would probably get whiny too. This section is all about how to fix common door and lock problems.

A BRIEF HISTORY OF DOORS

Years ago, doors were made on an individual home basis. Extremely tall people had extra-tall doors, wheelchair-bound people had wide doors, children had low-handled doors, and rich people had hand-ornamented doors with a butler to open them. And the door needs of the people were met.

In the age of industrialization, the door options are few. Doors are made from softwood or hardwood, the latter of which is much heavier and expensive. Though doors may look different, the vast majority are softwood doors in one of two designs—"paneled," with four indented panels of wood, glass, or plywood, or "flat," with a level surface hiding a lightweight wood frame beneath. Custom hardwood and soft-wood designs are available, but are amply more expensive. Doors can also be either hollow or solid, with the latter providing a much better sound barrier. Most are sold as unfinished wood and then painted or glazed later. Many modern interior doors are sold preattached to the frame and come as one unit.

Exterior doors are just like interior doors, with the exceptions of thicker wood frames surrounding the door and a threshold at the foot of the door. Exterior doors also often have a third hinge, helping to support the heavier, hardwood door.

DOOR SPECIFICATIONS UNHINGED

Doors should swing open cleanly and shut with little force. If you suspect there is something wrong—perhaps you're hurling your hip against the door repeatedly, or the ear-wrenching *creeeaak* tipped you off—knowing the proper door measurements can help you identify and fix the problem.

STANDARD DOOR SIZES

- × Top and side clearance: 1/16 inch
- × Bottom clearance: 1/4 inch to 1/2 inch (more with thick carpeting)
- × Top hinge distance from top: 7 inches
- × Lower hinge distance from bottom: 10 inches
- × Height: 6 feet, 8 inches to 7 feet
- × Width: 2 to 3 feet (many safety codes require entrances to be 3 feet wide)
- × Thickness: 1¼ inch to 1¾ inch

TIP

If you are living in a very old residence, the door might be a custom size. You will have to have a replacement door specially sized to fit, or buy a bigger door and cut it down. Consider installing a sliding door or French doors instead.

HOW DO DOORS WORK?

Doors are attached to the wall by hinges, and work by swinging on the axis of the hinge pins, the vertical rods inside the hinges. Go look at a door hinge. If the three screws that attach each hinge plate to the wood loosen or move over the years, the pins will not be completely vertical and the door will not swing correctly. Weather, wear and tear, and incorrectly hung doors can cause misaligned hinges. The doorknob latch also needs to slide into the center of the strike plate (the little hole that the door latch goes into), so hinge adjustments must carefully keep hinge pins and doorknob latches aligned.

HINGED ON HOME REPAIR: TYPES OF HINGES

There are two kinds of hinges: "standard" hinges, which are capped with "pins" on both top and bottom, and "antirising" hinges, which have a pin on the top and a hole on the bottom. You can tell which kind you have by looking at the hinge: if it appears the same on top and bottom, it's a standard hinge. If not, it's an antirising hinge. Both effectively do the same thing.

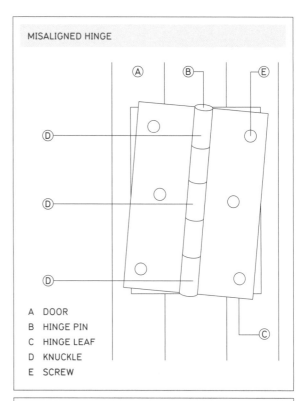

MISALIGNED HINGE

A DOOR
B HINGE PIN
C HINGE LEAF
D KNUCKLE
E SCREW

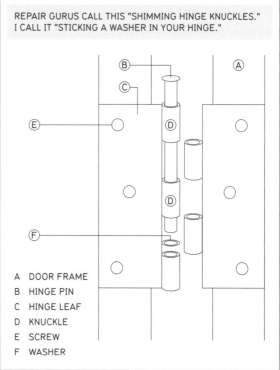

REPAIR GURUS CALL THIS "SHIMMING HINGE KNUCKLES." I CALL IT "STICKING A WASHER IN YOUR HINGE."

A DOOR FRAME
B HINGE PIN
C HINGE LEAF
D KNUCKLE
E SCREW
F WASHER

SQUEAKING HINGES

If your door squawks like a Siamese cat, your hinges need some oil. You are going to loosen the hinges, remove the door, oil the hinges, and replace the door. Yes, there is no lazy way to do this: the entire pin needs to be coated in oil. See instructions at right.

REPAIRING WORN HINGE KNUCKLES

While you are oiling your hinges, if you notice worn hinge knuckles—the circular pieces that rub together like intertwined knuckles—you can prevent further damage by placing a washer (a little O-shaped piece of metal) in between the knuckles. Washers cost pennies each, so take the hinge pin with you to the hardware store and purchase the thinnest washers that fit around the pin. Back at home, place the washers in between the worn knuckles before reinserting the pin.

MY DOOR IS CROOKED

After years of use (read: slamming), door hinges loosen. You can tell that the hinges are loose if your door is hitting the top or bottom of the door frame. You can also check by lifting the doorknob-side of the door—if you can lift it up, the hinges are probably loose. Lucky for you, hinges don't often loosen at the same pace, so if the top of your door is hitting the door frame, you know that the top hinges are loose, and vice versa. To tighten them:

1 Locate the 3 screws attaching each hinge plate to the wood.

2 Get someone to lift the doorknob-side of the door.

3 While the door is being held up, tighten the offending screws with a flathead screwdriver (righty tighty, lefty loosey), or a power drill. (You might need to stand on a chair for the top hinges.) That's it!

If the screws appear to be tight but the door is still at an angle, the above instructions for Repairing Worn Hinge Knuckles can subtly shift a leaning door back to center. You want to place a washer in the hinge that is diagonally across from the rubbing door corner.

YOU NEED

- × Longish nail or a screwdriver
- × Hammer
- × Paper towels
- × Hardware oil (WD-40 is ideal)

STEPS

1 If you have a standard hinge, catch your screwdriver on the part of the hinge that sticks out over the top of the hinge (the pin) and gently hammer the screwdriver handle upward. If you have an antirising hinge, put a nail through the hole at the bottom of the hinge and hammer the pin upward.

2 If the pin doesn't give way, you might need to oil it a bit while still attached. This is best done with WD-40, an oil canister with a very thin head attachment, or by using whatever means possible to get oil into the hinge, such as a Q-tip and oil. Be creative.

3 Release the hinge pins and carefully remove the door. Keep in mind that leaning a door against a wall is a great way to damage the wall, so lean it against a wall you don't care about, or throw a blanket over the top of the door.

4 Oil each pin with your paper towels and oil. Oil the hinges themselves. This is like body lotion: you want it to be moist, but not a slip-and-slide. Wipe everything off.

5 Replace the door and hammer the hinges back into place. Door fixed!

FILLING IN OVERSIZED HINGE SCREW HOLES

YOU NEED

- × Longish nail or screwdriver
- × Hammer
- × One plastic golf tee
- × Utility knife or scissors
- × Carpenter's glue

STEPS

1 After you have removed the door from the frame (see Squeaking Hinges, page 61, steps 1 through 3), unscrew all 3 screws and remove the hinge plate.

2 Dip your plastic golf tee in carpenter's glue and hammer it into the large hole.

3 Let the glue dry.

4 Come back and cut off the visible section of the golf tee.

5 Reinstall the door, inserting a screw directly into the golf tee. The golf tee will be surprisingly malleable, effectively filling the area around the screw and creating a tight fit.

OVERSIZED SCREW HOLES

A door misaligned for years can sometimes cause the door weight to pull against one or two screws. That pressure is placed directly on the wood around the screw, and the screw hole can get very large. This means that when you try to tighten the screw, it won't work because the hole is too big. There is an unusually fun solution for this problem.

MY DOOR CHANGES SIZES

Your roommate told you you were crazy. Your landlord ignored you. Your dog looked at you like you were wacky. Never fear, you're not imagining things: your door does indeed suffer from Seasonal Affective Disorder. It changes sizes with the weather. Wood shrinks during the winter in dry air, and expands during rainy and humid seasons in moist air, making your door change sizes. If you're too lazy to fix the door itself, an easy way to relieve a door that rubs against a rug in the summer and closes easily in the winter is to remove the rug during the summer.

Otherwise, try sanding the door bottom: buy some sandpaper at the hardware store and place it on an old newspaper or novel underneath the door, holding the edge in place with your foot. Swing the door back and forth a bunch of times to sand it down.

If the problem is beyond sanding, it is possible to take some wood off the edge of the door with a hand plane (a wood cutter), but you want to be very careful to not take off too much wood in the wrong season.

The basic idea is this: during wet weather when the door is expanded, mark the door with a pencil at the place where the door rubs against the door frame. *Wait until the dry season*, remove the door from the hinges (see Squeaking Hinges, page 61), and hand plane the edge of the door where you marked it. Remember that door clearance should be only ¼ to ½ inch, so you are not removing very much wood. Rehang the door and pat yourself on the back.

CURVY DOORS

If your door has obviously warped—years of hanging wet towels on it will do this—rather than buying a new door, remove the door from the hinges (see Squeaking Hinges, page 61), and place it on a table that you won't be using for a while, convex side up (like a frown, not a smile). Put cement blocks on the curved part, and leave it there for a week or two, until it returns to shape.

SLIGHTLY STICKY DOORS

If your door sticks a bit when opened, wait until dry weather and paint sealant on the edges of the door. The newly smooth door will slide in and out of the frame cleanly. Just go to the hardware store, ask for door sealant and an appropriate brush, and follow the directions. It should take fifteen minutes to paint and a day to dry.

DRAFTY DOORS

Everyone has had a door that resembles a wind tunnel. Rather than piling blankets by the door, go buy a "threshold seal." These are particularly important on exterior doors, but can also keep heat in bedrooms. Measure the bottom edge of the door and go to the hardware store. The simplest versions are adhesive strips with a rubber lip that reaches the floor. While they are cheap and functional, adhesive versions wear out quickly and may fall off on a carpet floor. More durable threshold seals are made of plastic or aluminum, and are easily screwed into the door at either end with a screwdriver or power drill. The seal can be made of rubber, metal, or brushes that resemble those on a street-cleaning truck.

SLIDING DOORS: SILICONE SPRAY TO THE RESCUE

If wrestling with your sliding door is a way of life, the door needs to be lubricated and/or adjusted. The below repair applies to metal or wood sliding doors, including modern interior sliding doors that hang from above, "accordion" doors, which open up to look like a scrunched-up accordion, and "bifold" doors, which open from the center and use central hinges to fold against the wall on each side. To adjust:

1 The door may simply be in desperate need of lubrication. Any supply store will sell silicone spray, which you can apply to the track after opening the door fully. For a sliding door on a track, spray one side, then move the door to the other side and spray. Also spray any plastic or metal rollers that you can see.

2 If troubles persist, close the door three- quarters of the way and stand back to look at it. The door is probably not hanging symmetrically. It should be completely parallel to the floor, and if it has both top and bottom tracks, evenly spaced between the tracks.
    – On the bottom edge of most slidey doors, there is a screw surrounded by a little metal plate. This is the adjustment screw. Placement differs from door to door, so find it.
    – With a screwdriver, turn the screw to the right to lower the region that the screw is on. Turn it to the left to lower the opposite region. You might need to wedge something thin under the door to help you turn the screw to the left.

3 If you have a metal track on the floor, make sure that the track itself isn't bent from years of people kicking it. If it is bent, put a wooden block in the track, step on it, and while stepping, hammer the edge of the track flat.

TIP

Sliding doors are ideal for small rooms where space is an issue. Regular doors require around 6 square feet of empty floor space. If you don't have that, consider a sliding door instead.

LOCKS

Some people will go out of their way to avoid fixing glitches. Like the woman who has mice, but instead of getting rid of them, avoids sleeping at home. Or the woman who clicks her turn signal manually for two years instead of bringing the car to the shop. You know that woman: she doesn't fix the glitch; she learns to function *with* the glitch.

Doorknobs tend to represent the epitome of this life strategy: until it falls off and refuses to go back on, you don't respond. In an effort to make your life glitch-free, this section is all about how to deal with the lock malfunctions in your life, so you can focus your energies on more productive pastimes—like lounging in front of the television.

HOW DO LOCKS WORK?

You probably have no idea how your front-door lock works.

When you place the proper key in the keyhole, the keys lift up a row of four or five pins with springs above them. The key slides in alongside a "plug," which is a metal piece with specific metal grooves, attached to the latch. When the pins match the shape of the plug, the plug will move and the latch will slide in and out.

AT THE STORE: WHAT KIND OF LOCK SHOULD I BUY?

If you're out doorknob shopping, know the doorknob categories: "keyed" (uses a key), "privacy locks" (interior locks with a little push button that blocks the plug from moving), and "passage" (no lock, the plug moves freely). You can also get a lever handle, which is easier for the young, disabled, and Fido to use. "Warded" locks are the ones with the old-fashioned lock keys associated with handcuffs and prison wards.

GOLDEN LOCKS

Dead bolt locks increase your personal safety, particularly if your neighborhood is prone to break-ins, or you just think it is. Lock installation is very feasible, so don't assume that it's too complicated—just go

to the hardware store and purchase a new lock. Each kit comes with full installation instructions for that lock, so I won't waste space here. Some installation kits also helpfully include the required tools.

Installing the lock should take about an hour. While this is not a simple repair, the steps are quite logical. The major challenge often comes after you have installed the door lock and need to place the hole for the dead bolt perfectly in the door frame. The trick is to smear lipstick on the outside edge of the dead bolt. "Unlock" the bolt and shut the door. There will be an exact imprint on the frame where you need to install your hole and strike plate.

 TIP

Before you install your lock, you want to make sure that it is nowhere near any windows, door windows, or pet doors—locks are futile if someone can reach in and open the door.

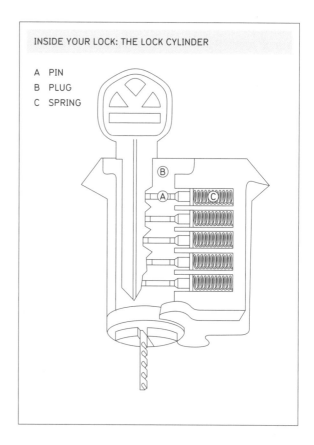

INSIDE YOUR LOCK: THE LOCK CYLINDER

A PIN
B PLUG
C SPRING

STICKY LOCKS AND STUCK KNOBS

Locks naturally delube themselves over time, making keys and knobs hard to turn, and invariably locking you out right when you *really* need to get inside. For minorly dry locks in nonhumid regions, a trick is drawing all over your key with a pencil. (You could also purchase graphite powder, but a pencil, which is also graphite, works just as well.) Completely cover the key in pencil, and then stick it into the lock, turning the key around a few times. In humid regions, spray lock oil into the keyhole and place some on the key.

If the pencil or oil trick doesn't work, adjusting your lock to open and close with ease is easy and requires only oil and a screwdriver. You need to take apart the lock, oil it, and put it back together. Remember that this is an ideal time to practice the golden rule of placing parts on a flat surface in the order that you remove them, so you know how to put them back together.

UH-OH, HALF OF MY KEY IS STILL IN THE DOOR

Half of your key disappeared inside the lock, and you're holding the other half. Locksmiths will charge you a bundle to reunite your halves. Instead, with your new understanding of locks, you can get it out yourself. The front end of the key is sitting under springed pins, so you will stick something small (like a sturdy needle) in there above the key, pushing up slightly on the pins in your way, and slide the key out. (See the illustration opposite.)

TIP

Major Money Saver Tip   There is something very wrong with the inner workings of your doorknob or lock and you have no idea how to fix it. Rather than calling a locksmith for a house call, remove the entire doorknob mechanism (see Sticky Locks and Stuck Knobs, above), dump it into a resealable plastic bag, and take it to the locksmith. You will save yourself ample cost on a home visit and pay only a basic maintenance fee. The same applies to a lock for which you have lost the key: rather than purchasing a new lock, bring the whole lock to the locksmith, and he or she will insert new parts to match a new key. For safety reasons, never give a locksmith your address—make one up.

LUBRICATING A DOORKNOB OR DOOR LOCK

YOU NEED

- × Screwdriver
- × Non–water-based hardware oil
- × Paper towels or rags

STEPS

1   Remove the knobs or locks from both sides of the door with a screwdriver. Most doors have a very hidden tiny hole underneath the base of the knob that you press your screwdriver into, before pulling off the knob. Some models have more obvious screws on one or both sides to loosen. Pull off the knob and the decorative ring against the door. If there is another set of screws underneath the knob, loosen those as well.

2   Oil all metal parts that seem to move, shifting them around against oiled paper towels or rags.

3   Oil up the key and turn it in the lock a few times.

4   Blot any excess oil.

5   Reassemble the lock or knob.

RETRIEVING A BROKEN KEY FROM A LOCK

YOU NEED

- × Small, serrated saw blade
- × A key stuck in a lock
- × Long-nose pliers, or if you don't have those, cosmetic tweezers

STEPS

1 Go down to the hardware store and explain that you need a very small, serrated blade. They will probably hand you a blade for a "coping saw," which is an extremely small electric saw.

2 Back in front of the lock, first make sure that the key is vertical in the lock. Nudging it with the saw blade will flip it to vertical.

3 Insert the blade into the keyhole, going over the top of the broken key. You will be pushing the pins that are holding the key in place upward.

4 Apply slight downward pressure on the key to pull it out. As soon as it has passed the edge of the lock, grab it with your pliers or tweezers.

OTHER LOCK PROBLEMS

PROBLEM A small child has locked herself in my bathroom.

SOLUTION Look for the indented hole on your side of the knob. It's an emergency release, usually opened by sticking a small piece of wire or a hairpin in the hole. A complex doorknob may have come with an "emergency key," which will also open the door.

PROBLEM It's cold out, and my lock appears to be frozen.

SOLUTION Hair dryers unfreeze anything, though you may have to borrow your neighbor's and an extension cord. For future troubles, buy deicing spray, which also works on car locks.

PROBLEM I came home today and my key wouldn't fit in the lock anymore.

SOLUTION If your key didn't experience unusual bending trauma today, this often means that the lock was tampered with while you were gone, damaging the keyway. You need to replace the lock and increase your safety precautions.

PROBLEM My doorknob is almost falling off.

SOLUTION Tighten the outside screws that hold the doorknob in place.

PROBLEM I have to slam the door to get it to stay closed.

SOLUTION The latch is not properly aligned with the door frame. Buy a metal file, stick the file in the hole, and file away, testing regularly as you file.

WINDOWS

WHAT DO WINDOWS DO?

Windows were called lights before Edison came along. They provide ventilation and light, and in many cases offer an emergency exit, which explains why apartment codes require a window in every bedroom.

The frame holding the window glass in place is called the sash, and the sash either runs on tracks or opens with a hinge. "Sash" is a weird word, because it is both singular and plural. The pieces of glass inside the sash are called panes. The frame of the window (the surrounding part that's attached to the wall) is almost always made of wood, though sometimes attached to an aluminum window track.

TYPES OF WINDOWS

See illustrations right and on page 68.

WINDOW CLEANING

A variety of window cleaners can be found on the shelves of your local grocery store. Cleaning not only helps you see, but greatly lengthens the life of the window. If you're adverse to cleaners manufactured in corporate chemical plants, try mixing together 2 parts white vinegar, 1 part ammonia, and a couple of spoonfuls of cornstarch. Using old newspapers instead of rags will reduce streaking. Clean away, reaching your arm out the window to get outside panes, but not if doing so will create a safety hazard.

MY WINDOW LETS IN MORE COLD AIR THAN AN AIR CONDITIONER

If you can feel a window draft, you're wasting ample money on your heat bill every month. First, make sure the storm window is in place. If that doesn't help, get your fingers wet and hold them in front of the window to determine where the draft is coming from. Visually locate the gap causing the draft.

TYPES OF WINDOWS
WHAT DOES YOUR WINDOW LOOK LIKE?

1   DOUBLE-HUNG WINDOW

The Model T of windows. Both the top and bottom sash can be opened.

2   SINGLE-HUNG WINDOW

A cheaper version of the double-hung window, where the top sash does not open. This limits ventilation and cleaning options.

TYPES OF WINDOWS
WHAT DOES YOUR WINDOW LOOK LIKE?

3 CASEMENT WINDOW

A window that opens like a door, with hinges on one side. For safety specifications, make sure that larger windows have more than one lock, and that the window opens wide enough for an emergency exit.

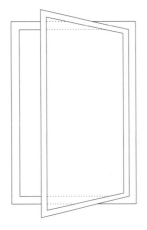

4 SLIDING WINDOW

These are double-hung windows on their side. They are often quite difficult to clean.

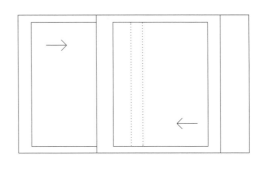

5 AWNING WINDOW

Just like a casement window, but smaller, with the hinges on top of the window.

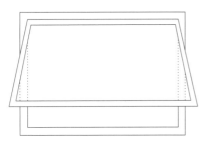

6 BAY WINDOW

Usually a set of three windows that extend out beyond the exterior walls. Bay windows make rooms seem much larger than they are, but need good curtaining at night, lest everyone see everything you do inside.

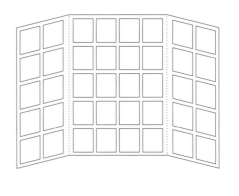

TROUBLESHOOTING SUGGESTIONS
FOR DIFFICULT WINDOWS

PROBLEM My metal window tracks are impossible.

SOLUTION Lubricate. Spray the sash channels with silicone spray. This also works on screen and storm window troubles.

PROBLEM The previous owner appears to have painted the window shut.

SOLUTION Using an X-Acto knife, cut around the edges of the window, creating a slice through the paint in every seam. Then gently whack a block of wood with a hammer, knocking evenly around the edges of the window frame, which should jar it enough to get it open.

PROBLEM The window is completely stuck.

SOLUTION First make sure that the previous owners didn't install a window pin, nailing the window shut. If they did, pull out the pins or nails. Otherwise, hold a block of wood over the sash frame and give a couple of light hammer whacks, which should jar the window enough to get it open and lubricated.

PROBLEM It feels like the tracks are too tight for the sash to move up and down.

SOLUTION Rather than disassembling the window, try enlarging the channels. Take a block of wood and a hammer. Hold the block against the inside edge of one of the channels, and whack it a few times. Start conservatively, especially if the channel appears to give easily. Open and close the window to test. Repeat in each channel that seems to benefit. This will work noticeably in metal windows, and faintly in wood windows.

PROBLEM There's lots of paint and other gunk in the window tracks. I think this is why it's so hard to open.

SOLUTION Years of paint may have built up along the channels of older double-hung windows. Gently chipping off some of the paint with a utility knife might help, as will dampening a rag with paint thinner and removing the offending paint. Be careful in houses built before the late 1970s, as many paints have high lead content. Use gloves and clean up thoroughly.

PROBLEM My wooden window tracks are impossible.

SOLUTION WD-40 helps wooden tracks, as does rubbing the end of an old candle along the tracks, distributing the wax.

There are a variety of solutions for this, but my favorite is the use of "expanding foam," which is like shaving cream that hardens into place. Ask for some at the hardware store, follow the directions, and spray it into the gaps causing the draft. Wait for it to dry, and cut the edges smooth to align with the window frame.

Weather stripping is also an option. Weather strips are rolls of very thin foam with adhesive on one side. Professionals place weather stripping on the external side of the window tracks, directly against the tracks. Though not the most cosmetically sound repair, if you're cold and don't feel like hanging out your window, you can simply place a piece of weather stripping along the inside edge of a drafty window edge during the winter, and pull it off when the weather warms up again.

BROKEN GLASS: DAMAGED WINDOW PANES

Fixing a broken glass window is not hard, but requires working with broken jagged glass, a lot of expensive tools that you probably don't own (a glass cutter, for one), and either repairing against a nonsecure upper-floor window or removing your window, which you don't want to attempt in cold or rainy weather. In summary, you need someone who knows what they're doing, or a professional.

In the meantime, start off by going to the hardware store and buying waterproof tape and a sheet of polyethylene to tape over the broken pane from the outside for weather protection. This will buy you some time. If the pane is just cracked, apply the clear waterproof tape directly over the crack, which will give you a few days of weather protection. Masking tape will hold the glass intact, but will not hold up against rain.

WINDOW DRESSINGS

SCREEN AND STORM WINDOWS

Most windows have both screen and storm options. Screens are useful for letting in bug-free summer air. Storm windows protect the external window frame during those long winters—no household part benefits from five months of being caked with snow and ice—while further insulating your room from cold air. Modern windows are often triple-track models, with interchangeable external screen and storm windows. To switch, open your window, pull up the screen, and pull down the storm window. You should go through your entire house as winter or bad storms approach and pull down the storm windows.

MY SCREEN HAS A HOLE IN IT

There are three options for repairing screen holes:

1   If your finger can't fit through the hole, you might be able to use a darning needle to pull the wires back in place. Look closely at the wires, and note that none of them are actually damaged; they're just bent to one side. Use your needle to nudge them back into place. Then cover the area with a couple of layers of clear nail polish.
2   For larger holes, buy a "screen patch" at the hardware store, and place the adhesive side over the hole. You can also make a patch from extra screen, cutting the patch at least an inch larger than the hole on all sides. Place the patch over the hole and bend the wire ends of the patch through the screen to secure it. Secure the patch with acrylic glue or clear nail polish.
3   If there's more hole than screen, buy a new screen. Screen is sold by the foot, so buy enough to overhang the metal frame by a few inches. Screens can be sharp, so wear gloves. Remove the old screen by prying it out of the frame grooves with a screwdriver. Be careful when pulling out the "spine," which is the rubbery black string around the edges that holds the screen into the frame grooves (unless the spine is old and brittle, in which case you can purchase more at the hardware store). Lay out the new screen on top of the frame. Place the spine over the screen, along the edges of the frame, and use a spine roller, which resembles a pizza cutter, to roll the spine and new screen into the grooves of the frame. Cut away any excess with a utility knife.

HOW DO SHADES WORK?

You know that window shade that hasn't worked in years? The one you either always leave down or manually roll up and down as needed? Once you understand how the shade works, you can stop overcompensating and fix it for good in three minutes.

Inside the roller is a big horizontal spring. When you pull down the shade, the spring expands until it is very long and tense, just waiting to spring back together. The shade is held down by a little metal "ratchet tooth" on the roller that catches on a little metal piece (the "arm") every time the tube rotates 360 degrees, stopping the roller from turning. When the shade rolls up, the lock mechanism releases and the spring bounces together, pulling up the shade and releasing tension. The roller is held in place by a bracket on either side of the window.

Based on this understanding, you can fix most problems.

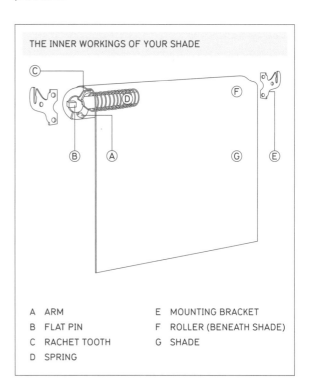

THE INNER WORKINGS OF YOUR SHADE

A ARM	E MOUNTING BRACKET
B FLAT PIN	F ROLLER (BENEATH SHADE)
C RACHET TOOTH	G SHADE
D SPRING	

TROUBLESHOOTING SHADES

PROBLEM My shade doesn't lift at all. It's stuck all the way down.

SOLUTION Your spring probably has no tension. Remove the roller and pop off the cap at the end with the flat pin. Hold the roller still with one hand, and with the other, take pliers and twist the flat pin clockwise until you feel tension. Rehang; adjust if needed.

PROBLEM The shade doesn't seem to "catch" and hold itself up at various heights.

SOLUTION You need to oil and clean the little tooth-and-arm locking mechanism. Take down the roller and pull off the cap at the end with the flat pin sticking out. Clean off the area and lubricate the little tooth and metal piece with any non-water-based lubricant, like WD-40.

PROBLEM My shade doesn't lift at all. It's stuck all the way down.

SOLUTION Your spring probably has no tension. Remove the roller and pop off the cap at the end with the flat pin. Hold the roller still with one hand, and with the other, take pliers and twist the flat pin clockwise until you feel tension. Rehang; adjust if needed.

PROBLEM My shade rolls up with the force of a NASA launch. Sometimes it does this by itself.

SOLUTION The spring is too tight. You need to loosen the tension of the spring by taking down the roller, unrolling it halfway, and rehanging it.

PROBLEM My shade won't pull down. It's stuck all the way up.

SOLUTION It sounds like the lock mechanism is stuck. Remove the roller and pop off the cap at the end with the flat pin. With pliers, twist the flat pin a bit. This will cause the lock to release. Adjust as needed and rehang.

PROBLEM I keep getting cold drafts through the shade.

SOLUTION Check to see that the shade unwinds *behind* the roller, close to the window. This will save you money on heating by providing more insulation. If you care more about looks than temperature, flipping the shade so it unwinds in front of the roller will hide roller ugliness from view.

PROBLEM My shade falls down altogether.

SOLUTION There is something wrong with your brackets, which attach to the wall. Each bracket should have one little groove for the roller pin to sit in. Is the bracket falling off the wall? Tighten its screws. Is the metal bent, allowing the pin to fall right out? Gently unbend the metal with a hammer. If the brackets are too wide apart to hold the roller, unscrew one bracket, place a thin piece of wood between the bracket and the wall, and rescrew the bracket.

PROBLEM The shade is crooked.

SOLUTION Either the shade is rolled up unevenly, or the brackets on either side of the window were installed asymmetrically. Take down the roller and completely unroll and reroll it evenly. If that doesn't work, put a carpenter's level on top of the installed roller. (If you don't have one, just eyeball the roller—is it level?) If the bubble is not centered, one of the brackets needs to be moved by unscrewing the bracket and reinstalling it slightly higher or lower.

PROBLEM My shade is ripped.

SOLUTION Tape the rip from the back with white cloth tape so no one can see the rip or the repair. Or purchase a new roller and shade. They are sold in standard roller widths, measuring from tip to tip of the pins at either end of the roller, and the shade should measure the height of the window plus 8 inches. If you're creative, you can either glue attractive fabric on top of the old shade, or make your own shade with nonfraying fabric. Cut the ripped shade off the roller. Cut the fabric to match the old shade size, glue the fabric to the roller, and hem a wooden stick into the bottom for a handle.

BLINDED BY THE LIGHT

Venetian blinds occasionally get out of whack—one side pulls up more than the other, some slats close more than others, or the whole thing falls on you. Whatever the problem, take the blinds off the window and *lay them on a table to adjust them*. It's much easier to see what's wrong that way, because some cords will be obviously more slacked than others. To adjust, just even out offending blinds and cords, and hold the new adjustments in place with the buckles on the cords.

HOW DO VENETIAN BLINDS WORK?

The two strings or tapes going through every blind are called ladders, and they hold the blinds together. The cord that you pull to adjust the blinds (the "lift cord") is threaded through the center of every single slat and controls how much space there is between slats. The wand (sometimes it's a cord) that angles the slats is attached to a horizontal "tilt tube" across the top of the blinds. When the tube tilts, it pulls one side of both ladders, causing every blind attached to the ladder to tilt in one direction.

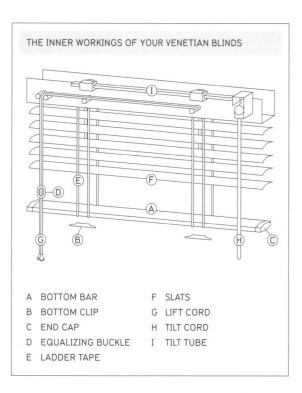

THE INNER WORKINGS OF YOUR VENETIAN BLINDS

A BOTTOM BAR	F SLATS
B BOTTOM CLIP	G LIFT CORD
C END CAP	H TILT CORD
D EQUALIZING BUCKLE	I TILT TUBE
E LADDER TAPE	

TIP

REPLACING OLD CORDS

If you frequently change your venetian blind adjustments, the strings and cords will wear out much faster. This is usually obvious upon inspection, because the strings and cords will look fraying and thin, or because one broke and the blinds are at a 90-degree angle with one another. Take the measurements of your blinds and go purchase replacement cords at a window or blinds store.

The trick to this is to exactly mimic the placement of the old cords and ladders. The specifics of how cords and ladders are wound and attached can differ; just mimic whatever knots or staples attached the old cords, and remove the old cord or ladder slowly, following slat-by-slat with the new cord or ladder.

To replace any worn or fraying cords:

1 Put the blinds on the table.
2 Remove the end caps on the bottom bar; slide the whole bottom bar right out.
3 You should be able to see the bottom of the cords and ladder tape.
4 Unknot the old cord.
5 Tie or tape the new cord to the old cord, and pull it all the way through the top of the blinds. If you are replacing central cords, you will be pulling the cord through the holes in the slats. Leave the same amount of excess cord as the old cord had, erring on the side of too much cord—you can always cut later.
6 Knot the cord at the bottom and replace the bottom bar.
7 Rehang the blinds and adjust the buckle on the cord that you pull to lift the shade.

Ladder tape is the two vertical strips that attach to every single blind. Not all blinds have tapes—some have only cords, in which case you follow the above directions. To replace the ladder tapes:

1 You probably have two tapes, so replace one side at a time so you can look at the other for reference.
2 Look carefully at the old ladder tape, and then detach one end from its clips at the top of the bar.
3 Attach the new ladder tape.
4 Slowly remove the old ladder tape a few slats at a time, while replacing it with new ladder tape.
5 When you reach the bottom, remove the old ladder tape from its clips and replace it with the new ladder tape.
6 Continue until you have completely replaced one tape, then repeat on the other side.
7 Replace the bottom bar and rehang. You can see, you can see!

If you happen to mess up midstream and have no idea how to fix what you've done, pack the venetian blinds into a bag and go to a window store. A nice person there will probably help you for a nominal fee.

TIP

String Safety You probably never considered venetian-blind strings a safety risk until you heard about a small child wrapping her neck in one. If you or anyone you know has a child with a head small enough to fit through the cord, install a small "cleat" on the wall at adult-arm height. A cleat is a metal piece with two arms for wrapping cords around, which you probably associate with flagpoles. The cleat can be installed high on the window frame. All you need is a cleat, a screw, and a screwdriver, and you simply screw the cleat into the window frame. (A power drill to make a screw hole will make this easier, but isn't pivotal.)

DRAPED IN COLOR: CURTAIN RODS

We all know people in apartments with bare windows because the place didn't come with curtain rods. This is a lame excuse. Curtains are easy to install, and equally decorative and functional. As long as the curtains aren't leaning against a heater, you're in business.

REASONS WHY YOU SHOULD HAVE CURTAINS

× They're pretty.
× They insulate from noise, drafts, heat, and sunlight.
× Privacy: just because you can't see them doesn't mean they can't see you. If you don't have curtains or shades, chances are you're putting on a show for your whole neighborhood.
× If you're a nondecorator who nevertheless wants a cool atmosphere, curtains are the easiest and cheapest way to give a room a personal touch.
× Safety: drawn curtains seriously limit the chances of the local creepy peeper knowing what you look like.
× They're portable. Unlike many decorations, which become donations to the apartment, curtain rods and curtains are completely transportable.

Curtain rods are made from aluminum, steel, or plastic, and are available in an array of styles and sizes, ranging from hand-ornamented bronze to cheap plastic. The most basic are the truly portable "tension-mounted" versions, expandable pieces of plastic or metal with rubber tips that are wedged into place across the window, much like a portable pull-up bar. Beyond the $8 range, you will find two varieties: rings-on-a-rod or the more complex pull-cord-and-track. If you're a low-maintenance type, I would highly suggest the basic rings-on-a-rod variety. Magnetic rods are also available if your window frames are metal.

All curtain rods (except the portable kind) are supported by two brackets. To install, you screw the brackets into the wall surrounding the window with screws.

1 Mark with a pencil where you would like to install the brackets on the wall, making dots for each screw hole. If you are installing above the window, you can draw a straight line across the top of the window with a carpenter's level.
2A For a wood-frame wall, you need to install the brackets into beams of wood behind the wall. Most windows—especially large ones—are surrounded by horizontal beams ("casing") behind the wall. Knock on the area above the window with your knuckles, listening for a solid sound (as opposed to a hollow "pop"). You can install the curtains

anywhere in the solid area. Simply use a drill to make drill holes into your dots, and use a screwdriver to insert the bracket screws into the wall.

2B If the wall is cement, brick, or other masonry, you can drill holes anywhere around the window. See Hanging Pictures on Nonwood Walls (page 53) to learn how to drill holes, place anchors in the holes, and insert the bracket screws. This, too, is a fast and easy process.

3 Attach your curtain onto the rod and place the rod in the brackets.

FLOORS

FLOORED, GROUNDED, AND LEVEL: WHAT'S IN A FLOOR?

Look at your bare floor. Below the wood, tile, or vinyl surface there is a "subfloor" holding you up. The subfloor is flat sheets of plywood, which sit directly on top of "joists," the beams of wood going from one side of the room to the other, usually 16 inches apart. The joists are part of a horizontal wooden frame that looks just like the wood in your wall. The exception to this design is the concrete basement floor that is often part of the foundation of the house or building.

The top floor layer that you see was chosen after the "subfloor" was in place. If hardwood floors are in order, floorboards are nailed directly on top of the subfloor, in thicknesses ranging from less than ½ inch to more than 2 inches. The floorboards are painted with a finish, which gives them an attractive, protective coating against your future abuse. Or, if the builders know that the floor is destined to be hidden under vinyl, wall-to-wall carpeting, or tiling, they will often install sheets of particleboard (compacted chips of wood), which is much cheaper than hardwood floor-boards. Cost is of the essence: a high-quality, large hardwood floor with a lush carpet can cost more than a university degree, while cheap parquet flooring—thin tiles of decorative wood—will equal only your annual rent.

Certain rooms lend themselves to different kinds of floors. Bathroom floors are often covered with ceramic tiles for their waterproof quality, while kitchens often have vinyl, which is both affordable and easy to clean.

Carpeting and vinyl can be laid in full sheets or squares, while ceramic tiles range in size. Landlords often insist that tenants cover any open hardwood floors with carpeting to prevent floor damage.

SQUEAKY FLOORS

Your wood floor gives an enormous creak every time you walk by. This was probably the main struggle of your childhood—parents purposely don't fix floors because these squeaks tell them when their children are sneaking around the house.

If you don't have children and could do without the squeaking, the easiest fix is carpeting, which muffles floor squeaks. Carpets are often required in multi-unit buildings, to spare neighbors below. For a more permanent fix, first you need to determine if the squeak is coming from the surface of the floor, where one floorboard is rubbing against another, or below the surface, from under the floorboards. The easiest way to determine this is to throw yourself down, ear-to-floor, and make someone walk repeatedly over the creaky area. Listen carefully; you'll be able to tell whence the creak comes.

If it is a surface problem, a dousing of dance floor wax in the spaces between boards might do the trick. Greasing the offending floorboards won't stop them from moving, but will stop them from emitting sound. Local dance studios can tell you where to purchase it if your hardware store doesn't carry it. Follow the directions on the package. I suggest you use gloves—preferably latex—when using this product.

If the sound is clearly coming from below the surface, you have a bit more work to do. The problem is most likely that either the subfloor or joists are rubbing against a nail. Wood loses moisture and changes shape within its first couple of years, causing these little gaps and spaces that screech when you land 100 to 250 pounds on them. To prevent this, you're going to screw the floorboard more securely to the underlying floor beams. "Spiral" or "ringed" nails have spirals going down to the sharp tip of the nail, almost like screws but with a sharp tip, making them grip the wood and prevent future creaks. They are usually lubricated to help them go into the floor, and need to be inserted with a power drill, like a screw. A hardware store worker will help you find what you need.

FIXING A SQUEAKY FLOOR

YOU NEED

- × Stud finder
- × Pencil
- × Safety goggles
- × Power drill
- × 2-inch spiral nails or ringed nails
- × Wood filler

STEPS

1 First you need to locate the joists near your creaks with a stud finder. Most creaks are directly on top of joists, but use the stud finder's light as a guide for the beginning and end of each joist. Mark the beginning and end of the joist with a pencil, and then mark the center point with a dot.

2 Pick up your power drill and put on a drill bit that is slightly smaller than your ring-shank nail. Put on safety goggles, then drill a hole straight down through the floorboard and into the joist below. This should make an approximately 2½-inch-deep hole.

3 Place your spiral or ringed nail onto the end of your drill, and drill it down into the hole, at least 1 inch into the joist. The top of the nail should be an inch below the surface of the floor.

4 You now have a little hole in your floor surface, above the nail. Fill the hole with the wood filler, which is pasty stuff that cleanly fills in small wood holes. Wipe the surface flat.

5 For a floor that squeaks in multiple places, repeat Steps 1 through 3 on each joist. For very noisy floors, repeat Steps 1 through 3 on both ends of a joist in a room or hallway. No more squeaky floor!

TIP

Wood filler is not always a perfect cosmetic match with your beautiful floorboards. Try first in a corner or under a carpeted area, and make sure you are comfortable with the look.

TEARS AND HOLES IN VINYL FLOORS

You know your floor is made of vinyl by elimination: if it's not hardwood, tile, cement, or carpet, but is clearly covering a floor layer below and feels kind of rubbery but smooth, your floor surface is vinyl. And you probably know that accidentally tearing vinyl is not hard. A dropped kitchen knife can leave a 2-inch gouge.

Fixing this is easy. If the cut is truly tiny, a bit of liquid seam sealer, which is sold at hardware stores or floor supply stores, will close the hole invisibly. Smear it on, press on the tear, and wipe off excess. Hold it down to dry for 10 minutes, then leave the room alone for a day.

If the cut is bigger than ¾ inch but still clearly qualifies as a cut (as opposed to a gash or hole), we're going to take the creative route and use glue.

The glue trick won't work for a real hole. For this repair you will need a scrap of vinyl that matches the pattern of the damaged area. You are going to cut out the damaged area and patch it with the extra vinyl. If you don't have an extra scrap, go to a flooring store and see if they still sell the same pattern. Otherwise, cut some off the floor of a closet or an equally unnoticeable area.

FIXING BROKEN FLOOR TILES
See Killing Chip (page 51).

STAINS: FLOOR AND CARPET BLEMISHES

It is surprisingly easy to dump enormous amounts of a staining liquid on your favorite carpet while completely sober—let alone while throwing a kegger with eighty of your closest friends. Floor stains happen, and now you'll know how to remove them.

REMOVING STAINS ON HARD FLOORS

FIDO PEED AGAIN If you're lucky enough to own a

REPAIRING A TEAR IN A VINYL FLOOR

YOU NEED

- × Scrap of matching vinyl
- × Masking tape
- × Utility knife
- × Ruler
- × Putty knife, as needed
- × Vinyl adhesive
- × Paper towels
- × Latex or rubber gloves
- × Liquid seam sealer (optional)

STEPS

1 Cut a piece of the scrap vinyl that is bigger than the damaged area. Tape it over the damaged area with masking tape so that the pattern matches the surrounding edges exactly.

2 Using your utility knife, cut a rectangle through both the new and old vinyl, using a ruler to guide a straight line.

3 The new patch will come right off. The damaged area might come right off, or it might be adhered to the floor. If it is glued, use a putty knife to scrape the damaged area off the floor.

4 You are now looking at a hole in the vinyl, some bare floor below, and a new patch.

5 Spread your vinyl adhesive into the hole, using gloves.

6 Place your patch into the hole, pressing it flat and quickly wiping away any adhesive that sneaks through with a paper towel. Hold the patch down for a minute with your hands.

7 Let the area dry for 24 hours.

8 If you are adventurous, you can apply liquid seam sealer to the edges of the patch the next day to further aid the adhesive. However, this isn't usually necessary, unless the floor is in a high-usage area.

PATCHING A HOLE IN A VINYL FLOOR

YOU NEED

- × Extra scrap of vinyl
- × Food grater
- × Small bowl
- × Acrylic glue
- × Rubber gloves
- × Paper towels

STEPS

1 Take an extra piece of vinyl (if you don't have one, buy some of the same color at the store) and dump a few square inches in your food grater.

2 Grind the life out of it.

3 Pour the vinyl into a little bowl and mix it with acrylic glue to form a very thick, mostly vinyl paste.

4 Wearing rubber gloves, smear the pasty goo over the tear until the surface is flat.

5 Make sure to wipe up quickly any excess glue with a paper towel. Let the area dry.

6 Clean the heck out of your food grater before you use it again for food.

wood floor and a dog with a bladder control problem, purchase a bottle of wood bleach. Follow the directions, and place the bleach mixture on the stained area immediately. If you wait, the wood will stain permanently. You should also keep around a can of wood finish, because after you use the bleach, you need to paint that area with another coat of finish. Before disaster (or Fido) strikes, test the bleach and finish in a corner, to make sure the color matches.

SNEAKER MARKS Scuffs on floors are not attractive. Place a rag dipped in mineral spirits (the stuff painters use to clean brushes) or household bleach on the stain, being careful not to accidentally damage your clothes. As always, test it on a back corner to make sure you don't damage the floor, particularly vinyl. Lay a plastic bag flat over the area; leave it for a few hours. When you return, you should be able to wipe the scuff mark right up.

NAIL POLISH Try to avoid using nail polish remover to clean up that overturned bottle, because the polish remover can also eat right through the seal on your floor (which is very similar to clear nail polish). Instead, blot up what you can, let the stain dry, and then use steel wool and a kitchen cleaning powder to unpeel dried flecks. Be careful not to rub the wet stain, or it will spread.

INK STAINS Rubbing alcohol will work to remove ink stains, but you don't want to dump it on the floor. Instead, use a thin cotton swab stick dipped in alcohol and try to absorb as much of the ink as possible. If the stain is large, upgrade to a larger cotton swab.

TIP

An easy solution that many forget is the possibility of cutting off the tops of stained "pile" (the upright carpet threads). There are thousands of pieces, and no one will miss the five you cut out.

REMOVING CARPET STAINS

For carpet stains, first blot the area with a white cotton cloth, trying to suck up as much of the stain as you can. Next try a carpet stain remover product or a detergent and water combination. Glass-cleaning

---

REPAIRING A STAINED CARPET

YOU NEED

- × Big carpet stain
- × Circular rug cutter
- × Unused piece of carpet
- × Scissors or utility knife, as needed
- × Double-sided carpet tape
- × Seam adhesive or clear nail polish

STEPS

1 Take the circular rug cutter, which resembles a cookie cutter, and place it over the stained area. Press down and turn to cut through the carpet, careful to not cut the padding and floor beneath.

2 Cut the extra carpet swatch to exactly match the circular piece of carpet you just removed. Depending on the carpet, you can do this with scissors, a utility knife, or a carpet cutter.

3 You are now looking at a hole of visible floor (or padding) below the carpet. Cut a piece of double-sided carpet tape a few inches longer than the hole's diameter. Place the tape flat onto the floor below, extending underneath the carpet on either side of the hole.

4 Fit in your replacement patch into the hole, making sure you have a pattern match.

5 You are now looking at the top side of the patch placed in the hole. Smear seam adhesive around the edges of the patch, at the bottom of the pile, to prevent the patch or carpet from unraveling. If you don't have seam adhesive, clear nail polish will also do the job, but you'll need most of a bottle, as the carpet will absorb most of it.

6 Let the area dry for a day. Play the game Bet You Can't Guess Where My Stain Was with friends.

sprays have also been known to work. Just because a product once removed a stain on a different rug doesn't mean it won't ruin the currently stained rug, so always test first on a corner.

REPAIRING BADLY STAINED CARPETS

Severely stained carpets can be fixed with relative ease. If the big burn mark or nail polish puddle refuses to fade, just replace the whole area. For this, you need to have an extra carpet patch. If you don't, see if there's a hidden place where you could cut off a swatch—try the back corner of a closet, or underneath a couch that you know is permanent.

DIRTY CARPETS

Carpets are like your hair. Imagine if someone walked back and forth, laid on, and sometimes accidentally dumped stuff on your hair for years. Yes, it would get pretty nasty, and some shampoo would be in order. So it is with rugs. To shampoo your rugs, you can either pay for a professional to do it, or rent a rug-shampooing machine from the local hardware store or supermarket. Purchase the shampoo and follow the directions—the machine itself will apply the shampoo—and then let the area dry. Any supermarket sells cheaper versions of spray-on shampoo, which you spray on, rub in with a big sponge, and then vacuum up. This is more feasible on a low budget, but doesn't clean as well.

Shampoo annually and vacuum weekly, and much more often for popular, pet-treaded, or child-crawled areas. Vacuuming will also help asthmatics, for whom rugs contain a veritable army of dust mites. As always, test a corner with any new product to make sure it doesn't remove the carpet color.

SMELLY CARPETS

It's not broken, but it sure smells funky. If you have a funny smell in your room and you can't figure out what it is, it might be in the carpet. To remedy this, sprinkle baking soda all over the carpet, wait for 15 minutes, then vacuum it up. If the baking soda alone doesn't work, try a solution of 1 part white vinegar, 4 parts water. Spread it on the carpet with a spray bottle and let it dry.

MY CARPET IS A SAFETY HAZARD

Carpets should always be secured to the floor, either held down tight by furniture or by actual devices meant to hold down carpets. Rather than tripping over your carpet for all eternity, take the plunge and buy some carpet tacks and tape.

There are two easy ways to secure carpets (and doormats!): carpet tacks and double-sided tape. Not surprisingly, I am a proponent of the double-sided carpet tape. It is like duct tape, but for rugs. It is recommended for rubber-bottomed carpets, but if you're only using it on the corners of a nonrubber rug, you should be okay. Place the tape facedown around the rug perimeter, or just under the corners that you want to adhere. The faceup side of the tape is covered by protective film, so when you're ready to attach the rug, tear off the extra layer and press the carpet down.

The other option is carpet tack strips, which are strips of metal with little tack ends that catch on the bottom of the carpet. Place the strips along the edges of a room, and nail in each side with one nail. Then put the carpet down and press.

REPAIRING FRAYED EDGES OR TORN SEAMS

An obviously ripped or fraying carpet doesn't mean that you need to get a new one. Instead, go buy an upholstery needle.

For a fraying edge, use the thickest thread you can find that matches the carpet color. Starting before the fray, do a wrap stitch around the edge, so that each stitch touches the entire previous stitch. Sew right over the fraying, making the stitch as long as you need, continuing on an inch past the end of the fraying.

For a carpet tear or seam that has come loose, thread the upholstery needle with a lightweight "monofila-ment" thread (just ask at the crafts store). This time, you're going to simply sew the two broken edges together, with stitches approximately a half inch apart. If the base of the carpet is thick, you might need to pull the needle through with pliers. When you have sewed the entire seam, reverse direction to reinforce the seam. Rub the rug surface when you're done to fluff it up and hide your stitches.

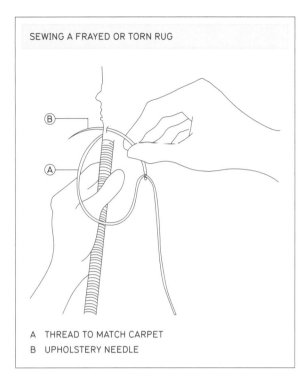

SEWING A FRAYED OR TORN RUG

A   THREAD TO MATCH CARPET
B   UPHOLSTERY NEEDLE

MOVING IN AND OUT

Much of the damage discussed in this chapter is caused by moving in and out, and can be avoided with some simple tips.

×   When moving large objects through doors, either tilt the object in the direction that the door swings open, or take the door off its hinges and remove it altogether. This will give you the extra few inches you need to squeak—not scrape—through.

×   Never roll anything heavy—particularly refrigerators—over linoleum. To put in a refrigerator, place plywood boards on your kitchen floor and roll the refrigerator over the boards.

×   Cover all sharp points and edges with an old blanket or sheet to save your walls damage. This includes couches, stereos, and objets d'art that you aren't planning to slam into your walls, because you will.

×   If the furniture is taller than the door frame, as is often the case with big couches, you need to stand the couch on an arm. Have a very strong person stand behind the couch, and tip it 45 degrees backward onto the person's arms. Someone in front of the door should pull the lower part of the couch through the door, while the person in back allows the couch to angle low enough to clear the top of the door frame.

×   Dragging things across a floor is asking for damage If you can't move your bed or dresser by yourself, wait until someone can help you, or ask the movers. You might need to pay extra, but your kitchen table is useless in the hallway.

×   Always keep a ball of twine around, which will be invaluable when the couch, bed, or La-Z-Boy starts opening while on the stairs.

A WORD ON PROFESSIONAL MOVERS

Professional movers are a godsend. They carry heavy things while you sit and gesture. However, they don't care about your walls or your new paint job and can cause quite a bit of damage. Feel free to watch carefully and warn them of impending collisions.

If you're concerned that a box or two might disappear, clearly number each box on three sides with a big permanent marker. In your new digs, you will be able to do a quick eye-scan of the boxes and ask for Box #14. Movers can sense who has nice stuff and who doesn't, and while you can't hide the obvious opulence of your new digs, it's in your best interest to appear like a pauper. Pack yourself and tape all your boxes closed, giving no indication of where the valuables lie. Writing "Fragile" on a box is a big hint of valuables within, and movers break fragiles anyway, so move breakables yourself. Tip well, offer water, and if you like your movers, request the same folks next time.

CHAPTER 3

HELP, IT'S DARK! ELECTRICITY AND LIGHTING

Wires! Volts! Electricity! Ah! Home electricity seems complicated only because it is behind walls. The hardware store doesn't help: poorly labeled wires and gadgets seem meant to confuse and to highlight the fear that if you mess up, something *really bad* could happen. Thus, you continue pretending that you don't really need to understand. But electrical outages happen all the time. Here is a three-page summary of everything you need to know about electricity in your living space:

HOW ELECTRICITY WORKS

Electricity, put simply, is the flow of electrons through a material. The tiny electrons move easily through some materials, like copper wire, and barely at all through other materials, like plastic and wood.

Materials that easily allow electron movement are called conductors. Copper wire is incredibly conductive, and is the main material in your household wires. Wires are wrapped in plastic or rubber coating because plastic and rubber are "insulators," which don't allow electron movement, and keep the electrical current moving along the copper wires—rather than through every nearby object, including you.

There are three main units used to measure the movement of electricity. (I'm telling you this because appliance labels use these units to tell you how much electricity an appliance uses.)

AMPS, or AMPERES, which measure the electron rate of flow.
VOLTS, which measure the electron pressure forcing the movement.
WATTS, which measure the electron power, or the amount of work that the electrons do.

Because some appliance boxes don't give you information in the units that you need, I will give you the formulas for calculating from one unit to another:

Volts = watts ÷ amps
Amps = volts ÷ ohms

Watts = volts × amps
Ohms = volts ÷ amps

Ohms are less useful to you, but they measure the resistance to electricity, and are used on packaging.

ARE ALL OUTLETS THE SAME?

To help standardize appliances, American electrical systems deliver electricity to your outlets at either 120 volts or 240 volts. So some of your home outlets are wired with a capability of handling 120 volts and others, 240 volts. Large appliances need 240 volts to run, while smaller appliances and lights need 120. This is why when you buy a deluxe entertainment center, you need to read its voltage label, which will tell you whether your 120-volt living room outlet has the proper capacity. This is also why you need to use converter kits when traveling abroad: the decision to use 120- and 240-volt systems was completely arbitrary, and many other countries made different decisions.

CIRCUIT WHAT?

In order for electricity to successfully power your light or toothbrush, its wires must travel in a complete circle, from the power source to an outlet and back again. This loop is called a circuit. If there is any break in the circuit, the electricity's flow is broken and the appliance you want to use will not work. An unexpected break in the loop is called a short circuit. Incidentally, your light switch, when you turn it off, is creating a break in the loop, thereby purposely creating a short circuit.

Your circuit box or fuse box—depending on the age of your living space—is the Mission Control of your electrical system. Mine was for many years named Mission Impossible. The box monitors the electrical supply from the outside powerlines and funnels that electricity toward individual circuits in your home. Each switch or fuse monitors one circuit and is designed to allow a maximum amount of electricity into that circuit. Each circuit controls one outlet or area of outlets, such as a bedroom. There are three kinds of circuits:

The difference among the circuits are in their wires. Much like the difference between a superhighway and a small back road, the wires in a 240-volt

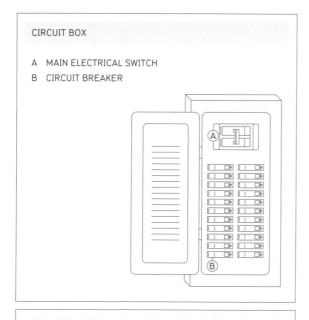

CIRCUIT BOX

A   MAIN ELECTRICAL SWITCH
B   CIRCUIT BREAKER

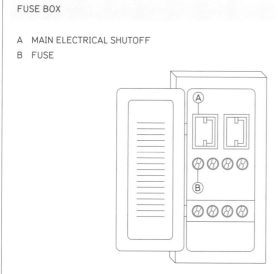

FUSE BOX

A   MAIN ELECTRICAL SHUTOFF
B   FUSE

PURPOSE	VOLTAGE	AMPERES
LIGHT CIRCUITS	120 VOLTS	15–50 AMPS
SMALL-APPLIANCE CIRCUITS	120 VOLTS	20 AMPS
INDIVIDUAL-APPLIANCE CIRCUITS	120 OR 140 VOLTS	25–50 AMPS

individual appliance circuit are much thicker than those in a 120-volt light circuit, and can handle a larger influx of speeding electrons.

For this reason, you need to know the wiring capability of various outlets in your living space. Otherwise, when you go to the store and come home with a 240-volt air conditioner, you won't know that all the outlets in your bedroom are 120-volt, and the big heavy air conditioner you just carried home will be useless. If you haven't yet followed the instructions in The Art of Labeling (page 18), ask a friend or expert to label your circuit or fuse box for you, so that you know exactly which switch controls each room. This will save you hours of staring at the panel in the dark with a flashlight.

Sometimes one circuit will demand more electricity than its wires can safely manage, usually because you turned on multiple appliances at once. Or else, there might be a sudden short circuit in an appliance or on a circuit itself. In response, your circuit switch will cut off the electrical flow to the circuit, or a piece of metal inside the fuse will melt, also stopping the flow of electricity. An overloaded circuit will "blow" a fuse or "trip" a circuit breaker. Thus the teenage lingo "Don't blow a fuse, man." You will know this happened because you will be plunged into darkness.

A blown fuse or tripped switch is not a "break" at all, but an automatic safety feature. For those of us who enjoy electronic equipment and don't pay attention while plugging it in, overloaded circuits are a regularity. More intelligent people evenly distribute appliances throughout their homes, preventing most tripped breakers.

OTHER ELECTRICITY TERMS THAT COME UP A LOT

GROUNDING This is not of much consequence to you, but you might hear it mentioned. Safe electrical systems are "grounded," which means the whole system is attached to wire leading to a metal rod in the ground near your house or building. This ensures that abnormal currents escape the system and enter the earth, rather than start a fire and/or electrocute you.

AC/DC It's not just a rock band. To further complicate things, there are two kinds of electrical currents, alternating current (AC) and direct current (DC). The difference is the direction of electron movement. In an AC current, which supplies households, the electrons change direction 120 times each second. In a DC current, which is used by batteries, the electrons move in only one direction. The decision to use AC currents for households was also somewhat arbitrary, and simply means that when using an electrical battery charger, the charger is converting the current from the outlet into DC. For your purposes, make sure that appliances you're going to plug in say "AC" on them.

TOOLS FOR TESTING ELECTRICITY

There are two tools for testing electrical flows:

VOLTAGE TESTER Voltage testers consist of a plastic shell a few inches long, attached to two wire probes. You simply place the probes in an outlet, and if a little light turns on, you know there is electricity flowing. It is electrical testing for beginners.

VOLT OHM METER An easy-to-use tool that tells you not only how much power is flowing at a receptacle but also whether an appliance is electrically sound or a battery has remaining power. This author is a major fan of the volt ohm meter, because it helps you quickly identify where problems lie. When you buy one, try an electronics store for more model options. Keep in mind that though home outlets are wired at 120 and 240 volts, they are rarely *exactly* 120 or 240 volts. Readings of 123 or 232 volts are normal, particularly if you bought a cheap volt ohm meter.

When using the voltage tester or volt ohm meter, you are harnessing powerful electrical flows into a tool in your hands. If you are a novice, a voltage tester is a much safer tool—you have to work *hard* to mess up a voltage tester—but it won't give you numerical readings. With either device, never touch the metal parts of the probe directly while in use; instead hold the insulated grips. Also, make sure that your volt ohm meter is set to the appropriate unit: if you want to test voltage but set the meter to ohms, the meter will break. You can only test ohms on a circuit that is not attached to electricity. Models differ, so follow accompanying instructions carefully.

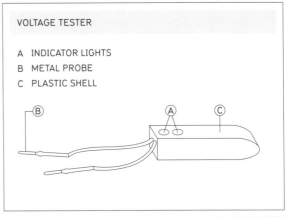

VOLTAGE TESTER

A INDICATOR LIGHTS
B METAL PROBE
C PLASTIC SHELL

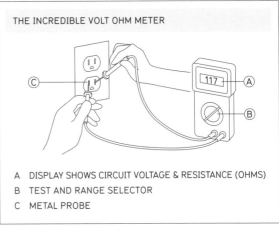

THE INCREDIBLE VOLT OHM METER

A DISPLAY SHOWS CIRCUIT VOLTAGE & RESISTANCE (OHMS)
B TEST AND RANGE SELECTOR
C METAL PROBE

MAPPING YOUR CIRCUITS

If you're like most people, you probably have no idea which outlets in your home are on which circuits, nor the wiring capability of each circuit. This information will become pivotal during the Dog Days of Summer when you are sweating in front of the air-conditioner aisle at the store, wondering which size appliance your outlets can handle. And, if you plug in the air conditioner and have a short circuit, you will be in the dark—both literally and figuratively. So we will learn how to map the wiring of your home.

TIP

If you're not sure where some of your outlets are—a common problem if much of your wall space is covered by heavy furniture—be aware that the National Electrical Code requires one receptacle for every 12 feet of wall space, one on any wall longer than 2 feet, and one within 6 feet of each door. Use these rules to deduce where the nearest outlets must be, not forgetting about floor outlets that might be hidden by rugs. As you might suspect, the mapping process is much faster if you begin with a general idea of your circuit layout.

HOME ELECTRICAL CIRCUIT MAP

Now you have a complete map of the wiring capability of your entire living space and may purchase and plug in appliances with ease.

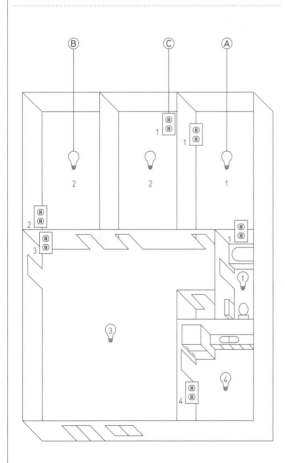

A   EACH NUMBER IS ONE ELECTRICAL CIRCUIT
B   LIGHT FIXTURE
C   OUTLET

COMMON ELECTRICITY TESTS

Testing receptacles: does my outlet work?

SOLUTION Make sure you set the volt ohm meter for "AC" current and "voltage." Place each probe in a vertical outlet slot, and the number on the screen will tell you the voltage of the outlet. If the number is much lower than 120 or 240 (such as 54 or 196), then you might have a low-voltage problem on the circuit. Turn off the circuit and call an electrician.

Testing appliances: does this appliance work?

SOLUTION If you suspect that there might be a short circuit within an appliance, unplug the appliance and turn its power switch to "On." Set the volt ohm meter to "Ohms." Place a volt ohm meter probe on each of the flat plug prongs. If the number on the screen is 0 or near 0, that means that the appliance circuit is okay, because ohms measure resistance. If the reading is a high number, that means that there is a great amount of resistance for electricity—i.e., a short circuit within the appliance.

Testing a circuit: I just plugged in a huge appliance.

SOLUTION Perform this test when you want to know whether a circuit is doing okay with a new appliance, such as an air conditioner or portable heater. First, do the basic receptacle voltage test above and jot down the voltage reading. Then, plug in the new appliance and turn it on. Holding onto the insulated grips, place the probes into the unused socket. If the voltage reading stays the same, the appliance is fine. If the voltage reading drops by more than a few volts, the circuit is quite overwhelmed by the appliance and will eventually short-circuit. You need to put the appliance on a different circuit or unplug other appliances on that circuit.

Testing battery power: are these batteries dead?

SOLUTION Set the volt ohm meter to "DC" voltage. Touch the red probe to the (+) side of the battery, and the black probe to the (−) side of the battery. The number should be relatively close to the voltage rating on the package of the battery; if the reading is more than 30 percent off, replace the battery.

MAPPING YOUR ELECTRICAL CIRCUITS

YOU NEED

- × Paper
- × Pencil
- × Voltage tester or small lamp or night light
- × Volt ohm meter (if you want the voltage of each outlet)
- × Permanent marker

STEPS

1 Draw a bird's-eye view of your apartment or house, showing rectangles for each room, and X marks for each outlet or light fixture. If you live on more than one floor, draw separate pictures for each story. This is not the time to play Picasso.

2 Turn off any expensive, important, or sensitive electrical equipment, such as computers.

3 Go to your fuse box or circuit box. Unscrew one fuse, or flip one circuit to "Off." This means that all the outlets on that circuit won't work.

4 Go around from outlet to outlet with your voltage tester or a small lamp and plug it in. For every outlet that doesn't work, mark it as "A" on your map. Don't forget to check ceiling light fixtures by trying to turn them on.

5 Return to your control panel and rescrew the fuse or flip the switch back to "On."

6 Repeat Steps 2 through 5 for each circuit, labeling the next circuits B, C, D, etc. You now have a full map of every circuit in your living space.

7 Return to your fuse box and clearly label each fuse or switch with the letter for each circuit, in a permanent marker alongside each switch and fuse. Tape a copy of the map next to the control panel.

8 If you are ambitious and want to know the voltage of each circuit, go to each outlet with a volt ohm meter. Place each of the meter's probes into the outlet holes, and the meter will give you a number—128 or 235 or 115, for example.

9 Mark each circuit 120v or 240v accordingly on your map. You don't need to bother testing the outlets of major appliances such as washing machines or your hot water heater—those are 240-volt outlets.

CIRCUIT POINTERS

Some simple guidelines will help you keep your electrical system healthy.

× As a general rule, appliances that involve temperature—air conditioners, hair dryers, water heaters, etc.—require the most concentrated electricity and are the most taxing on your circuit system—and your electricity bill. This is why teenage girls are known for blowing fuses by plugging in a hair dryer, a curling iron, and a crimper alongside a TV, a boom box, and a cordless phone. A blown fuse is an electrical system's way of protecting you (and teenagers) from burning down residences.

× As a general rule, older rooms that still have two-prong outlets indicate a lower wiring capability, usually 120 volts and 15 amps.

× People often have many items plugged in to one outlet for years, and are suddenly surprised to overload a circuit. Simply plugging in items won't trip a breaker; turning on all of them at once will.

× If you suspect an electrical wiring problem, unplug any valuable items, such as computers or stereos, before trying to fix it. You can't hurt it if it's not plugged in.

× A major sign of impending electrical doom is heat: heat around a receptacle or switch of any kind, around wires, or undue heat from an appliance. If this is the case, turn off the electrical circuit and call an electrician or turn off the appliance and have it fixed.

ELECTRICITY-REPAIR SAFETY

Any time you are working with electricity, you need to:

× Turn off the power to the circuit, and double-check that you have by plugging in a lamp or using a voltage tester. If you are not sure which circuit breaker or fuse to switch off, temporarily turn off all power with the fuse box or circuit box main electrical shutoff.

× Use only tools with insulated handles—the rubber coating protects you from shocks.

× If you're having major electrical problems and are near a pipe, don't touch it. Electrical systems usually use a long metal pipe (often the cold water pipe) already in place to provide "grounding" for the system. You probably don't know which pipe is being used, and you don't want to find out.

× If you're exposed to an electrical short, you won't be able to let go. Push yourself or the person being electrocuted away with anything that doesn't conduct electricity—a rag, a board, anything.

× To prevent inadvertent electrocution, experts recommend standing on a wooden plank while working with a control panel, and using only one hand while changing fuses, leaving the other hand in a pocket or behind your back. (You need two hands to complete the electrical circuit.) Never use metal, such as a coin, to help insert a fuse. If you are concerned about inserting a new fuse, err on the side of safety and turn off the main power switch for your fuse box.

× Keep water—condensation on pipes, water lines, and puddles—far away from any electrical repair.

× Wear rubber boots. They're not just a fashion statement. Rubber boots prevent you from potentially transmitting electricity if you accidentally touch a live wire.

× Avoid using aluminum ladders, which are the equivalent of standing on a lightning rod.

 TIP

One more reason to always call a professional for all electrical troubles: if a fire starts after you tried to repair a problem, your fire and home insurance can refuse to cover the damages. The professional is cheap by comparison.

FIXING BLOWN FUSES AND TRIPPED CIRCUITS

A blown fuse or a tripped circuit is the most frequent living-space issue you will ever encounter, so we will spend a few extra pages teaching you how to respond.

HOW DO I KNOW I TRIPPED A CIRCUIT OR BLEW A FUSE?

If you lose electricity directly after plugging in or turning on an appliance, chances are that you tripped a circuit or blew a fuse. Another sign is that you still have power in other sections of your living space, but everything on the same electrical circuit has no power.

 TIP

If you suspect that a larger power outage may be to blame, call the electric company to ask about local power disturbances before you begin repairing.

If a circuit breaker trips multiple times, you may have a problem with one appliance. This is your electrical system's way of telling you that the electricity isn't flowing back from the appliance correctly. You could test a suspect appliance with a volt ohm meter (see page 84), or, if you're not sure which appliance is to blame:

1 Unplug every item on that circuit.

2 Flip the circuit back on.

3 One-by-one, plug in each power cord individually and turn on the power. After a few seconds, turn off the power. If a circuit blows with one item, you know you have a faulty appliance.

If the circuit continues to trip repeatedly, turn off all power in that area and call an electrician immediately.

YOU NEED

× Flashlight
× Box of new fuses (if you have a fuse box)

STEPS

1 Turn off and unplug everything in the area that the circuit controls. If you are not sure which appliances are on the circuit and which aren't, unplug everything in the area, just to be safe.

2 Go to your circuit or fuse box and find the troubled fuse or circuit. A tripped circuit will look like a light switch out of line with all the other switches; a blown fuse will be a small round ball in a different color than all the other balls. Most blown fuses are gray in color, but not always.

3 Reset the circuit or replace the fuse. To reset a circuit, flip the circuit switch back to "On." To replace a fuse, unscrew the discolored fuse and screw in a new one. Always keep a flashlight and a box of new fuses (the same size as your old fuses) stored next to your fuse box.

4 If you can't locate the blown fuse or tripped circuit, electricity may have been cut off by a "secondary panel," which is a separate minipanel located near the main panel. If this is the case, find the appropriate fuse or circuit on the minipanel and repeat Step 3.

5 Test the circuit. Return to the circuit area, and plug in a small lamp to test your handiwork.

PLUGS AND WIRES

After years of being plugged in, unplugged, and replugged, plugs stop working—and make you think that you need a new appliance. Remember that lamp with the old cord that you threw out last year? A simple plug replacement probably would've done the trick. Replace a plug that has cracking around its protective shell, loose prongs, or any signs of burning. To replace, cut off the old plug, purchase a new plug, and thread the appliance's electrical wires into the new plug. Note that plug models vary, and each will come with its own instructions.

REPLACING THREE-PRONG PLUGS

To replace three-prong plugs, the directions are the same as for Replacing Two-Prong Plugs, except that you will need to strip a bit more insulation off the wires—almost an inch—and there are three wires instead of two. Wires are standard colored, usually white, green, and black. The screws inside the plug center will be gold, silver, and green. Wrap the white wire around the silver screw head, the green wire around the green screw head, and the black wire around the gold screw head. If your wires are different colors, a quick call to a local electronics store should help alleviate your confusion.

THE WONDERS OF CONTACT CLEANER

No, we're not talking about saline solution.

Older electrical or battery-powered appliances can often appear to be broken, when really one of the electrical contacts has simply corroded and power cannot get through. One of the best examples is the Walkman that you've taken running every day, rain or shine, for five years, or the electric toothbrush that no longer charges in its electrical charger. Look at the Walkman's battery connection, and note the extreme rust and corrosion. Look at the toothbrush charger's surface. It is probably covered with bathroom grime.

To fix these and similar problems, purchase some electrical contact cleaner, which comes in an aerosol can with a thin nozzle attached. Turn off the appliance and unplug it or remove the batteries. Conservatively spray the contact cleaner wherever you suspect that the electricity isn't getting through, such as the backs of entertainment consoles, where dust can dirty electrical connections. Wipe off any moisture and let the surface dry for an hour before using. Contact cleaner cannot bring electrical components back from the dead—badly corroded parts need to be replaced—but it can clean things up. When in doubt, if opening up an appliance, follow the electrical wires to places they meet with conductive metals and make sure all areas of contact are clear and clean.

PROTECTING AGAINST THOSE SURGES

You're probably familiar with surge protectors, aka power strips. Not only are they convenient (one tiny plug becomes eight!), but they also protect valuable appliances from electrical surges due to power outages. For example, if you lose power during a storm, your beloved computer plugged directly into a wall will fry itself when power resumes in a flood of electricity.

Contrary to popular opinion, a maze of power strips is indeed a fire hazard. You will have fun explaining yourself to the fire chief: "One plug became forty-two plugs! It was amazing! . . . And then there was a fire." In order to maintain your reputation as an intelligent individual, limit yourself to one strip per outlet.

HIDING VISIBLE WIRES

Ideally, wires are hidden behind walls. However, in the World of Nonrepair Folk, people typically stretch extremely long cords from one room to another, such as snaking a living room Internet cord up a flight of stairs and down a hallway into an office. In addition to being a visual atrocity, these wires are a fire hazard, as stepped-on and pulled-on wire insulation can erode.

The intelligent response is to install so-called raceways, the white plastic rectangular tubes that neatly and safely carry wires along a wall. Raceways have two parts: a flat base piece that you attach along your wall, and a three-sided plastic cover that you snap onto the base. They come in long strips that you cut to the size you need.

See illustration on page 91.

YOU NEED

- × New plug (see Step 1)
- × Multipurpose wire tool or very good scissors
- × Small screwdriver (depending on plug model)

STEPS

1 Turn off and unplug the appliance or light. Look at the plug you're replacing. How many prongs are there? Are the 2 flat prongs the same size or different? If they are different, the plug is "polarized," and you need to buy a polarized plug with the same number of prongs and prong sizing.

2 Holding the *unplugged* cord in your hand, cut through the cord just before the plug with a multipurpose wire tool or very sharp scissors. Take the plug with you to the electronics or supply store and purchase a new plug.

3 Detach the outer shell of your new plug. Depending on the model, you will either be able to pull the center right out, or you will have to unscrew the little screws holding the plug center in place with a small screwdriver.

4 Identify the 2 main wires inside the cut cord. You want to remove the outer insulation from about ½ inch of both cords, which is called "stripping." There is a wire-stripper tool, but you can usually do this with your fingers—just pull off the rubber or plastic coating until you have ½ inch of two bare wires.

5 Thread the stripped wires through the bottom of the plug protective shell.

6 Tie the stripped wires in an underwriter's knot with insulated wire, as shown, and pull it just tight enough that the knot rests cleanly between the prongs. The knot prevents a hard cord tug from jerking the wires out of the plug (and also explains why you're not supposed to do hard cord tugs).

7 Look at the plug center. You will see the heads of 2 screws, called terminal screws, somewhere on the plug center—location differs by model. Take one of the stripped wires and thread it around a terminal screw, twisting it so that it wraps around the screw head. Some plugs have a little indentation next to the terminal screw, meant for the wire to be wrapped around.

8 Repeat with the second wire.

9 Reinsert the plug center into its protective shell and attach screws with a screwdriver if necessary.

10 Carefully test your new light or appliance.

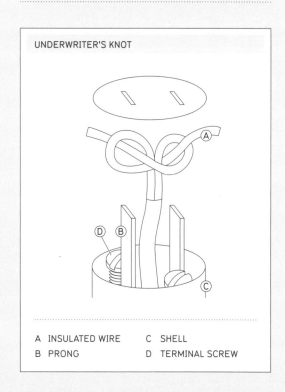

UNDERWRITER'S KNOT

| A | INSULATED WIRE | C | SHELL |
| B | PRONG | D | TERMINAL SCREW |

WIRE RACEWAY SYSTEM

Ⓓ

Ⓒ

Ⓑ

Ⓐ

A   NEATLY CONCEALED WIRES
B   PLASTIC RACEWAY COVER
C   RACEWAY BASE
D   WALL

INSTALLING ATTRACTIVE RACEWAY SYSTEMS

YOU NEED

- × Measuring tape
- × New raceways
- × Raceway screws and/or nails
- × Good scissors
- × Carpenter's level (optional but good)
- × Pencil
- × Hammer (or power drill and safety goggles for masonry wall)

STEPS

1   Measure the distance that the wires travel along your walls. Add a few feet to be safe.

2   Go to a supply store to purchase the requisite length of raceways and accompanying screws or nails. Each package has its own installation instructions, but generally you need to do the following:

3   Cut the raceway base and cover pieces to match the length of your walls.

4   Use a carpenter's level to mark a straight line where you would like to attach the base. Most people put raceways along the bottom of the wall for visual purposes, but anywhere is fine.

5   Place a nail or screw through the proper nail hole in the base, and gently nail the base into your wall with a hammer, or screw the bases onto your wall with a power drill. (Most raceways are lightweight enough that you don't need to bother finding the vertical wall studs on a wood-frame wall, but follow the directions on the package.)

6   Place the wires into the base and snap on the plastic covers.

LIGHTS AND LIGHT REPAIRS

Lighting is associated with electricity only because plunging into darkness typically indicates an electrical problem. "Help, it's dark!" = short circuit. And everyone knows to avoid unwanted darkness. However, lights are prone to glitches other than mass power outages, and there are many tricks to avoiding faulty lights, to lowering electricity bills, and to achieving superior room lighting.

ILLUMINATION: HOW DO LIGHTS WORK?

INCANDESCENT LIGHTS Filament is the thin wire that you see light up inside a lightbulb. Incandescent bulbs consist of a glass chamber of air around a piece of filament wire, which is connected to metal wire on either side. When the electricity goes through the wire into the filament, the filament heats up and its atoms light up. Over time, the atoms get so hot that they detach from the filament, and float up to the top of the glass, blackening the bulb. Eventually, so many atoms leave the filament that it no longer works.

HALOGEN LIGHTS Halogen lights are just like incandescent lights, but better. When the atoms get old and detach from the filament, the gases inside the bulb react with the atom so that it floats around for a while, and then reattaches to the filament. The filament will eventually develop holes and stop working, but lasts three times longer. The filament is also hotter, creating a brighter light.

FLUORESCENT LIGHTS There is a reason that department stores insist on using fluorescent lights in dressing rooms, despite their tendency to turn your mirror image into a human mound of cellulite. Fluorescent lights use five times less electricity than incandescent bulbs. A typical 100-watt incandescent bulb costs around $7.20 to run twelve hours a day for a month, while an equally bright 20-watt fluorescent bulb costs just $1.08. (Yes, that's a savings of $73.44 per year per light, which, in the world of department stores, is millions.)

Fluorescent tubes contain a mixture of chemical gases. When you turn on the light, an electrical current is sent directly into the tube, which charges the gases. This creates a glow. The inside of the tube is coated with phosphor, which magnifies the light. After the initial surge of current, the light drops its voltage intake to just enough to maintain the glow.

SHOPPING FOR LIGHTBULBS

Lightbulb packages contain a mind-numbing array of numerical information. Bulbs are rated fundamentally in watts, which is the amount of energy that the bulb uses. Packaging also uses lumens, a unit that measures brightness, as well as hours, how many hours the bulb should last for. To save yourself time, keep bulb packaging so next time you can quickly pick the same brand.

To simplify the process, you have four main concerns to weigh: fire safety, energy usage, light output, and initial cost.

FIRE SAFETY Many light fixtures say something like "To reduce the risk of fire, use MAX 60 watts, Type A." Type A means the typical bulb shape you know. If your light fixture doesn't have a warning, replace it with the same wattage as the current bulb. Never go over 100 watts on a normal fixture; 60 watts is usually safe. Desk lamps trap much more heat than table lamps, so be conservative. A burning-hot bulb means that you need to use a lower wattage bulb.

ENERGY USAGE You can choose a 20-watt, 40-watt, 60-watt, or 100-watt bulb. A 20-watt bulb is often too dim, while 40- to 60-watt bulbs are standard, though maybe not enough for tired eyes in a dark room. The exception is fluorescent lights, for which 20- to 40-watt bulbs are plenty. While one bulb won't devastate your electric bill, remember that you use ten to twelve bulbs regularly. Consult the electricity usage chart on page 96 and do the math.

LIGHT OUTPUT Once you've chosen your wattage, double-check that the lumens are reasonable from brand to brand. Bulbs can vary enormously.

INITIAL COST Like every other product, there is a big price range for bulbs. The easiest way to decide whether you're getting ripped off is to check the expected hours of bulb life, and compare that to the cost, remembering that multipacks are not always cheaper per bulb. The exception is for lights that you hate changing, like the super-tall ceiling light. In that case, buy the one that will last the longest.

VARIATIONS Lights also come in three-way varieties for lamps, with dim, medium, and bright settings, as well as in softer tones and colors. Children are big fans of colored lights, while softer lights tend to flatter adults by hiding blemishes and giving the impression of a natural glow.

TIP

Low-Voltage Kits *Though household systems work on 120- or 240-volt wiring, many electrical devices need fewer than 120 volts to work. With this in mind, you can purchase a low-voltage kit and have it installed by a friend or professional. Low-voltage circuits are common on doorbells, indoor track lighting, and some outdoor lights, which need only 10 to 12 volts. Over the years, you'll save a bundle.*

LIGHTING TROUBLESHOOTING

Your light won't turn on. It worked yesterday, but today, nothing. Lamps and lights are somewhat simplistic in their structure, and therefore easy to fix. Before tinkering, always *turn off and unplug a light*, or *turn off power* to a ceiling fixture's electrical circuit.

INCANDESCENT TROUBLES

Most incandescent troubles involve a lightbulb that you simply tighten or replace. Before repairing, try a new bulb.

On light fixtures, the most common problem is wiring that is no longer touching the "terminal heads," which look like screw heads with wire curled around them. The terminal heads are inside the socket, which is the cylindrical metal piece that you screw the lightbulb into. If bare electrical wires aren't directly touching the screw heads, the light can't work.

Models vary, but *turn off power to the room* at your circuit or fuse box, unscrew the decorative fixture covering, and remove the lightbulb. Loosen the

screws attaching the socket to the ceiling and it will come off with a bunch of wires in tow. Look inside, and make sure that each terminal head has a wire properly wrapped around it, comparing terminal heads with each other. Signs of damage include frayed wires, cracked insulation, or burn marks. If these exist, stop using the fixture and have it replaced.

On a broken lamp, check that the electrical outlet is still working by plugging in another light or appliance. There are a limited number of potential lamp defects. Chances are, you're dealing with a defective lamp plug, an old power cord, or a bad on/off switch. If the plug looks old or damaged, follow the instructions under Plugs and Wires (page 89). For a defective switch—often signaled by a visibly damaged switch or a switch that spins freely without catching—remove the lamp shade, take out the lightbulb, and remove the metal shell around the socket by pulling upward. Loosen the screws attached to the lamp socket and switch with a screwdriver. Pull off the socket and switch (they're attached). You'll know you've removed it if you're holding the switch in your hand, wires in tow, and only a metal base with wires is left on the lamp. Uncurl any wires attached to the inside of the socket. Bring the socket and switch to the store to be replaced, then reassemble.

FLUORESCENT TROUBLES

Fluorescent bulbs don't just stop working the way that incandescent bulbs do. Instead, they partially light or flicker madly for hours on end, leading you to think that something is horribly wrong and you need to replace the whole light fixture. Instead, turn off the light and look at the tube. Gently wiggle it out of its socket. If there are black circles on either side of the tube, it needs to be replaced. *Handle the tube carefully*, as dropped tubes have been known to explode.

If your light won't turn on at all, chances are that the trouble lies with the starter or the ballast. Older models have a "starter," which is the cylindrical knob on one end of the fixture that you probably think is a button. Move it around to make sure that it's in contact with the tube. If that doesn't work, turn off power to the light and remove the starter by turning it a quarter turn counterclockwise. Bring it to the store and replace.

If your fluorescent light doesn't have a starter and the rest of the tube and fixture look okay—no corrosion or loose parts—the problem is probably the ballast, the big gray or black box with tubes coming out of it that's hidden behind the tube (and sometimes a protective plastic cover that you need to pop off). That familiar humming sound is often caused by a bad ballast. You either need to replace the ballast or replace the whole fixture, which is sometimes cheaper and/or easier.

TIP

Fluorescent lights are not made to be constantly turned on and off, which greatly decreases their life span. In fact, given the surge of energy required to initially light a fluorescent bulb, it is sometimes cheaper to leave them on for a couple of hours, rather than turn them on and off.

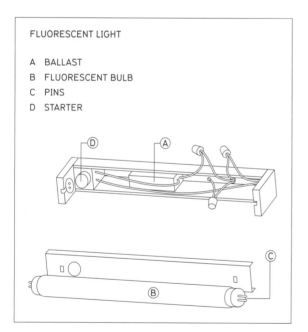

FLUORESCENT LIGHT

A   BALLAST
B   FLUORESCENT BULB
C   PINS
D   STARTER

THE POTATO TRICK: REMOVING BROKEN BULBS FROM FIXTURES

So something went wrong and now there's jagged glass sticking out of your light fixture. Don't throw out the light.

YOU NEED

×   1 raw potato

STEPS

1   If you're working on a ceiling fixture, turn off the electrical circuit. For a lamp, turn it off and unplug it.

2   Cut your raw potato in half.

3   Press the cut side of your potato right into the broken glass, toward the socket. On a ceiling lamp, stand slightly to the side, in case a piece of glass falls.

4   Turn the potato to the left to unscrew the bulb.

5   Safely throw out both the potato and the embedded bulb.

6   Replace the bulb.

HOW TO CHANGE A REFRIGERATOR OR OVEN LIGHTBULB

Changing the little bulb that goes on when the door opens may be the easiest repair in this book. Before you begin, *turn off power* to your refrigerator or stove by shutting off power to the whole circuit from your electrical control panel or, for the refrigerator, by unplugging it. While many bulbs have been successfully changed with the power on, in a dirty oven or refrigerator, a tug in the wrong direction can cause the fixture behind the light to come out, accidentally exposing live wires.

MY LIGHTING ISN'T LUMINOUS: SUGGESTIONS FOR LIGHTING

As you know, lighting can set the mood for a room. Before you attack your walls with a brighter color paint (which will also help), here are a few simple tricks to turn a room that eats light into a bright, happy place.

×   A well-placed horizontal mirror on a wall can reflect light threefold around a room. Strategically place the mirror with both window light and night-time fixture light in mind. You should not be able to see the light directly when looking in the mirror.
×   The instinct to fix all lighting problems with one very strong overhead light is often misconceived. Overhead light is very harsh, and tends to form shadows on faces and floors. Lights on walls or furniture are often more effective.
×   "Indirect lighting" is the technical term for light meant to highlight one part of a room, such as a nice decoration or painting, or lights hidden under a shelf to illuminate a working area.
×   Nothing accentuates flaws like harsh, direct lighting. If either you or your room is feeling shabby, a lower-light solution may fix the problem.
×   Lights for bedside tables or seats should be placed below seated eye level, so that they don't shine directly in the eyes. Use higher wattage bulbs than for overhead lights, but use "soft" bulbs, so that the light doesn't reflect off the page.
×   If you feel like you're living in a shadow, you're probably frequently in front of your light source. Install another light on the side of the shadow. Desk lights should be placed in front of you.

CHANGING AN OVEN OR REFRIGERATOR LIGHTBULB

YOU NEED

×   Flathead screwdriver
×   Rubber gloves or rubber jar opener
×   New lightbulb

STEPS

1   Locate the bulb in the refrigerator, and if there is a protective case, remove it. Some plastic cases slide or snap out, while glass cases protected by a piece of wire need the wire pulled off. Some cases are held in place by obvious screws, which you loosen with a flathead screwdriver.

2   Unscrew the lightbulb. This may not be as easy as it sounds if your refrigerator is incredibly dirty. Stove bulbs can become caked with grease, so rubber gloves or a rubber jar opener might be helpful. Don't break the bulb by accident.

3   Replace the lightbulb with a bulb of the same wattage. Usually this is 10 watts; if you're not sure, wait until you remove the bulb and bring it with you to the store, or find the owner's manual.

4   Screw in the new bulb and reattach the protective case.

ELECTRICITY USAGE CHART

APPLIANCE	WATTAGE (WATTS)	TYPICAL HOURS PER MONTH (HRS)	TYPICAL KWH PER MONTH (KWH)	AVERAGE COST PER HOUR ($)	AVERAGE COST PER MONTH ($)	AVERAGE COST PER YEAR ($)
KITCHEN APPLIANCES						
Blender	386	3.2	1.24	0.07	0.21	2.52
Coffemaker, brewing	1,400	5.0	7.20	0.24	1.22	14.64
Coffeemaker, warning	85	240.0	20.40	0.02	3.47	41.64
Freezer, 15 ft³	341	262.0	99.60	0.06	16.90	202.80
Freezer, 15 ft³, frostless	440	334.0	147.00	0.07	25.00	300.00
Garbage disposal	445	3.0	1.35	0.08	0.23	2.76
Microwave	1,500	11.0	16.50	0.26	2.80	33.60
Oven, baking	2,833	8.0	22.70	0.48	2.86	46.32
Oven, broiling	2,900	6.0	14.70	0.42	2.50	30.00
Refrigerator/ Freezer, 15 ft³	326	291.0	94.90	0.06	16.10	193.20
Refrigerator/ Freezer, 15 ft³, frostless	615	248.0	152.50	0.10	26.90	322.80
Stove, 6 inch burner	1,400	15.0	7.90	0.09	1.35	16.20
Stove, 8 inch burner	2,600	15.0	14.10	0.16	2.40	28.80
Toaster	1,146	3.0	3.40	0.19	0.58	6.96
Toaster oven	1,500	2.0	3.0	0.25	0.51	6.12
Waffle Iron	1,161	1.6	1.90	0.20	0.32	3.84
AROUND THE HOUSE						
Clock	2	720.0	1.44	0.0003	0.25	3.00
Dishwasher	1,200	25.0	30.00	0.20	5.10	61.20
Dryer	4,856	17.0	83.00	0.83	14.11	169.32
Fluorescent light (20w)	20	150.0	3.00	0.003	0.51	6.12
Fluorescent light (40w)	20	150.0	6.00	0.007	1.02	12.24
Incandescent light	100	150.0	15.00	0.02	2.55	30.60
Iron	1,100	5.0	5.50	0.19	0.94	11.28
Vacuum Cleaner	630	3.0	1.90	0.11	0.32	3.84
Washing machine	512	10.0	5.12	0.90	0.87	10.44
Water heater	4,500	35.0	157.50	0.77	26.80	321.60

TOTAL PER YEAR: $1,040.04*

OTHER ENERGY-SAVING TIPS

× Hot water is a double whammy, costing you on both your water and electricity bills. When washing your dishes, hands, or face, use a sink stopper to catch hot water and turn off the flow. Install a low-volume showerhead and forgo baths.

× A microwave uses about half the electricity or gas equivalent of a stove per minute, and it cooks faster. If you must go gourmet, use proper-size pans and keep them covered.

× Room temperature can be an expensive proposition to maintain. During the summer, keep the temperature as warm as is comfortable before allowing an air conditioner to cut in. During the winter, set your thermostat at 65 degrees.

× As a writer, I am pained to point out that roommates who work at home or have excessive downtime are expensive. You will inevitably end up splitting monthly utility bills, thereby footing the bill for Diana's daily thirty-minute showers, Arthur's endless hours of television and video game lounging, Becky's gourmet cooking fests, and the eight lights all three leave on through these activities.

I'M POOR: LOW ENERGY BILL TIPS

As you well know, electricity usage is directly related to how much money you shell out to the electric company. Most people have no idea how much each of their appliances costs them every month. To remedy this, here is a chart with common appliances and monthly rates. Reference this chart before purchasing new appliances—for example, the extra freezer that many families keep in a garage can cost up to $300 per year in electric bills. And you are now justified in kicking slowpokes out of the shower: a couple of people taking long daily showers can run an extra $200 per year.

* USING SMALLEST REFRIGERATOR OPTION, AND 8-INCH STOVE BURNER / THIS CHART IS BASED ON NEW YORK CITY ELECTRICITY PRICES OF $0.17/KWH. LOOK ON YOUR ELECTRIC BILL; IT WILL TELL YOU THE COST PER KWH IN YOUR TOWNSHIP. RATES CAN CHANGE FROM SUMMER TO WINTER.

CHAPTER 4

HELP, IT'S NOT WORKING! APPLIANCES

HOW TO REPAIR APPLIANCES

Appliances can break in two ways: electrically or mechanically. Mechanical breaks usually involve only one part or connection, and are more obvious—pieces that don't move as they're supposed to, very loud grinding noises, et cetera. Electrical troubles show themselves in the form of appliances that are short circuiting or won't turn on altogether. For the latter, please see Chapter 3, Help, It's Dark! Electricity and Lighting.

As a general rule of thumb, bigger appliances are easier and cheaper to fix, while small appliances are more complex to fix and cheaper to replace. Broken digital clocks most always need to be replaced.

While staring blankly at a broken appliance, remember that appliances are nothing more than a bunch of parts stuck together, any of which can be removed and replaced. Broken appliances often have only one damaged component, usually a small plastic piece, and it is well worth it to fix it yourself if you don't have a warranty or long ago lost the receipt. Handy types like futzing around with this stuff, so friends are also a viable option.

If you have a landlord, he or she will theoretically take care of all living space repairs: the walls, plumbing, electricity. Depending on where you live, some large appliances may also fall under landlord domain. But if your personal air conditioner or dehumidifier breaks, you're on your own. Frankly, unless your breaks are belligerently loud, the landlord doesn't care. (His or her feelings are similar toward your personal life.)

In Apartment Land, with the heavy work taken care of, it's the little things that become bothersome—the air conditioner that makes funny noises, the refrigerator that leaks, the microwave with food permanently melted on. It's all functional, sort of, and yet you have no idea how to fix it without buying a new one.

One of the major tragedies of the Western world is that small appliances are so darn expensive to fix. Electronics and department stores charge top dollar from the moment the repairperson picks up a tool. It is usually cheaper to buy new than fix old, resulting in thousands of barely broken appliances filling local landfills. In this chapter we will talk about easy solutions for common problems you have to deal with yourself: basic appliances, such as refrigerators and microwaves, as well as the mystical, magical world of humidifiers and dehumidifiers.

It should be noted that in some states, landlords are required to deal with some of the issues discussed in this chapter. However, regulations vary by location, so contact your local government for a list of tenant's rights and a brochure on your legal obligations under a lease. As a general rule, your personal belongings will always be your own responsibility.

A WORD ON MANUALS

Contrary to popular opinion, the manual that came with your appliance is not window dressing, packaging, or recycling. It's important, explaining the appliance and who to call for help. I suggest designating one drawer as Manual Dumping Ground, a collection that should also include receipts and warranty information. Before you start tinkering, read to make sure you can't get the company to do the repair for free.

HOW DO MOTORS WORK?

All appliances have motors. Despite this, few people know how they work. The center of the motor is called the "rotor," which is magnetized metal attached to an outside shaft. Electrical wires are all around the rotor. When electricity pumps through the wires, a constantly changing magnetic field around the wires is created, causing the rotor to spin in an effort to make its north-south ends align with the shifting magnetic field of the wire.

The energy generated from the spinning rotor is used to power the appliance. A fan motor is the most direct application of a motor: the spinning arms of the fan are attached to a shaft that is directly attached to the rotor.

Motors seem confusing only because they are hidden by a cover. Motor repairs are complex, and will usually require a handy type, but you should understand the concept.

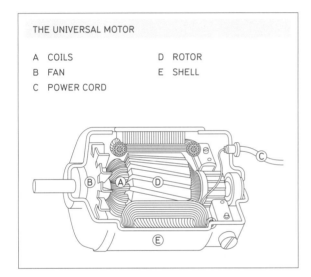

THE UNIVERSAL MOTOR

A COILS   D ROTOR
B FAN   E SHELL
C POWER CORD

FOUR FABULOUS REPAIR STEPS

× Appliances usually have power cords, so always disconnect the appliance before working on it.
× Keep loose clothing, long hair, fingers, and jewelry far away from moving parts—small motors can be surprisingly strong!
× Set up a clean counter or floor space and lay down a mat, blanket, or piece of plastic to prevent greasy part stains. Lay out your tools next to you.
× As you open your appliance, at each layer, spend a minute *looking* at the parts to see how they work. Understanding what moves what will be invaluable, and once you've fixed a couple of appliances, you'll begin to realize that they're all the same.

TOOLING AROUND: APPLIANCE TOOLS

If you decide that you need to open up an appliance, your first step is to figure out how to do that. Manufacturers are experts at hiding the entries to appliances: look for plastic caps, screws hidden behind dials, labels covering screws, or plastic parts that can be pried to show hidden tabs. Hopefully your basic two screwdrivers will get you in, but if not, there are three useful tools you might have to run out and purchase in the correct size to help you:

NUT DRIVER A hollow-ended tool, a nut driver loosens a variety of nuts, bolts, and six-sided screws. The trouble comes in happening to own the perfect size for the nut at hand. If you have a power drill, buy a "nut driver kit," which contains a variety of nut driver bits to put on the end of your drill.

HEX KEY Also known as Allen wrenches, a hex key turns a variety of hexagon-shaped set screws. You place the short end of the key in the screw's indentation and turn.

TORX DRIVER Like a screwdriver with a star-shaped tip, a torx driver is necessary for removing those tiny screws with a star-shaped indentation.

The other useful appliance supply is *lubricant*, which can quickly solve all matters of grinding appliance parts and gears. If noises indicate that a moving part is scraping against another part, often the fix is as simple as pulling off the lid and adding a bit of lubricant to the parts in question. As a general rule, all metal appliance parts should never be bone dry, so while you are tinkering around, adding lubricant can't hurt. WD-40 is appropriate for metal. For other materials, go to the hardware store and explain what you are fixing; the employee will help you choose from the myriad of material-specific lubricant options.

FIXING PLASTIC PARTS

Once you've identified a broken part, you need a replacement. Most larger and more expensive appliances come equipped with an outside label including the serial number, model information, and electrical ratings to tell you how much energy the appliance uses. This information is required when calling either the manufacturer or one of the hundreds of parts suppliers listed in the phone book.

```
MICRO AIR CONDITIONER
XX VOLT, XX AMP

SERIAL # 4398606
```

PAINTING CHIPS

Old appliances tend to have various chips in their paint coat. Instead of staring at them for years, why not fix them? Find the manufacturer's label (see example above) and call the manufacturer directly to ask for the color code. ("It looks like it's white" won't work.) It is usually easier to order the paint directly from the manufacturer, but if that's not possible, visit a local appliance or paint store.

Most appliance paints come in a small bottle that includes a little brush, much like nail polish. If a brush isn't included, go to a local hardware store, explain what you're doing, and an employee will hand you a cheap little brush. Clean the area well before applying paint, and then wait at least one or two hours before adding a second coat, if needed.

MICROWAVE TROUBLES

Microwaves function by inundating your food with electromagnetic energy. Your food becomes hot because the energy causes food molecules to move quickly, making your frozen pasta vibrate and generate internal friction from the movement. The radiation that microwaves use to cook can be dangerous to humans, so your microwave is *not* the appliance on which to test your repair skills.

Even minor door adjustments should be made by a professional to prevent electromagnetic leaks. Yes, the phrase "electromagnetic leak" should shake your soul with fear.

If your microwave isn't working, it's probably because one of the microwave's own safety devices worked properly: a blown fuse in response to a power surge or an automatic shutoff in response to overheating or a fan failure, for example. Microwaves include an automatic door switch that prevents them from operating while open: if yours does operate with an open door, stop using it immediately.

Keep in mind that microwave repairs often exceed the costs of purchasing a new one, so a new microwave (with more power and more options!) might be the best solution.

TIP

Safety Tip *Never test an empty microwave, or you might damage the magnetron, which produces those electromagnetic rays. Six ounces of water in a mug or bowl serve as an adequate tester "food."*

MINOR TROUBLES

Microwave Dependency Syndrome (MDS) is a common affliction, particularly among young, noncooking hungry types. If there is something wrong with the way your microwave cooks—it takes a very *long time to cook food*, it's *sparking* for no apparent reason, the inside is badly *chipped*, or the window is *cracked*—you need to take the microwave to a professional or buy a new one.

Otherwise, in an effort to continue your dependence, here are some micro-tips:

× After years of abuse, the inside of your microwave is a living testament to all the foods you have cooked in it. To get the *residue* off the walls and ceiling, microwave a cup or bowl of water on "High" for around three minutes, and leave it in there for another five minutes. The steam buildup will loosen the food deposits and you can wipe them off with a sponge. Feel free to do this repeatedly—steam is strong stuff. (Anything that can fix your pores is worth trusting.) *Never use steel wool or scouring powder on the inside of a microwave.* You can damage the finish, which can lead to radiation exposure.

× If your microwave *sparks* and you aren't cooking something metal—thermometers and Chinese food containers contain metal, folks—you have a problem. Mix together some warm water and dish soap, and wash off any grease that might be congealed along shelves or corners. Also make sure that any cooking racks are securely fastened. If this doesn't fix the problem, you need to have the unit checked by a technician.

× Your microwave *reeks* and you're not sure why. Try mixing together a cup of water and a cup of concentrated lemon juice and cook it on "High" for five minutes. Take it out and wipe out the inside of the microwave. Repeat if necessary.

× You want to know if a container, dish, or bowl is *microwave safe*. To find out, put two ounces of water in the dish in question, and put it in the microwave on High for twenty to thirty seconds. If the dish is too hot to touch, don't touch it. It's not microwave safe. If it's warm, use it to microwave things for under four minutes. If the dish is cool, you can use it endlessly.

REFRIGERATORS

Refrigerators and air conditioners work by the same principle: a compressor repeatedly forces refrigerant through two pairs of connected coils. In one set of coils (external coils) the refrigerant is under high pressure, and is a liquid that loses heat. In the other set of coils (internal coils) the refrigerant is a gas that absorbs heat. This way, the coils internally absorb heat and keep your food cool, while externally releasing the heat generated by the process. On the inside of the refrigerator, a fan spreads the cool air around. Both the refrigerator and freezer have an internal thermostat that allows you to control the temperature manually.

Your freezer and refrigerator have separate sets of coils. If you have a freezer-on-top refrigerator, the freezer coils are behind the back freezer wall or hidden internally between the two sections, and the refrigerator coils are at the bottom of the unit, behind the grille.

TIP

Safety Tip No, the "refrigerant disposal" fee on your repair bill is not a joke. Refrigerant is a highly

toxic substance that also happens to have a variety of restrictions on its disposal. Refrigerant is well concealed inside your refrigerator coils, but if by some catastrophic misfortune it leaks into your kitchen, you need to stay away and call a professional immediately.

ALL ABOUT DEFROSTERS AND DEFROSTING

If your refrigerator didn't have a defrost system, the coils would naturally build up with frost and fail. Newer refrigerators will say "frost-free" on the label, which means that a few times a day, a small heater next to the coils turns on and dispels any frost that may have formed on the coils. Other models, called cycle-defrost refrigerators, have a heater in the refrigerator that turns on repeatedly through the day and sends the resulting water to a pan in the bottom of the unit, where it evaporates. You know this is the case if your freezer often seems consumed by the frost monster: the freezers in these models have coils in the top, bottom, and side walls, which makes for a very cool freezer but no defrost system, so you need to defrost periodically.

TO DEFROST

× Wait until you are running low on frozen foods, remove your food from the freezer, and turn the thermostat inside the freezer to "Off" or "Defrost."

× Leaving the freezer door open, allow the frost to melt. This should take a few hours. Never attempt to pry the ice off a freezer with a knife, not even a butter knife. If you pierce a coil, you'll have to buy a whole new freezer. This is the voice of experience.

× To clean, wipe down the freezer with a mixture of hot water and baking soda before you reload your food.

THE RUNNING REFRIGERATOR: CLEANING CLOGGED COILS

Your refrigerator runs so much that you wouldn't know what to do without the background hum. The biggest culprit of a refrigerator that runs all the

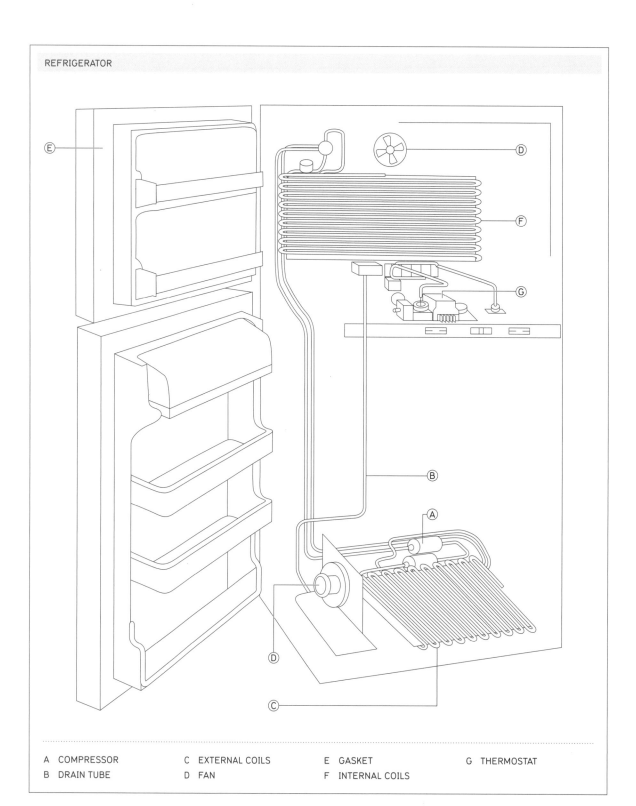

REFRIGERATOR

A COMPRESSOR   C EXTERNAL COILS   E GASKET   G THERMOSTAT
B DRAIN TUBE   D FAN   F INTERNAL COILS

time, stops running, or runs inordinately loudly is clogged coils: there is so much dust, lint, hair, and other nastiness that the airflow of the coils is blocked, causing your refrigerator to work overtime. To fix this, you just need to vacuum the coils. A vacuum extension tube is useful for this. Just *unplug* your refrigerator, remove the bottom grille with a gentle tug, and stick your vacuum tube inside. Vacuum everything you can, while being careful not to damage the coils. If the coils are located on the back of the unit, you will have to carefully pull the refrigerator out from the wall with a friend before vacuuming the obvious coils in front of you. (To protect your floor, roll the refrigerator out onto two plywood planks.) People who live in very dusty areas, or with an excessive number of pets or hairy people, will need to do this a few times a year.

MY REFRIGERATOR DOOR IS AT AN ANGLE

Your refrigerator door isn't closing properly. The freezer door touches the refrigerator door and you have to lift it manually to close it, or the fridge door is touching the floor. The problem probably lies in the door hinges. Hinge systems differ from model to model, but repairing this is a simple matter of tightening whichever hinges are loose:

× Locate the cap covering the hinge on the top or bottom corner of the door. Pop it off. In some cases, a metal sheet is bolted over the hinge, which you will have to loosen with a wrench or adjust appropriately.
× With a flathead screwdriver, tighten the hinge by turning it to the right, while holding the door in the correct position with your left hand. Continue until the door opens and closes smoothly.
× Replace the caps or coverings.

Some refrigerators feature screws between the freezer and refrigerator doors. These can be visibly loose. If you can't fit a screwdriver between the doors, gently remove your freezer door by carefully loosening the screws on top of the door. Have a friend lift up the door while you tighten the offending middle screws. Slide the door back into place, and replace all the screws. The key is to keep track of which screws go where.

MY REFRIGERATOR DOOR LEAKS

If you suspect that a door might be leaking cool air or not getting a solid seal, try shutting the door on a scrap of paper. You should feel resistance when you try to move the paper around the perimeter. Try it in a few different places. If the paper moves with no resistance, you need to have the door gasket (that rubbery material the seals the door shut) replaced. Professionals will charge a bundle for this repair, so it's worth it to try yourself, replacing the gasket one section at a time.

 TIP

Before you take the time to install a new gasket, you might want to try washing and softening the still-attached old gasket. Wash it with a rag, hot water, and detergent. An old, worn gasket can be softened with a bit of petroleum jelly.

THE COOLEST REFRIGERATOR

Whether you use your fridge to store old pizza and beer or wine and caviar, you need it to be functional, since fridges are a key part of surviving past noontime without a dining service. Here are the solutions to the most frequent fridge problems:

× If your refrigerator is noticeably stinky, beyond the funk of one fermenting food item, wait until you are going away and empty and unplug the unit for at least a couple of days. When you return, wash it out with a rag and a mixture of baking soda and water. Plug it back in.
× Food, especially good food, is odorous. As a general rule, an open box of baking soda in your fridge will absorb the most noxious odors. Consider this baking soda a sacrifice to the Gods of Hygiene, and don't use it for actual cooking purposes.
× If the fridge light isn't coming on and you'd rather not use a flashlight when you're looking for last week's leftovers, you most likely need to replace the bulb. If you're not sure what kind of bulb it is, unscrew it and bring it to the hardware store (see How to Change a Refrigerator or Oven Lightbulb, page 95).
× Periodically check the temperature of your refrigerator and freezer. In the freezer, cram a

thermometer between two foods that have been there for a few days. It should read between 0 and 6 degrees Fahrenheit. Place a cup of water in the refrigerator, and after a few hours, check the temperature. It should be between 34 and 42 degrees Fahrenheit. Supply stores sell special thermometers for this purpose.

MY REFRIGERATOR'S CROOKED: ANGLING A REFRIGERATOR

Refrigerators purposely stand angled toward the back. Pools of water on the floor around your refrigerator, ice forming on the bottom of your freezer, or doors that won't close by themselves are all signs that the unit is probably not tilted slightly backward as it should be.

To determine if this is the culprit, place a carpenter's level along the front edge of the refrigerator. If the bubble is not centered between the middle two lines of the level, you need to adjust one front foot of the refrigerator to match the other, with an adjustable wrench. Turn the carpenter's level 90 degrees. The bubble should be off center, toward the front of the refrigerator. If it is not, you need to either lower the back feet or raise the front feet.

 TIP

You can level any appliance that is off kilter, though refrigerators are most commonly in need. Washing machines and dryers are also frequent offenders. Any appliance that seems to vibrate and shake more than necessary is probably off level and can be tested with a carpenter's level. Propping an off-kilter appliance with a small scrap of wood is often easier than struggling with feet adjustments.

REFRIGERATING FOR CHEAPSKATES

Fridges eat up a lot of electricity each year. Here are a handful of easy ways to lower your monthly electric bill:

× Put your refrigerator someplace cool, not in direct sunlight or on top of a heating vent.
× Avoid overfilling your fridge, which takes more

INSTALLING A NEW REFRIGERATOR DOOR SEAL

YOU NEED

× New gasket
× Flathead screwdriver
× Refrigerator caulk (optional)

STEPS

1   Equipped with the measurements of your current gasket, go to your local general supply or refrigeration supply store. You should know the model and make of the refrigerator, which can often be found on a label hidden somewhere on the side or bottom of your refrigerator.

2   Purchase a new gasket and the smallest tube of refrigerator caulk that the store sells. You will use the caulk like glue at the door corners.

3   Back at the ranch, turn off the refrigerator or just unplug it. Set yourself up on a chair in front of the open door.

4   Begin at the top of the door. Lift up the old gasket and locate the first 2 screws hidden underneath. Loosen the screws with a screwdriver, but don't remove them—you don't have to.

5   Loosen the first few feet of gasket with your fingers. It is held in place by a plastic strip called the retainer. Slide a foot of the old gasket out of the retainer, and install a foot of the new gasket directly behind it. Tighten the screws.

6   Repeat this process all the way around the door, until the new gasket is installed.

7   A new gasket is sometimes awkward to work with, and might not conform to corners. To help this, use the refrigerator caulk like glue: place a bead of caulk in the retainer going into and out of the corner. Insert the new gasket and hold it in place for 2 minutes. Be very gentle to not pull out the corners as you continue installing the gasket. When finished, let the area dry for 4 or 5 hours.

LEVELING A REFRIGERATOR
(OR OTHER APPLIANCE)

YOU NEED

- × Adjustable wrench
- × Carpenter's level
- × Screwdriver (if necessary)

STEPS

1 Most refrigerators hide the front feet behind a grille at the bottom of the refrigerator. Pull off the grille to gain access. If screws are holding the grille in place, remove them with a screwdriver.

2 Look at the 2 visible feet. Refrigerators on wheels often have a screw to adjust height (instead of wrench-adjusted feet), so you might need a flathead screwdriver instead. Have a friend lift the fridge slightly backward from the top of the refrigerator, so you can lengthen the front feet with a wrench or screwdriver. Adjust longer or shorter as needed.

3 After each adjustment, check your progress with a carpenter's level to make sure the front feet are the same length, lest you have water leaking out sideways.

4 If you need to adjust the back feet as well, empty the refrigerator, carefully pull out the refrigerator with a friend, and adjust the feet accordingly. (Repeat Steps 2 and 3.) Heavy refrigerators, especially on vinyl floors, are best rolled onto wooden planks to protect the floor.

energy to cool. Ideally, there is plenty of space for cool air to circulate around your food.
- × Wait until food is cool to put it in the fridge.
- × Keep your freezer full—already-frozen items are cheaper to cool than warm air and will benefit from being in contact with other frozen items.
- × You can always store your higher-alcohol-content beverages, such as hard liquors, in the freezer, because they won't freeze.
- × Dry containers before putting them into the fridge, because the defrost heater uses a lot of energy.
- × Some units have a "humid weather" switch, which keeps humidity low during muggy weather. In most climates, turn off the switch from September through May.

GARBAGE DISPOSALS

The pressing question of our time is how does the garbage disposal work: where does the food go? Most people look down into their garbage disposals every day and see a quickly spinning blade. You probably think that the blade annihilates the food, and then the food goes away. Wrong-o.

That blade is actually called a flywheel, and its purpose is to hurl your former food against the interior wall of the disposal. The wall is a shredder lined with little blades, much like your cheese grater. The shredder is what annihilates your former food.

Below the flywheel is a motor, and when you turn on power, the motor makes the flywheel spin. The remains of your food, now near liquefied, exit the disposal through the same drain that your sink water exits, leading to your main waste pipe. Your sink drainpipe juts down off the side of the disposal, above the disposal motor. You can see all of this by looking below your sink.

Proper disposal use: turn on the *cold* water and place a moderate amount of food in the disposal. Turn on the switch and continue adding garbage as needed. (Never jam your disposal full of food.) When you're finished, turn off the switch and let cold water run for thirty seconds to clean out any remaining grease.

GARBAGE DISPOSAL

A MOTOR
B MOUNTING RING
C MOUNTING SCREW
D SINK
E PLASTIC SHELL
   (DECREASES NOISE)

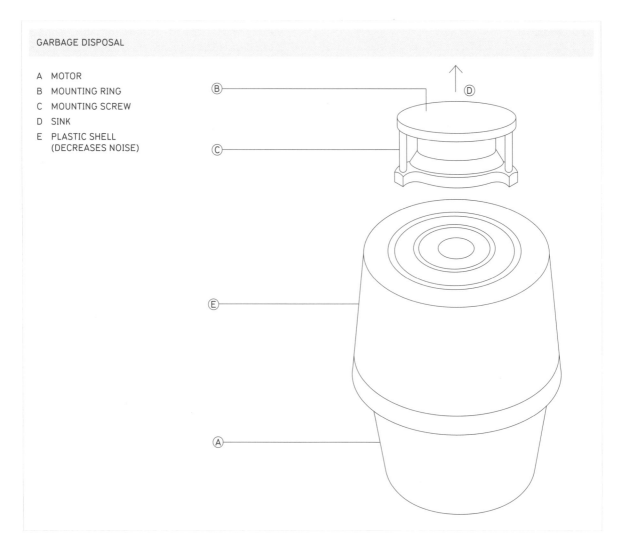

WHAT CAN I DISPOSE?

Nonperishables never belong in your garbage disposer. Fruit and vegetable products are fine, with the exception of foods that might be considered "stringy," such as corn silk. If you're not sure, throw out the waste.

TIP

Both mice and lost pets seem to find the darkness of a garbage disposal comforting. If either of these scenarios apply to you, be careful before you turn on the disposal. Or be prepared to say a violent good-bye to Fluffy, Snakey, etc.

WE BE JAMMIN': CLOGGED DISPOSALS

The most common garbage disposal problem is a jam. You'll know you have one when the disposal either stops altogether or makes a low, buzzing noise. Whatever the scenario, *never ever put a hand in the disposal, no matter what.*

NOTE

Bad clogs might extend into the drain trap, meaning that your disposal is not the problem. To clear these normal sink clogs, follow the directions for clogged sink and tub drains (page 126).

DETACHING A GARBAGE DISPOSAL

YOU NEED

- × Bucket
- × Pipe wrench
- × Screwdriver

STEPS

1 Turn off power to the kitchen from the circuit or fuse panel. Place a bucket under the disposal to catch any accidental goop falling from the U-trap.

2 Detach the trap (U-shaped pipe) from the disposal by loosening the big nut holding the U-shaped drain in place with a pipe wrench.

3 Pull off the dishwasher hose, which is the smaller hose on the top of the disposal.

4 While holding the bottom of the disposal, turn the whole unit to the left. You should be able to remove it.

5 Some units are attached to the sink bottom with screws. Use a flathead screwdriver to loosen the screws, then perform Step 3.

6 Now the disposal is still attached to its power cord. To remove the cord, pop off the plastic panel on the bottom of the disposal. Unscrew the screws holding in the cord. Remove the cord and wires.

DECLOGGING A GARBAGE DISPOSAL

YOU NEED

- × Broom handle
- × Cooking tongs
  Hex key (maybe)

STEPS

1 Turn off the disposal and find a broom handle, plunger handle, or other handle of that ilk. Use the broom handle to push around the flywheel and release whatever is caught.

2 Use a pair of cooking tongs to take out the item causing the jam.

3 If that doesn't work, go below the sink. There is a small hole in the center of the garbage disposal. Place a hex key in the hole and turn it back and forth, to rotate the flywheel. Repeat Step 2.

4 Sometimes a garbage disposal won't restart after a bad jam. Go take a walk to give the unit time to cool and then press the "Restart" button, which is usually hidden inside an indentation on the bottom of the disposal.

WHAT CAN I DISPOSE	
OKAY	**NOT OKAY**
× Meat bones (thin and within reason) × Fruit and vegetable rinds or products × Fruit pits × Ice × Any soft food	× Glass × Plastic × Bottles × Silverware × Seafood shells × Banana peels × Corn silk/husk × Gum

DRIPPING DISPOSALS

There's a small lake forming under your kitchen sink and all signs point to the disposal. Water leaks coming from the disposal are usually a matter of loose connections to and from the disposal. These can be fixed by tightening the connections between the sink and disposal, and the disposal and drainpipe. Under your sink, look at the metal contraption between the disposal and the sink, called the "sink mounting ring." The disposal is usually connected to the mounting ring by screws that can be tightened with a hex key. To tighten the drainpipe connection, look at how the pipe is connected to the disposal. Depending on the shape of the connecting screw or nut, you will need either a wrench, screwdriver, or nut driver to tighten the connection.

 TIP

It is good practice to leave a small bucket sitting permanently below your sink, giving you ample time to find leaks before water damage takes place.

MAJOR GARBAGE DISPOSAL REPAIRS

Unlike most appliances, garbage disposals, once disconnected, are handheld. This means that you can remove one, try to fix it yourself, and if that doesn't work, take it to a friend or repair shop to identify and replace old parts. It also means that installing a new disposal is relatively easy: just remove the old one and follow the instructions in the manual for installing a new one.

To remove, you need to detach the two hoses going into the disposal and loosen the nuts holding the disposer to the sink bottom.

TRASH COMPACTORS

Trash compactors are one of the great Completely-Unnecessary-but-Very-Useful inventions of our time. They can be quite helpful in smaller apartments, particularly walk-ups or small kitchens where emptying the trash daily is annoying. Your local garbage truck has a similar mechanism, allowing the crew to smush an entire neighborhood's worth of trash into one truck. Trash compactors work by taking your freeflowing garbage and smushing it into a little bundle. After you place your trash in the drawer and close the door, a big rectangular ram above the drawer rides down two shafts on either side of the drawer and presses the garbage downward. The shafts are "threaded," or spiral grooved, so two nuts spiral down the shaft, holding the ram steady under increasing power.

The ram is powered by a motor tucked away at the top of the compactor, behind the drawer. The bottom of the motor is attached to a chain, which loops around each shaft and spins it, so that the two nuts are forced to travel downward, bringing the ram with them. When the ram is very low, the motor switches directions and the nuts spiral back to the top, completing the compacting cycle. Due to the wide potential for injury in an appliance that smashes objects to a pulp, compactors contain a variety of built-in safety devices. All models have a switch that prevents the compactor from working when the drawer is open, while most have a childproof drawer lock and/or an "On-Off" switch operated by a key. Keep children far away; if you're concerned, unplug the compactor altogether.

TRASH COMPACTOR SAFETY TIPS

Never compact anything that strikes you as "toxic." Chemicals, bug sprays, paints, spray cans, and related products are best left to the regular garbage or safe disposal. Flammable products are also not suggested—placing your old lighter into a hot appliance with a motor is stupid.

CAN I COMPACT GLASS BOTTLES?

If recycling doesn't happen in your neck of the woods, glass can be compacted. Always place it in the drawer with ample other garbage, and place the bottle flat in the middle, surrounded by other trash.

TRASH COMPACTOR REPAIRS

Always unplug the compactor before doing any repair.

If your trash compactor is installed under the counter, try to locate the plug behind the counter—your dishwasher or electric stove probably uses the same outlet. If you can't find it, turn off the entire electrical circuit from your circuit box or fuse box. Test the compactor's power switch to make sure the electricity is off.

Freestanding compactors are much easier to repair: simply unplug and open the drawer for full access.

COMMON TRASH TROUBLES

The general sign that a trash compactor is broken is quite simple: it's not compacting well. A few basic repairs can bring it back from the dead.

LOOSE CHAINS The chain coming from the motor should not be slack—it needs to be wound tightly around the bottom of the two shafts to spin them and bring down the ram. If you touch the chain and it gives by more than ¾ inch, you need to tighten the chains. You do this by moving the motor back a bit. The motor is bolted to the same frame as the drawer. Simply loosen the bolts holding down the motor with an adjustable wrench, slide the motor back a bit, and tighten the bolts. On some models you will need to tip the unit on its side to loosen the bolts, which may be along the underside of the unit.

WORN POWER NUTS The nuts that spiral down the shaft to carry the ram up and down undergo quite a bit of pressure and frequently wear out. If they look worn, stripped, or otherwise in poor repair, you need to replace them. Models vary, but you'll need to remove the top panel of the compactor, usually with some combination of screwdriver and wrench. The nuts that you need to replace will be hidden beneath two "nut retainers," which prevent the nuts from spiraling beyond the top of the shaft. Loosen the retainers with a wrench, remove them, and you should find yourself face-to-face with the damaged nut. Unscrew it and take it to the hardware store for an identical replacement. Replace the nut and reassemble the unit.

DRY SHAFTS If the shafts are bone dry, chances are that it's hard for the two nuts to travel up and down the shafts smoothly. All you need to do is lubricate the shafts a bit, which is the equivalent of putting lotion on your arm. Call up the manufacturer and ask which lubricant they suggest. Go purchase that grease, and with a rag, sparingly rub the grease onto the shafts. When in doubt, WD-40 always works.

DIRTY PARTS After years of compacting trash, it's not surprising that trash compactor parts can have so much grime along the shafts and ram that they no longer function well. To clean, you basically need to remove all the grime you can, any way you can. Scrape off gumlike substances with a flathead screwdriver, scrub down the drawer and ram bottom with soap and a sponge, and clean off the shafts with a bristled brush. Keep in mind that you're cleaning an appliance with moving and electrical parts, so be careful not to drop pieces of trash near the motor and to allow the whole unit time to dry out.

DISHWASHERS

The dishwasher is the most amazing invention of the twentieth century. Not only does it wash the crusty remains of your noshing for you, it also dries the dishes afterward. Now all we need is a robot to put the dishes back in the cupboards again—unless you're efficient and store your dishes in the dishwasher in the first place.

When you hit the "Start" switch, the dishwasher fills up with two gallons of water, supplied from your main hot water pipe, with pressure from a pump at the base of the dishwasher, and mixes with detergent. The two rotating spray mechanisms—one on the top of the dishwasher and one on the bottom—

PROBLEM The dishwasher smells like it's on fire.

SOLUTION This is very common. If you don't see smoke, a dish is probably touching the heating mechanism, which dries the dishes. The heating mechanism is the hot tube located either on the top or the bottom of the chamber, so either move the object from the top rack that is touching it or find what dish or utensil fell to the bottom.

PROBLEM My twisty straw has fungus.

SOLUTION Dishwashers clean with steam and streams of water, so items that are either deep or twisted, such as a deep vase or a twisty straw, cannot be adequately cleaned in a dishwasher.

PROBLEM My glassware keeps coming out of the dishwasher cloudy.

SOLUTION Your glassware is not dishwasher safe. The cloudiness is microscopic cuts on the glass.

PROBLEM My favorite wooden spoon cracked.

SOLUTION Wood cracks and disintegrates in dishwashers. Chopsticks, wooden spoons, and knives with wooden handles need to be hand washed.

PROBLEM I have streaks on my dishes.

SOLUTION The cause is either the detergent or hard water. Change detergents or use less. If you experiment with detergents and still have streaks, you probably have hard water from your local water supply. Fixing this for your residence is a major undertaking—you would have to install a water softener either on all hot-water pipes or the entire water system. Other signs of hard water are white rings around bathtubs and sinks, and soap and shampoo that don't lather well. Antistreak products exist, though they tend to cost quadruple the price of detergent.

PROBLEM The food is still stuck on my plates.

SOLUTION Older and weaker dishwashers sometimes need dishes to be rinsed before dishwashing. Food left on plates for long periods of time will stick no matter what. When in doubt, run just the prewash cycle on dirty plates, and run the regular cycle a day or two later when the rest of the machine is full.

PROBLEM The pictures of Winnie the Pooh washed off my favorite plates.

SOLUTION Designs created with meltable materials, such as the cartoon characters on children's plates, should never go in the dishwasher. Any soft plastic items will also melt.

PROBLEM My plates are dyed colors from my food.

SOLUTION The dyes in some foods are extremely strong and need to be rinsed off immediately after eating, such as the yellow from runny egg yolks, or blueberry remains. The dishwasher heat can sometimes make these stains permanent. Oops.

suck in water and hurl it back out at the dishes. The center of the spray mechanism features a vertical spray pole that hurls more water at the dishes.

The process is run by a timer mechanism, and after a few minutes, the soapy water drains, and the process is repeated, this time without detergent. The round coil at the bottom of the dishwasher is the heating element, which maintains a water temperature of at least 140 degrees Fahrenheit, which is the minimum for melting grease. The unit empties again, and the drying cycle begins. Depending on the model, the heating element alone increases the air temperature to dry the dishes, or a small fan mechanism works in tangent with the heating coil.

DISH ISH

Dishwashers are so great that most dishwasher problems are due to human error. Opposite is a chart to solve all your dish "ish."

DISHWASHER LOADING SKILLS

People seem to have remedial dishwasher repair skills, so here are some tips:

× Glasses should go between the prongs, not on top of them.
× Big pots or plates can block the water flow or detergent release altogether. Stick your head inside your dishwasher: large items are best placed in the back corner opposite the draining apparatus.
× Much of the spray comes from the center of the dishwasher, so face dishes in that direction.
× Leave enough space between dishes that the water spray has a vague chance of spraying the dish with force.
× Place pointy utensils facing downward, far away from the door or any inner hoses and parts. Accidental punctures in hoses or door seals cause leaks.
× Don't load
  – Disposable aluminum pans
  – Anything you would classify as "fragile," " antique," "very expensive," or "of great sentimental value"

PROBLEM Grease doesn't wash off my dishes.

CAUSE Water temperature might be too low.

SOLUTION Fill a cup with the hottest water that your sink can muster. Use a cooking thermometer to measure the temperature. If it is under 140 degrees Fahrenheit, your dishwasher is too cool to melt grease. You need to either increase the thermostat setting on your hot water heater (see Hot Water Heaters, page 143), or better insulate your home's hot water pipes (see Insulating Pipes, page 143). Households with children, disabled, or elderly purposely leave water temperature low to prevent accidental scalding.

PROBLEM My dishwasher door leaks.

CAUSE Your door is misaligned or you need to replace the gasket.

SOLUTION If the door is visibly off kilter, use a screwdriver to tighten or loosen the hinges at the base of the door. Some hinges are obscured by caps, which you'll have to pop off. Otherwise, the rubbery stuff around the edge of the door that creates a waterproof seal, the "gasket," is leaking and needs to be replaced. See My Refrigerator Door Leaks (page 105) for instructions. Before you repair, try wiping down the gasket with a warm sponge—grime can cause minor leaks.

PROBLEM There's a lot of dirty water at the bottom of my dishwasher.

CAUSE There's a huge clog in your drain hose.

SOLUTION Before you call a professional, if your model has a big strainer on the floor of the dishwasher, remove it and clean it. If the clog remains, you need a handy friend or a professional.

PROBLEM My dishes have food stuck on them.

CAUSE The water sprayers are clogged or the water pump is broken.

SOLUTION The water sprayers are clogged or the water pump is broken. Try pulling out the rack and using a piece of wire or toothpick to poke around the spray mechanism holes. More serious water pressure problems are caused by faulty water pumps, which require a professional to replace.

- Plastics that you're not convinced were manufactured with 160 degree Fahrenheit temperatures in mind
- Dishes with designs you would like to continue looking at
- Steel wool
- Things that don't say "dishwasher safe"
- Items made of iron or tin that are not fully enameled
- Hollow-handled silver utensils

 TIP

If you live in a small space, consider a countertop dishwasher. At around 2 x 3 x 3 feet, these small nifty dishwashers can fit in the smallest of counter or floor spaces and plug directly into your sink.

Keep in mind that while weak plastics and metals might come out of the dishwasher looking okay, you may have just melted a thin coating of plastic across all the dishes you eat from.

I'M POOR. CAN I AFFORD TO USE MY DISHWASHER ALL THE TIME?

Ideally, it is more energy efficient to use few dishes, and then wash them by hand, using one tub for washing and one for rinsing, then air-drying. However, if like most people, you use lots of dishes, pile them up, and then scrub for ten minutes at a time at full-faucet capacity, yes, hand washing will cost you more than dishwashing in water and energy bills.

To save a bit on bills, use your dishwasher at night during the summer, and turn off the drying cycle—just open the door and let the dishes air dry. Only run a full washer, and always run the light wash if it's sufficient.

BASIC DISHWASHER REPAIRS

The most common complaint about dishwashers is that they don't clean well. Good cleaning is dependent on two factors: high water pressure and high water temperature. A lack of either could cause a perfectly good dishwasher to fail miserably.

AIR CONDITIONERS

Air conditioners work under the same mechanics as refrigerators. (We're learning stuff like crazy, folks.) A pump forces chemical refrigerant through two connected coils, one interior and one exterior. In the interior coils, the refrigerant is a gas that absorbs heat; in the exterior coils, the refrigerant condenses into liquid and emits heat.

A big fan draws room air into the unit through side vents and over the interior coils, which absorb the heat in the air. The coils also happen to attract moisture, thereby dehumidifying a room. The fan then expels the now-cool dry air out into the room.

Any condensed water is released into a thin drainage pan below the unit, and then outside, explaining why you always get dripped on in the city. An external thermostat measures room temperature and powers the unit on and off accordingly.

HOW TO BUY AN AIR CONDITIONER

One would think that buying an air conditioner would be much like buying anything else: you go to the store, pick something with fancy-and-yet-trustworthy packaging, and kick yourself for overspending. But the air-conditioner aisle at the store is overwhelming. Some are huge, some are tiny, some are affordable, some are not. And all the packaging looks good. A few concepts will help you identify which one you want:

Most packages classify the cooling "strength" in BTUs (British thermal units), which measure the amount of heat the air conditioner can remove in one hour. A quick formula will help you identify how many BTUs you need: multiply (in feet) your room's length by width by height by 4.

The answer is an approximation of how many BTUs your air conditioner should have. Rooms with particularly good insulation or little sun exposure can use few BTUs. Air conditioners with lower BTUs are cheaper, but a unit that is too small for the space it is cooling will quickly wear out, after months or years of running constantly. Conversely, an air

AIR CONDITIONER

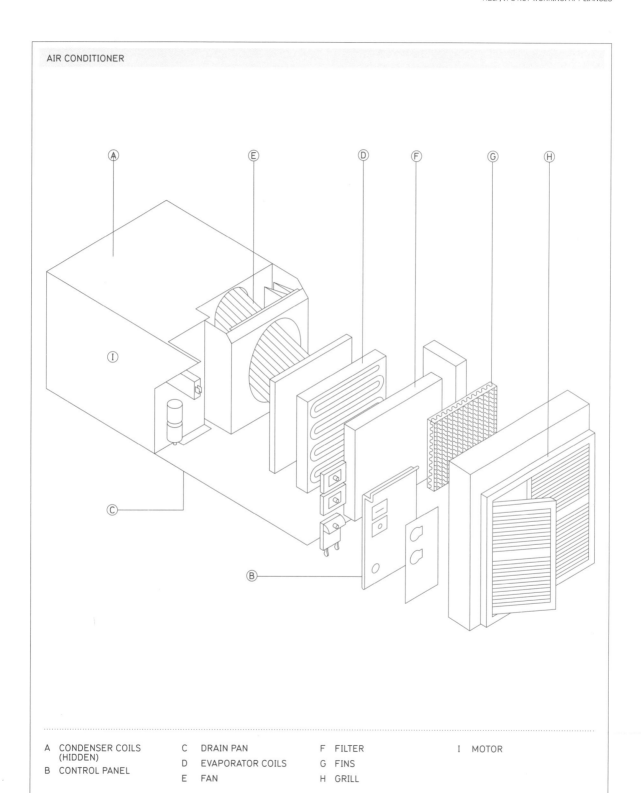

A CONDENSER COILS (HIDDEN)

B CONTROL PANEL

C DRAIN PAN

D EVAPORATOR COILS

E FAN

F FILTER

G FINS

H GRILL

I MOTOR

conditioner that's too large will, in addition to leaving the air feeling muggy, cost far more than necessary each month.

Unless you want to overload an electrical circuit, leaving your room both dark and overheated, you also need to determine where you will plug in your air conditioner. Air-conditioner packaging will say "120 volts" or "240 volts." Most normal three-prong outlets are 120 volts, while certain deluxe outlets, such as the ones for your kitchen stove and washer and dryer, are 240 volts. Mapping out your electrical circuits will help allay the mystery (see Mapping Your Circuits, page 84). If you have no idea, buy a 120-volt air conditioner and make sure that no other major appliances are plugged into the same electrical circuit. If the outlet you're considering has only two prong holes, you're out of luck: don't even think about buying an air conditioner.

Newfangled air conditioners include a variety of extras, including timers to allow you to come home to coolness, or use minimal energy overnight. Units with fans that can be pointed to best cool a room are also a good option.

Back at the ranch, keep the air conditioner away from furniture, curtains, shades, and other obstacles that can clog, confuse, or block the unit. Don't use the unit when it is under 65 degrees Fahrenheit, because the coils can freeze.

DISTURBING NOISES: AIR-CONDITIONER SPASMS

Your air conditioner sounds like a drowning lawnmower. Window-sized air conditioners are the answer for overheated budget-living types, and yet they can make quite a racket. If your air conditioner makes disturbing noises, try the following:

× Make sure the air conditioner is correctly tilted slightly *backward*, toward the outside. A nonlevel unit can make some funny noises as it gurgles on water that is not draining properly. You can also end up with a steady stream of water dripping into your window frame or down your wall, which will be hard to see and will ultimately cause water and mold damage.
× Turn on the air conditioner and press your hand

against the front grille of the unit. If the noise stops, duct tape the grille tightly to the unit, or creatively use picture hanging wire to better secure the grille.
× Many strange noises are caused from the air conditioner vibrating against the window itself, though it often sounds more complicated than that. With the air conditioner on, try pressing against various sections of the window, including the window sash and frames. Usually a well-placed small wooden wedge can stop the noise. If the noise stops while you are pressing on the glass itself, the glass is a bit loose—you can either reglaze the glass (ask at the hardware store) or be realistic and move the unit to another window.

IT'S GETTIN' HOT IN HERE: DIRTY AIR CONDITIONERS

Your air conditioner's sole purpose in your life is to make you comfortable. And yet you're sweating. Why?

Air conditioners filter air all day long, and city air can be pretty gross. As a result, the most common air-conditioner problems are due to dirt and grime, such as clogged filters and coils. Remember to clean the filter—hidden directly behind the front grille—every month during hot weather. (You just pull it out and scrape off all the gunk, much like a clothes dryer filter.) Some filters have an exterior handle for easy removal; if you need to remove the grille, most pop out by releasing small tabs, while some need a screwdriver to loosen screws. Filters made of metal or foam material can be washed with a bucket of soapy water. Some models have disposable filters that you'll need to change as often as recommended. A couple of times a year, remove the grille and filter and vacuum everything that you see inside. If your air conditioner sort of works, but not as well as you remember it working earlier, try the following:

× With a pointy vacuum nozzle, vacuum all the parts of the air conditioner you can get to with the grille removed, including the panel of fins. Cleaning will help more air pass through.
× Go to the hardware store and ask for a product with which to clean your aluminum air-conditioner fins. They will hand you a cleaning spray, which can effectively remove grime from the fins with a bit of water.

I'M HOT: THE NONWORKING AIR CONDITIONER

To the great joy of air-conditioner repairmen and their bank accounts, there is often nothing wrong with air conditioners that don't seem to work. If you think it's broken, try the following:

- × If it turns on but doesn't cool, the filter behind the front grille might be filthy. Clean or replace it.
- × If it won't turn on at all, you may have tripped a circuit or blown a fuse. Reset the fuse or breaker (see page 88), and turn the air conditioner back on.
- × You might be impatient. Some mobile units need to be powered on for twenty-four hours before use. Set the thermostat to around 10 degrees under room temperature, go visit a friend with a working air conditioner, and come home the next day.
- × Buy a "fin comb" from either a hardware store or an air-conditioner-supply store, and use it to straighten the aluminum coil fins, which can get bent over time, particularly if you recently bounced the unit around while moving. Bent fins effectively block air from coming out of your unit altogether and are worth fixing. There are two panels of fins, one for each set of coils. If you can find only one panel, behind the filter, don't worry about it.

Smaller air conditioners are now cheap enough that major repairs are often not worthwhile. Instead, find a moving sale and purchase yourself an affordable, working air conditioner.

SMELLY AIR CONDITIONERS

You've noticed that your air conditioner reeks. Chances are that the water in the draining pan isn't draining and is instead growing bacteria and fungus on the inside of your air conditioner. The solution is simple: you need to unplug the clogged drain hole, which is a small hole on the back bottom of the unit that regularly drips onto the passing pedestrians below. Jabbing a piece of wire around in the hole should do the trick.

SECURING YOUR AIR CONDITIONER SO IT DOESN'T KILL PEDESTRIANS

Window air conditioners are made to be wedged inside windows. While they can be carefully put in the grooves of your window track and held in place by a partially closed window, this places the full weight of the air conditioner on what might be an old, rotting windowsill and risks a visitor opening the window. Know that you have a major safety hazard, and at the very least, place a "Don't Move Me!" Post-it on the window.

Look for the screw-sized holes on the edges of the unit. Different models come with different securing systems, but air conditioners can either be bolted directly into wooden window frames (insert screws through the holes, into the window frame with a screwdriver or power drill); held in place by brackets that attach to the air conditioner and are bolted into the window frame (attach the brackets into the window frame or surrounding wall with screws, using a screwdriver or power drill); or secured with plastic that extends beyond the unit, bracing it against the inside wall (follow the brace directions). Large air conditioners, often seen in office buildings, are supported outside the window with a series of metal braces. If you inherited your air conditioner and any securing indications are long gone, go to the hardware store and explain your dilemma; you will quickly be supplied with a few dollars' worth of prevention.

HUMIDIFIERS AND DEHUMIDIFIERS

If you are experiencing air issues, you could probably benefit from a humidifier or dehumidifier.

Keeping the air appropriately moisturized sounds frivolous, but it is well worth your while. Not only will it be more comfortable for you, a 'midifier can also help reduce the number of times you need to pick up this book in a panic to repair something. Dry air dries out everything, including mechanical parts that are supposed to stay lubricated, while moist air can cause severe water and mold damage, as well as shorten the life of nice furniture. As an added bonus, 'midifiers also make good, gentle noise mufflers for sleeping.

HUMIDIFIERS

HOW THEY WORK All humidifiers have an external "humidistat," humidity's equivalent of a thermometer, which automatically switches the appliance on and off. Evaporative humidifiers work by placing a fan behind a sponged wheel or belt, which rotates through a tub of water. As you can imagine, the sponge has the potential to grow every kind of fungus imaginable, so clean it regularly. An old, worn belt needs to be replaced by calling the manufacturer.

WHAT THEY DO Exactly as their name suggests, they increase the humidity of the air.

WHY YOU NEED ONE If you're prone to a dry nose or throat, your air is probably dry and a humidifier in your room would help, especially in the wintertime. Humidifiers also protect wood furniture and string instruments, which can shrink in dry air. If you seem to have a strange problem with shocking yourself, humidifiers also reduce static electricity.

THE CHOICES There are four main kinds of humidifiers: evaporative, ultrasonic cool-mist, warm-mist, and floater filter. All four moisten air by spewing out the water in their tanks. If you are lazy when it comes to cleaning appliances, warm-mist models are highly suggested, because they boil water before spewing it, thereby killing bacteria and other harmful microbes. They also don't get dangerously hot like older models and don't need the frequent scrubbings and filter changes of other models. Most boxes give indications for appropriate room sizes. Some are geared toward humidifying entire floors, while almost-handheld units can handle small rooms.

Warm-mist humidifiers boil water, then expel the steam. Ultrasonic humidifiers use ultrasonic waves to cause undetectable water vibrations, which release mist. These need to be cleaned weekly. Last, floater humidifiers use floating filters to flick the water toward a fan, which expels vapor into the air. While arguably the coolest of the four, floating filters are disposable and need to be changed regularly.

MAINTENANCE Make sure to follow the maintenance instructions for your model, because otherwise you can spew molds and bacteria into your air. Most require frequent filter changes and cleanings with an antibacterial solution, as well as daily refills of the water tank.

Most humidifiers have only three to five primary parts: the fan, motor, water-spewing mechanism, filter, and humidistat. You can usually narrow down what is malfunctioning and call the manufacturer for a parts replacement.

DEHUMIDIFIERS

HOW THEY WORK The dehumidifier is yet another example of the coil system in both refrigerators and air conditioners. For this reason, unless you're in a rain forest, you should never run both the air conditioner and the dehumidifier.

Inside the unit, a pump forces chemical refrigerant through two sets of coils. In one set of coils, the refrigerant turns to gas and absorbs *both* heat and condensation; in the other set, the refrigerant is a liquid that expels heat. This time, the fan sucks room air across the cool coils, and condensation from the air attaches to the coils, then drips down into the water tank. Because dehumidifiers aren't concerned with air temperature, the hot and cold coils balance each other out. An external humidistat measures the humidity of the room and turns the appliance on and off accordingly.

If your dehumidifier won't turn on, keep in mind that dehumidifiers work only if the air is humid. If you're not sure, drag it into the bathroom while someone's showering, being careful to plug it in safely.

WHAT THEY DO The opposite of a humidifier, they remove condensation from the air.

WHY YOU NEED ONE If the air has a generally damp feel to it, or you are having mildew or mold problems in dark corners or on your cloth belongings, a dehumidifier will help. Low-lying rooms, such as basement apartments, can feature very moist, rain forest–like air.

THE CHOICES Dehumidifiers suck water from the air, emptying it either into a container or directly into a drain, depending on the model. Larger units remove significantly more moisture from the air and handle cooler temperatures much better—smaller models can freeze under 65 degrees Fahrenheit.

MAINTENANCE If you have a container, you need to empty it at least daily and occasionally wash it with water and bleach. Clean or replace the air filter monthly. Otherwise, you only need to vacuum the coils directly behind the grille and filter once or twice a year and carefully scrape off any goo with a toothbrush. If the fins are bent (see I'm Hot: The Nonworking Air Conditioner, page 117), a fin comb can be used to straighten them. Position the unit away from walls.

TIP

Most air-conditioner repairs apply to dehumidifiers, so see the Air Conditioners section (pages 114–117). In most cases, a thorough cleaning of the filter, coils, fin panels, and water tank, as well as a straightening of the fin panels with a fin comb, will fix troubles. As with most appliances, in a total failure, chances are that only one part has failed— probably the fan or compressor—but a repair will cost you more than replacing the unit.

5

CHAPTER 5

HELP, IT'S LEAKING! PLUMBING

THE PIPE SYSTEM BEHIND YOUR WALLS

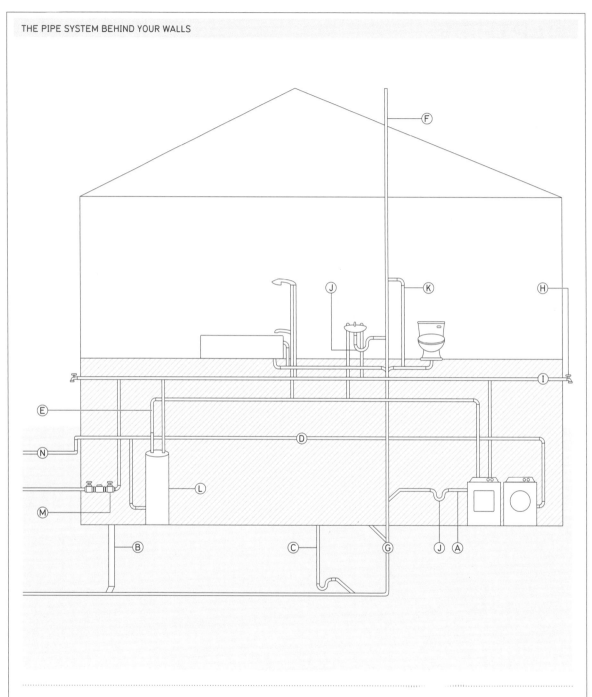

A DRAIN	E HOT WATER SUPPLY	I TRUNK	M WATER METER
B EMERGENCY DRAIN ACCESS	F MAIN VENT STACK	J U-TRAP	N WATER SUPPLY
C FLOOR DRAIN	G MAIN DRAINAGE LINES	K VENT	
D GAS LINE	H SPIGGOT	L WATER HEATER	

Some breaks are rather dependable characters—clogs, leaks, and drips will appear repeatedly in your life, even if you're lucky. Rather than a curse, these breaks are actually a good thing, because you can learn how to fix the repeat offenders. After the third drain clog, you *really* have no excuse.

This chapter is chock-full of the simplest possible solutions to common plumbing problems, because not only is fixing your own living space convenient (you don't have to waste your precious time calling others), it's also much easier to scrape by on a low budget if you can repair things yourself.

HOW DOES PLUMBING WORK?

You probably have not a clue where all the dirty water and waste you send down your drains actually goes. Despite appearances, there is great logic to the zigzag of pipes hiding behind your walls. Every inch of the entire plumbing system can be condensed to four types of equipment: fuel pipes, water and drain pipes, vent pipes, and appliance or fixtures. (A "fixture" is a sink, toilet, or other nonelectrical or non–gas-powered part of your plumbing system.)

Most important is the water supply, which comes directly from the local water main and enters your home underground below frost level, where it immediately encounters a meter: your township's way of measuring your water use. (If you have a well, the water comes in at the same place, but you don't have a meter.) Once inside, the main water pipe usually commands a center path through the house or apartment called a "trunk." The trunk branches off into smaller pipes for specific appliances, such as sinks or toilets. Early on, the cold water trunk will send a small branch to the hot water heater. The hot water heater releases a hot water trunk, which travels alongside the cold water trunk.

TIP

For future reference, you should know that the main gas line mimics the water supply line with a

central pipeline through the home. The gas line branches off to specific appliances as needed, such as the gas stove or the water heater.

Once the water has been used in a fixture, such as a shower or toilet, a drainpipe carries away the waste product. Each home has a main drainage line that sends all waste to the sewer line beyond the property or to a nearby septic system line. The major danger of drainage systems is sewer gas, which is toxic and often present in high levels. To prevent the gas from entering homes, each drain is equipped with a "trap," which is a U-shaped pipe directly below a drain. The trap effectively seals household drains from gas by allowing waste to go through, but "trapping" just enough water in its U-bottom to prevent sewer gas from floating into the home. Homes are also equipped with a "main vent stack," which releases sewer gas through the roof, while equalizing pipe air pressure throughout the house.

TOOLING AROUND: PLUMBING TOOLS

Three tool supplies appear repeatedly in basic plumbing repairs:

PIPE WRENCH A large wrench that wraps around a variety of standard-size pipes and nuts. To loosen or tighten pipe attachments, two wrenches are often needed, so purchase a pair. Pipe wrench mouths are in a C shape, and a little-known fact is that you need all three sides of the C to touch the pipe. If you apply pressure with only the top and bottom sides, you'll crush the pipe.

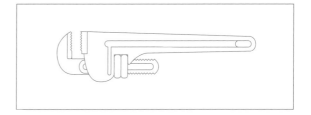

EPOXY PUTTY Also called plumber's seal or plumber's epoxy. Keep some around for emergency leaking pipes. Globbing some over a crack keeps things dry until a professional arrives. The putty can permanently repair minor attachment leaks, such as you might find below a sink cabinet. Always use with gloves, and keep it away from your freshwater supply—drainpipes are fine.

CLOSET AUGER A fishing pole-esque tool used to unclog drains and toilets instantly. You'll never flush-and-pray again. Highly recommended. Can be rented at the local hardware store for a few dollars, or purchased for $20 to $50. Drain augers are the narrower sibling of closet augers and ideal for small pipes, such as those below small sinks.

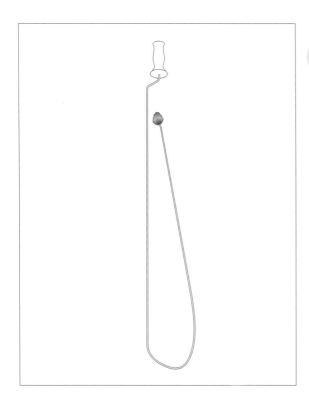

HOW TO DO PLUMBING REPAIRS

Begin with a quick prayer for calmness and comfort around potential sewer-related liquids. Then *turn off the water flow* to the area you're repairing; or turn off the main water shutoff, just to be safe. This

will severely limit the damage you can do—a toilet can't geyser without a water supply—and will always give you plenty of time to call a friend or a plumber if you feel overwhelmed. Shutoffs are often within a meter of a fixture, tucked in on the wall directly behind the fixture, or hidden in a nearby cabinet. *Sinks and showers have two shutoffs, one for hot water and one for cold.*

Remember that leaks are caused by nothing more than a small hole, which can be temporarily plugged with duct tape or a well-placed thumb. You can also often stop a leak in a freshwater pipe by turning off the water supply, and then turning on the nearest faucet to empty the leaking pipe. Remember to mop up the leak as soon as possible, to prevent water damage or possible slips.

TIP

Keeping small buckets below your sink drains will prevent the water damage that turns minor leaks into major water damage problems. One of your sinks will leak in the next few years, so put the buckets down now.

THINGS THAT CLOG

Clogs are just plain annoying. You wish the water in the sink would go down, but it won't. You want to go to the bathroom, but you can't. Thus the world of clogs.

Pipes throughout the home have little vents that equalize pipe air pressure. A clogged vent can cause pressure to change throughout the plumbing system, resulting in chaos: toilets won't flush, appliance drains overflow, traps let sewer odors enter your living space. For your purposes, you need to know only that vents prevent foul gases and vapors from flowing back into your living space. If you have a sewer odor in your house, it is probably not directly related to your toilet: you have a clogged vent somewhere and need to call a plumber. If you have a septic system, odors can also be indicative of a leaking septic tank, and you also need to call a plumber. In summary: when with odor, call plumber.

Fixing clogged drains is a rather unscientific process: all repairs consist primarily of trying to move the clog around, either by poking it or exerting pressure on it. It's not that hard, and you have a variety of options.

NOTE

If you are having difficulties with more than one drain at once, you probably have a larger plumbing problem located in the bowels of your plumbing system beyond the drains, and need to call a professional. Breathe deeply; you're off the hook.

TIP

If you're new to home repair, you might go to the store, buy some drain cleaner, and dump it down your drain. Don't do this! Most drain-cleaning fluids are highly toxic corrosives that function by eating right through whatever is clogging your drain. They also tend to severely damage your pipes by eating through the pipe metal as well, particularly if your clog is very bad and the acid has no place to go except through the pipe. They are also terrible for the environment and potentially dangerous to your health. ("Doctor, I was doing a great job cleaning my drain! . . . And then I burned my skin off.") If you value your skin, wear gloves.

IF YOU'RE LUCKY

Hopefully your sluggish sink or shower drain is the result of daily buildup of scuzz and small objects that you accidentally dropped down the drain, such as hairpins or marbles. Try sticking a bent hanger or a pair of pliers down the drain, and see what comes out. If you have a stopper or strainer (the thing partially blocking the drain hole that has saved you many earrings), remove it and clean it out. You might need to pull on a strainer with skinny pliers to remove it.

YOU COULD STILL BE LUCKY, WITH A PLUNGER

Plungers are women's best friends, second only to diamonds—which makes women's best-best friends diamond-studded plungers. Plungers are easy to understand and easy to use. They work because the plunging exerts force on whatever is plugging the drain, and all you have to do to be an excellent plunger-operator is push the plunger down and up repeatedly. You should own two, a bigger one for

toilets, and a mini one for sinks. Various models exist; make sure the one you buy fits your drain shapes.

When plunging drains:

- × Plug any sink or tub overflow holes with a wet rag.
- × Remove the drain stopper or strainer.
- × Put a bit of water in the sink or tub if there isn't stagnant water there already. You want enough water to cover half the plunger.
- × Slowly spin the plunger over the drain at an angle to limit air bubbles under the plunger. Smearing a bit of Vaseline over the plunger lips can also help.
- × Plunge forcefully while maintaining the seal.
- × Periodically pull the plunger off, and hopefully you'll hear the sucking sound of your plugged drain clearing itself.

Persistence pays with plunging. Sometimes you will plunge for a minute or two and nothing will happen—this is normal; keep going. Consider it your arm workout for the day.

YOU'RE NOT SO LUCKY

If poking or plunging your sink drain from above doesn't work, you need to go under the counter and find the U-shaped pipe (the "U-trap," which "traps" clogs). At the bottom of older U-traps should be a turnable cap, which is the "plug."

NOTE

- × *Older drains might not have a plug, in which case you need to skip to You're Not Lucky, But You'll Survive (page 128), and remove your entire trap.*
- × *Some very (very) old tubs have a trap located under a circular metal lid on the floor near the tub. You can pull open the cap and see if you can see the clog.*

TIP

In tubs, always clear clogs with an auger through the overflow hole, which leads directly to the trap, and not through the drain hole, which can be a good distance away. For a sink clog that seems to be farther down the pipe, try sticking the auger in through the U-trap's plug hole (see You're Not So Lucky, above).

UNCLOGGING A MINOR DRAIN CLOG

YOU NEED

- × Bucket or large tray
- × Adjustable wrench
- × Bent metal hanger

STEPS

1 Place a bucket or tray beneath the U-trap.

2 With your adjustable wrench, loosen and remove the plug.

3 Allow any caught water to flow down into your bucket.

4 Stick a piece of bent wire inside and poke around to break up or free the clog.

5 Rescrew the plug with a wrench (tightly!).

UNCLOGGING A SIGNIFICANT DRAIN CLOG

YOU NEED

- × A clogged drain
- × Trap-and-drain auger

STEPS

1 Feed your auger through the sink drain hole (the drain the water goes down) or tub-overflow hole (the porcelain hole that prevents overflows) by turning the auger handle to the right.

2 When you feel squashy resistance, you have hit the clog. If you feel firm resistance, that means you have hit a curve in the pipe and need to gently wiggle the auger around.

3 Crank the auger back and forth and move it around until the clog is broken up. You might have to do this a few times.

4 Remove the auger.

5 Partially fill the sink or tub with hot water, and let it flow down the drain, washing away the clog.

6 If the drain is still a bit clogged, you can use a plunger to further deteriorate the clog. No more clog!

UNCLOGGING A SEVERE DRAIN CLOG

YOU NEED

× Bucket or large water tray
× Electrical tape, duct tape, or a rag (optional)
× Pipe wrench (a wrench big enough to fit around the pipe)
× WD-40, as needed
× Bent metal hanger

STEPS

1 Place a bucket or water tray under the trap.

2 If you care about your pipe's appearance, place tape or rag over the pipe wrench jaws to protect the outside of your pipe.

3 Loosen the 2 pipe-size nuts at either end of the trap that hold the trap in place with your pipe wrench (righty tighty, lefty loosey). If the nut is difficult to loosen, spray it with WD-40.

4 While you are loosening, make sure to hold the trap so it doesn't fall. Depending whether your trap is made of plastic or copper and chrome, either remove the nuts or slide them down onto the trap.

5 Remove the trap, which may be gushing with nasty water and clog debris.

6 Remove into the bucket any clogs that you can see, and clean out all trap obstructions.

7 If you can see clogs in the open ends of the pipe under the sink, poke at them with your piece of bent wire.

8 Replace the trap and tighten the nuts.

9 Leave the bucket in place while you test for leaks by gently turning on the faucet. Tighten the nuts if necessary.

TIPS FOR PREVENTING CLOGS

Most drain clogs are caused by grease, hair, and soap. Yum. To prevent future drain clogs:

× **Avoid dumping food grease down your kitchen sink.** Instead, keep a Grease Jar in the freezer, and pull it out when you cook greasy foods, such as hamburgers or fried foods. Store all of your grease in this jar and you will not only protect your pipes, but if ever you have a delightfully eccentric houseguest who says, "Hmm . . . I'm really in the mood to drink about a pint of old, gelled grease," you will be 100 percent prepared. If you don't have friends like that, another way to dispose of the grease safely is to throw out the whole jar.

× **Purchase a hair guard for your shower drain. The average person loses a hundred strands of hair a day, most of which come out during showers and clog up your drain.** Hair guards cost less than $2 and protect your drain from both hair and large chunks of soap. The first time you use it, you'll be shocked by how much hair you lose, and will either save it to show others or find yourself paying attention to commercials for hair-replacement products.

× **Periodically fill up the sink or bath with boiling water or very hot tap water, and then let the water drain.** This will loosen up soap and grease residue. (Grease melts at 140 degrees Fahrenheit.) A more interesting remedy is baking soda and cola, which will foam everywhere as you dump it down your drain.

× **Don't pour anything down the drain that you wouldn't consider "natural" or water based.** For example, that goopy hair gel that holds your gorgeous strands in place also might stick to your pipes, holding drain scuzz in place.

YOU'RE NOT LUCKY, BUT YOU GET TO USE AN AUGER

If the above options didn't work, you get to use the mother of all clog tools: the auger. An auger is a long tube with a spiraled metal point at one end and a handle or motor at the other. You lower the spinning point into your clog. If you've ever had a plumber come to your home and use a "snake" on your drain, this is what he did, unless he was crazy and cruel to animals.

YOU'RE NOT LUCKY, BUT YOU'LL SURVIVE

If none of the above options work on your sink, congratulations: you have one heck of a clog. You need to remove the U-trap altogether.

RETRIEVING YOUR FAVORITE JEWELRY FROM YOUR SINK DRAIN

You did it again. Despite the acknowledged stupidity of handling small expensive metals over a big hole, there goes your favorite ring/earring/necklace. You probably shrieked something like "Noooo!" and did a slow-motion grab into the air, just missing your precious gem.

Immediately *turn off the water*, preventing the jewelry from being swept into the main drain. Stick your head under the sink, and look at the U-shaped pipe called the U-trap. Your jewelry is probably in there. To get it out, you need to remove the U-trap by loosening the two nuts at either end of the U-trap and dumping its contents into a bucket. Follow the complete directions on page 127 for You're Not Lucky, but You'll Survive, but dump the trap into the bucket, in search of your jewelry.

If the jewelry is not in the U-trap, there is always a chance that it is stuck in the space between the sink and the U-trap. Place the bucket below the drain and run water; hopefully the jewelry will appear. If not, it has already been swept into the main drainage pipe and is gone forever.

TIP

To avoid losing small items down your drain in the future, develop a reflex reaction to instantly cover the drain with your hand whenever you drop something, instead of trying to catch what you dropped in midair. Your hand will get there before the item you dropped. Or, close the drain before you begin fiddling with contacts or jewelry in the first place, and you won't need this section.

CLOGGED TOILETS

One of the worst moments in a human's life takes place when there is a line for the bathroom, you flush, and the water starts *rising*. Don't worry, we can help.

Since a drain is a drain no matter where it is, you may note that the solutions for toilet drains are suspiciously similar to the solutions for sink and tub drains above. The explanations below will be briefer.

THE OTHER LINE OF DEFENSE: FIBER

Dietary fiber makes everything run smoother. So do prunes, prune juice, milk of magnesia, and mineral oil.

YOUR FIRST LINE OF DEFENSE: THE PLUNGER

Plunge away. This is your opportunity to show the world how talented you are at plunging. If you naively thought that more flushing would help and the water level is now too high to plunge without spilling water, put on a pair of gloves, get a cup and a bucket, and put a few cups of water into the bucket before plunging. Later, disinfect or dispose of the gloves, bucket, and cup.

Plunge for up to two minutes at a time, and then break the plunger seal. You will know the plunger has worked if the toilet starts to drain without flushing. Sometimes it will make a cool gurgling noise.

YOUR SECOND LINE OF DEFENSE: THE HANGER

Unwind a metal hanger, and stick the hook part into the toilet hole, attempting to grab the clog. Poke around a lot. Be careful not to damage the porcelain.

YOUR THIRD LINE OF DEFENSE: THE AUGER

For a toilet, you need a "closet" auger. This auger is shorter than the kind you used for sink drains and won't damage porcelain. In a pinch, a drain-sized auger will work. Sometimes—i.e., usually—it is hard to get the auger into the toilet trap, in which case you will have to cover your hand and arm with a full-length rubber glove or a plastic bag, stick your hand into the nastiness, and push the auger where it needs to go. Fun!

THINGS NOT TO FLUSH

- × Tampons, pads, or other feminine inventions
- × Paper towels
- × Anything besides toilet paper that was not a creation of your body

TOILETS

Chances are that you underappreciate the beauty of your toilet, that modern meld of porcelain and plumbing ingenuity that whisks away your unmentionables with the touch of a lever. In the world of mechanics, toilets have redefined simplistic, effective function with just two parts: the bowl, which is anchored to the floor, and the tank, which sits on the bowl. As you read this section, go look at your toilet and remove the lid of the tank to follow along.

THE FLUSH

If you stick your head into the toilet bowl, you'll see that the rim of the bowl contains around fifty rim holes, all drilled at an angle. When you flush the toilet, the tank releases water through the rim holes, and the water streams out to clean the sides of the bowl in the spiral motion you're familiar with. Just out of sight behind the toilet hole is a U-trap, a pipe that uses its shape to form a water seal against sewer gases. The spiral motion is pivotal to the flush process because it provides enough force to siphon waste out of the bowl, over the U-trap, and toward the waste pipeline.

If you really crane your neck into your bowl, you will see another hole called the siphon hole, directly across from the drain opening. The tank also pumps water out through the siphon hole; this directly forces waste down the drain, ensuring that waste makes it through the U-trap.

The tank is just what it sounds like: a tank that holds water. There is an entrance for the water supply (the ballcock) and an exit (the flush valve; "valve" = hole with covering). When you flush the toilet, you are hitting a lever that opens the flush valve, a big flap at the bottom of the tank. The water rushes into the rim of the bowl. When the tank empties, the flap falls back down, sealing the flush valve. Inside the tank, there is also a big rubber balloon resting on the water surface called the ballcock float. It is attached by an arm to the ballcock, which is the freshwater entrance. As the water rushes out, the rubber balloon lowers with the decreasing water level, opening the ballcock. An incoming water-supply line refills both the tank and the bowl, until the float is again horizontal, at which point the ballcock closes and the flush is complete.

NOTE

When not in use, your toilet bowl maintains a water level, which serves two purposes: maintaining some level of cleanliness around the toilet drain opening while forming a seal against any sewer gases that might otherwise leak through the drain and into your bathroom.

SIMPLE TOILET TROUBLESHOOTING

In many cases, major troubles are fixable with minor adjustments to tank parts. These easy fixes will allow you to go to the bathroom without fear.

OTHER TOILET ISSUES

TOILET FUN: CLEANING TOILET RIM HOLES AND THE SIPHON HOLE

Sluggish flushes and a terminally dirty toilet bowl may be the culprit of something other than your roommate's personal habits: clogged rim holes commonly limit water pressure, and therefore a flush's natural ability to do good. To check, place a mirror below the edge of the bowl and look for blocked rim holes. Frequently, mineral deposits from local

FLUSH WITH JOY: SECRETS OF THE FLUSH

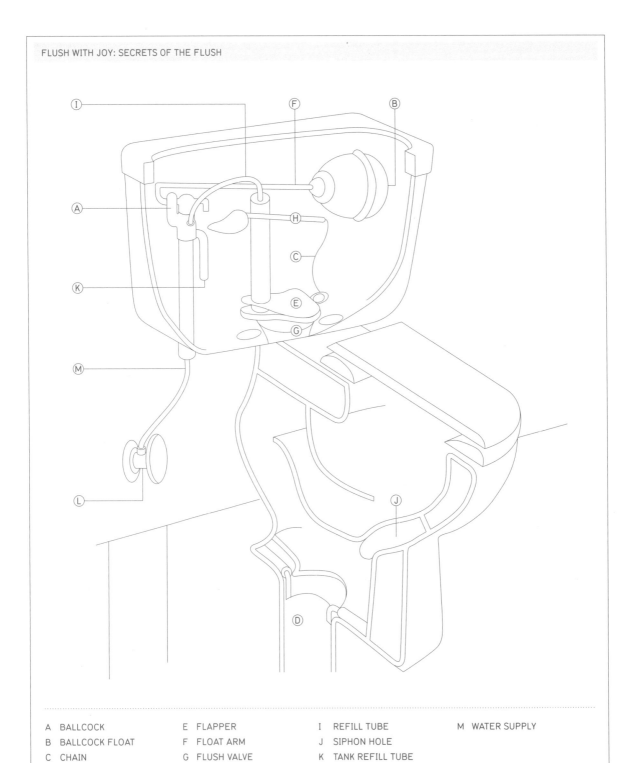

A BALLCOCK	E FLAPPER	I REFILL TUBE	M WATER SUPPLY
B BALLCOCK FLOAT	F FLOAT ARM	J SIPHON HOLE	
C CHAIN	G FLUSH VALVE	K TANK REFILL TUBE	
D DRAIN	H LEVER	L WATER SHUTOFF VALVE	

water supplies are to blame. Like most clogs, a bit of poking will do the trick: we suggest a strategically bent metal coat hanger, gently inserted and jiggled in the hole, being careful not to damage the porcelain. Hold a mirror with one hand to make sure you don't crack the porcelain.

Blocked siphon holes are, unfortunately, less mundane in their cause. Human waste regularly blocks siphon holes, which can be cleaned out with the same jiggling metal hanger method; again, be careful not to damage the porcelain.

WHY IS MY TOILET SWEATING?

The so-called sweat is not actually sweat, but condensation caused when cool water from your water supply pipe hits the warmer porcelain tank. The problem is not just cosmetic: sweating toilets create a chronic puddle, which will cause water damage over time. A well-positioned air conditioner or open window can prevent the sweating.

Otherwise, the most simple solution is to insulate the inside of the tank with a piece of Styrofoam or foam rubber.

HEIR TO THE THRONE: NEW TOILET SEATS

Whether someone broke it or you had an urge for a more interesting throne, replacing toilet seats is straightforward. The easiest way to size a toilet seat is to measure the distance between the two bolts at the back of the lid when closed. Though toilet seats come in neon, puffy, and glow-in-the-dark varieties, most people stick with white. Take the measurements to the store, and purchase the seat of your dreams.

PROBLEM I opened my tank to find Civil War–era parts. No wonder my toilet doesn't work well.

SOLUTION Wear, tear, and replacement is the normal cycle for moving parts. Signs of worn-out tank parts include cracked and hardened tubes and flaps and metal parts so caked with mineral deposits that they appear uncleanable. You can usually determine what's not working by watching a couple of flushes. Toilet parts are easy to disassemble, with most parts screwing, sliding, or unhooking. I suggest simply removing the old part and bringing it to the hardware store to request a properly sized replacement—this way, you don't even need to know what it's called.

If your toilet is older, make sure to ask whether they recommend replacing the part or replacing the entire assembly. Modern ballcock kits come with easy instructions and the installation shouldn't require more than an hour.

PROBLEM My toilet runs constantly. It's like the Energizer bunny: it never stops.

SOLUTION A running toilet means that water is somehow flowing from the tank into the bowl, either through the flush valve flap or the tank's overflow tube. There are two possibilities, the most likely being that the flush valve flap is slightly open because the outside lever is attached too tightly. To fix, remove the tank lid and slightly loosen the nut attaching the lever to the tank by turning clockwise (from above, to the right). This will slightly slacken the chain attaching the lever to the flush valve flap. If the chain seems too short, detach it altogether and bring it to the hardware store for a slightly longer replacement.

The other possibility is that the ballcock float, or big rubber ball in your tank, is slightly too high, causing freshwater to continually enter the tank and spill into the overflow (or plastic) tube. To fix, simply open the toilet lid and gently bend the metal armconnecting the rubber ball to the ballcock slightly, forcing the rubber ball downward.

PROBLEM My toilet won't flush. I hit the lever and nothing happens.

SOLUTION If you don't feel any resistance from the lever, your lever is probably no longer attached to the flush valve flap. Inside the tank, the lever arm should have holes for the hooks on the chain of the flush valve flap. Rehook the chain. If the lever is quite loose, it might have simply loosened over time. One sign of this is that you are afraid the lever is going to fall into your hand. To fix, open up the tank and, right on the tank side of the lever, locate the locknut that attaches the lever to the tank. Using an adjustable wrench, turn the nut counterclockwise (from above, to the left). If someone was recently working in your apartment, it is possible that the toilet water supply was shut off. (Landlords have a penchant for leaving without turning things back on.) There should be a water shutoff knob within a few feet of your toilet, often hidden under a sink cabinet. Turn it back on.

PROBLEM I own America's noisiest toilet.

SOLUTION Loud toilets usually mean that a water valve or pipe isn't allowing the water a clear path. Try turning off the toilet water supply and flushing the toilet to empty the tank. Then lift up the flush valve flap and clean it with plastic or brass wool. Make sure all tubes are kink-free and unclogged. Turn on the water and retry.

PROBLEM My toilet barely flushes. Toilet paper is a struggle.

SOLUTION Power flushes require ample water, and weak flushing that doesn't quite do the job can be a result of a low tank water level. To fix, perform the opposite of the preceding repair: bend the stick connecting the rubber ball to the ballcock slightly to force the rubber ball upward.

INSULATING A TOILET TANK

YOU NEED

- × Measuring tape
- × Foam rubber or Styrofoam, ½-inch thick
- × Utility knife
- × Silicone cement
- × Old towels
- × Another toilet to use for the next 24 hours

STEPS

1 Measure the inner dimensions of the larger tank wall. Go buy 2 pieces of foam rubber or Styrofoam of this size.

2 Turn off the toilet water supply, flush the toilet to drain it, and mop dry the inside of the tank with old towels.

3 Place the Styrofoam on the inside of the tank. Cut it smaller if necessary.

4 Glue the Styrofoam or rubber to the wall securely with silicone cement.

5 Allow at least 24 hours for drying, and consider your sweaty toilet a problem of the past.

INSTALLING A NEW TOILET SEAT

YOU NEED

× Flathead screwdriver
× Adjustable wrench
× WD-40 (sometimes)
× A new toilet seat

STEPS

1 Remove the old toilet seat by removing the bolts holding it down. Some bolts have plastic caps protecting them, which you need to pop off with a screwdriver or your fingers. Look at the seat with the lid down. The two white caps near the tank are the caps hiding the bolts. Sit below the seat edge, and use one hand to hold the bottom-side nut still with an adjustable wrench. Use the other hand to unscrew the top-side bolt with a screwdriver. (Righty tighty, lefty loosey.) Plastic bolts are easy to loosen; you may need WD-40 to help loosen metal bolts.

2 Repeat with the other bolt and remove the seat and lid.

3 Place the new seat and lid in line with the bolt holes.

4 Stick the bolts through the holes from the top, and twist the nut onto the bottom of the bolt.

5 Tighten the bolt while holding the nut in place with the wrench and turning the bolt tighter with a screwdriver. You want to tighten until the seat is secure, but not so much that you crack the porcelain. Repeat with the second bolt.

6 Enjoy your new throne.

FAUCETS

Faucets leak. They just do. Most people have at least one leaky faucet in their living space, if not two, wasting gallons of water a day and often rotting the surrounding sink area. Few people realize that it's important to fix leaking faucets quickly, because the common culprit—worn washers, the tiny metal doughnuts inside your faucet—will damage other pieces in the handle, requiring a much more complex repair.

Sink repairs are complicated only because of the variety of faucet models. There are three main kinds of faucets: "compression" faucets, which have separate hot and cold knobs, and "cartridge" and "ball" faucets, which have one handle for all temperatures. A fourth type, "ceramic disc" faucets, are an expensive hybrid between cartridge faucets and ball faucets. Though they rarely need repairs, when they do, they follow the same directions as ball faucets.

DOES YOUR FAUCET LOOK LIKE THIS?

Look at the illustrations on page 136 to identify which kind of faucet you have.

HOW TO DO FAUCET REPAIRS

Before attempting any faucet repair, you want to follow three steps:

1 Turn off the water shutoffs to the faucet. Many models have *two* shutoffs, one for hot and one for cold. Then turn on the faucets to empty out the pipes.
2 Put the stopper in the drain to prevent parts from from falling down the drain. If you don't have a real stopper, stuffing in a rag in the drain will work, as will a flat rubber jar opener.
3 Clear a flat area nearby on which to lay out the faucet parts in the exact order that you remove them. All faucet repairs follow the same trend: disassemble the faucet or spout until you reach the broken piece in question, replace the piece, and then reassemble.

COMPRESSION FAUCETS 101

A compression faucet, sometimes called a stem-and-seat faucet, is the oldest faucet model. The water flow is controlled by a washer that, when the water is turned off, moves down into a hole (the "valve seat") and prevents water from moving toward the faucet. When the water is turned on, the washer moves upward and allows water to pass.

LEAKY COMPRESSION SPOUTS

Leaks mean that the washer is not fitting securely into the hole. Either the washer or the hole is damaged, and most often it is only the washer. First you need to determine which knob is causing the leak by turning off the hot water supply to the sink from below the sink and seeing if the leak stops or not. Washers have many different possible shapes and sizes, depending on the faucet, and you probably won't know which shape you have until you disassemble the faucet handle. This said, your best plan is to take apart the faucet handle, bring the washer to the hardware store, and purchase an identical washer. Bringing in all handle parts will ensure that the correct pieces were used in the first place, which isn't always the case, while allowing you to replace any parts that look worn.

Disassembling a sink knob is rather easy. The strategy is to keep loosening downward as appears appropriate.

LEAKY COMPRESSION HANDLES

If your compression faucet *handles* leak, you probably have a loose "packing" nut, which is the horizontal nut hidden directly below the knob. They should only leak when turned on. This is simple to fix.

LEAKY COMPRESSION HANDLE BOTTOMS

For leaks from compression handle bases, you might need a new O-ring, which is the thin ring around the stem that prevents water from seeping out of the handles. The O-ring is the rubbery doughnut located on the stem, so the repair is the same as for Leaky Compression Spouts (above). You need to remove the stem, which is the major piece held in place by the nut below the knob. Bring the stem to the hardware store and replace the O-ring.

NOTE

In some sinks, the hole lining ("valve seat") is permanently attached to the sink. If this is the case, instead of replacing it, you're going to have to sand it down so that the metal is smooth again, because rough metal damages washers immediately and allows leaks to slip through. While this sounds complex, the grinding takes about 30 seconds. Go to the hardware store and ask for a "seat grinder" or a "seat dresser and cutter." Place the seat grinder into the valve seat and grind it down until smooth. Reassemble the handle.

THE CARTRIDGE FAMILY

A cartridge faucet has one handle for all temperatures, and uses an interior cylinder-shaped cartridge to control water flow. As you move the handle, the cartridge shifts to allow differing amounts of water to pass through the spout. You can identify one by a handle that juts off from a flat base—you need to pull it directly upward to turn on the water. There are a number of slight variations in parts, so if you don't see a part listed in the repair steps on page 137, just move on to the next step.

THE BALL FAMILY

Ball faucets work by controlling water temperature through a metal ball under the handle base. Depending on how the ball is positioned, different amounts of hot and cold water are allowed through the spout. You know you have a ball faucet if your sink control is a handle with a screw on the underside that you move around in circles to control water temperature.

LEAKY CARTRIDGE AND BALL HANDLES

Fixing a leaky cartridge or ball handle—water dripping from the handle—is really easy.

LEAKY BALL AND CARTRIDGE FAUCETS

To fix a leaky ball faucet—water coming out of the spout—first try the above repair. If that doesn't work, it is easiest to go to the hardware store and purchase a "ball faucet replacement kit." You could replace the individual parts, but identifying what needs to be replaced can be a headache.

YOU NEED

× Screwdriver
× Adjustable wrench
× Resealable plastic bag

× Vaseline, as needed
× Seat wrench, as needed (sometimes)

STEPS

1 Use a screwdriver to pop off any decorative knob caps.

2 Loosen the screw you uncovered just below the cap with a screwdriver and remove the knob.

3 A horizontal nut will appear below, holding down everything below. Remove it with your adjustable wrench (right tighty, lefty loosey).

4 The piece held in place by the nut is the "stem," which has the all-important washer attached at its bottom. Remove the stem by pulling it up with your fingers.

5 The washer will be attached to the bottom of the stem with a screw. This is the washer that blocks water flow. Loosen the screw; pop off the washer.

6 Put the washer or all the knob parts in a resealable plastic bag and head to the hardware store to replace them.

7 Back at the ranch, replace the old washer with a new washer of the exact same size, and reassemble in reverse order. In most cases, the washer replacement will cure the leak. If the leak continues, that means that the hole lining—the only handle part still attached to the sink, a 1-inch metal piece embedded in the hole where the handle once was—is damaged and not forming a clean seal with the washer. If this is the case, proceed to number 8.

8 Unscrew the hole lining (professionally known as the valve seat) with a seat wrench, which is a special tool with a screwdriver-like end that fits into the hole lining, just for this purpose. (Often an Allen wrench will do the trick, or if you're desperate, a screwdriver, but not always.) Bring the hole lining to the repair store to be replaced.

9 Install the new hole lining and reassemble the other handle parts in perfect reverse order.

10 As you assemble, if you want, you can grease the metal pieces that rub together with a bit (a bit!) of Vaseline to keep them working smoothly, making sure no Vaseline can contaminate the water flow.

11 No more leaky faucet.

COMPRESSION FAUCET

A   DECORATIVE CAP
B   SCREW
C   HANDLE
D   LOCKNUT
E   STEM
F   O-RING
G   SEAT WASHER
H   SPOUT

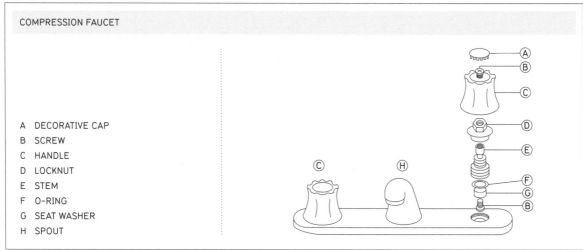

CARTRIDGE FAUCET

A   DECORATIVE CAP
B   SCREW
C   HANDLE
D   CARTRIDGE
E   RETAINER
F   SPOUT
G   O-RINGS

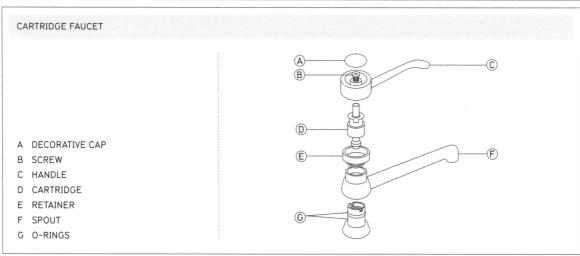

BALL FAUCET

A   HANDLE
B   SCREW
C   RING (REMOVE WITH SLIPJOINT PLIERS)
D   SPOUT
E   CAM
F   BALL
G   O-RINGS
H   SPRING
I   SEAT

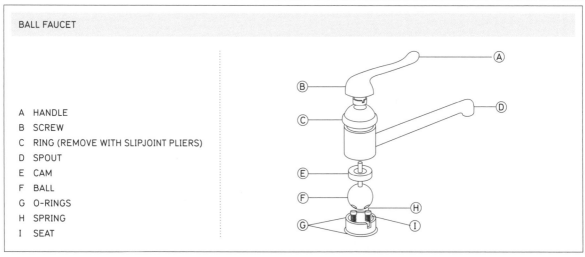

FIXING LEAKY COMPRESSION FAUCET HANDLES

YOU NEED

- × Screwdriver
- × Adjustable wrench

STEPS

1 Pop off the decorative cap.

2 Loosen the underlying screw with a screwdriver.

3 Remove the faucet knob you just loosened.

4 The nut directly in front of you is the packing nut. Tighten it with an adjustable wrench. (Righty tighty, lefty loosey.)

5 Reassemble in perfect reverse order.

6 Wash your hands.

FIXING A LEAKING BALL OR CARTRIDGE FAUCET SPOUT

YOU NEED

- × Screwdriver
- × Adjustable wrench
- × Long-nose pliers

STEPS

1 Remove the screw at the top of the base and take off the handle. Sometimes you first need to pry off a decorative plate or cover.

2 Remove the handle. Sometimes you will have to lean it backward and pull.

3 On most models, you will now be looking at a horizontal nut. Loosen it with an adjustable wrench and remove.

4 You are now looking at the cartridge itself, sometimes called a cartridge stem. Most models have a little vertical pole jutting out of the cartridge. Using pliers, pull the pole out straight upward.

5 Bring the stem to the hardware store and purchase a replacement, which will often come in a "cartridge replacement kit." Make sure the faucet on the package looks like yours.

6 Reassemble the pieces in perfect reverse order. You will know that you've correctly repaired the handle if it lifts smoothly. Test for leaks.

REPAIRING LEAKY CARTRIDGE OR BALL FAUCET HANDLES

YOU NEED

- × Screwdriver
- × Adjustable wrench or groove-joint pliers (big pliers), as needed

STEPS

1 Find and loosen the handle screw, usually hidden directly below the handle shaft. Remove the handle. If no tool you have fits the screw, go to the hardware store and say that you need a "faucet repair kit," which includes a tiny loosener for this screw.

2 Pull off the handle.

3 You will see either a horizontal nut or a horizontal metal ring directly in front of you. This is what is loose and causing the leak.

4 Thoroughly tighten the nut or metal ring (righty tighty, lefty loosey) with a wrench. For some rings, you may need to purchase a pair of "groove-joint pliers," which are like a wrench for round objects. To protect the outside of the faucet, wrap the nut or ring in cloth while you tighten.

5 Reassemble the handle. No more leaky handle.

It's easier to replace the whole kit and caboodle, and the kits themselves are extremely self-explanatory.

Before you leave for the hardware store, remove the faucet handle and underlying parts. You do this by loosening and removing consecutive parts with a screwdriver or wrench as you uncover them. Place all parts in a resealable plastic bag. You know you have removed all needed pieces when all that's left to remove is the spout. Take the bag to the hardware store to find a proper replacement kit, which will include specific ball faucet instructions.

On a cartridge faucet, the easiest bet is also to replace the entire cartridge. You could instead purchase an inexpensive "replacement seal," but they don't last very long—it's better to fix the real problem.

LEAKY BALL AND CARTRIDGE SPOUT BOTTOMS

If your spout leaks at the bottom near the sink, sometimes called the spout neck, you need to replace its O-rings. O-rings are the rubbery rings on the base of the faucet that prevent water from seeping out of faucets or spouts at the bottom near the sink.

1   Disassemble the handle parts as in the above repair, but instead of placing parts in a baggie, lay them out neatly on a counter.
2   When you get to the ball—the ball-like metal piece—remove it and the adjacent little springs. The ball is sitting on a cylindrical base of metal, surrounded by the spout. Pull up on the spout; it should come right off.
3   Now you are looking at a bare sink, except for a cylindrical base of metal with two rubbery rings wrapped around it. These are the O-rings. They probably look worn. Use a utility knife or sharp kitchen knife to cut them off.
4   Take the cut O-rings to the hardware store for replacements.
5   Replace the O-rings and reassemble the sink.

TUBS

The easiest repair in this book is caulking your tub or shower. This simple fix, which prevents water from leaking through small cracks between your tiles, is also the most cost-effective home repair: a $3 tube of caulking can potentially save you $5,000 in water damage bills.

Caulking—also called sealant—is the white pasty goo that water-seals the crevices of your bath or shower. To prevent water leaks, you simply line the edges of your tiles and tub with caulking and smooth it out to dry. The repair can be quite fun, as the caulking tube resembles a tube of frosting and your only job is to smear it around your shower crevices.

 NOTE

Never caulk directly around faucets and faucet handles. The water pipes behind the tile expand and contract with hot and cold water. If you caulk around the handles and spigot, that pressure is placed directly on the wall, which can result in cracked tiles or exploded water pipes.

TIP

Beauty Tip   Many people caulk purely for cosmetic purposes. New caulking cleanly hides broken grout and unattractive chips around the shower, while killing unseemly mildew that can grow behind old caulking. Caulking comes in different colors, including translucent, black, and silver, but most people stick with white.

CAULKING OTHER PLACES

Caulking belongs wherever different building materials meet, such as where window wood meets siding, or where chimney brick meets roof. Each material expands and contracts at different temperatures, potentially creating cracks. Caulking prevents this by flexibly filling the gap, thereby better insulating your residence from weather, water, and critters. Most outdoor projects require a caulking gun, which costs anywhere from $3 to $45 and resembles a glue gun.

YOU NEED

- × Tube of caulking
- × Scissors
- × Kitchen or putty knife (optional)

- × Utility knife
- × Roll of masking tape (optional)
- × Old rag

STEPS

1 Go to the hardware store and say, "I want to caulk my bathtub." If you are in a discount store, the underpaid worker will just stare at you blankly, so look for tubes that say "caulking" or "silicone sealant" and are labeled "for bath and kitchen use."

2 Go home and clean your shower or tub with shower cleaner and water, removing any dirt or grit.

3 Come back when the shower is dry. Most tubes of caulking have plastic nozzles that can be cut with scissors to match the diameter of your crevice. You probably will not need to, but cut accordingly for wider cracks.

4 Scrape off old tub caulking with a knife. (If you're lazy, this step is nonessential, but will lengthen the life of your caulking. Your old caulking is most likely a rubbery consistency, meaning that it is silicone caulking, and you can remove it with a kitchen or putty knife. If the caulking is rigid, it is probably latex caulking, and you need a utility knife or handled razor blade.) Hold the knife at a 45-degree angle to prevent scratching your tub or tile and simply cut off the old caulking, scraping off remaining bits.

5 For caulking perfection, place 2 strips of masking tape along either side of the crevice that you want to caulk—after you caulk, peel off the tape for a straight, smooth line.

6 There's an old wives' tale that the tub should be filled with water before you begin to caulk, so the caulking is applied while the tub is seated correctly.

Logically speaking, if the tub moves more than ¼ inch when filled with water, you've got much bigger problems than caulking. However, many home repair divas continue to insist on filling the tub. Use your discretion.

7 Holding the tube at a 45-degree angle, neatly release a strip of caulking. Caulk along any dry cracks where the tub meets tile or wall, both inside and outside the tub, or where grout is missing between tiles. In an all-tile shower, put caulking along the crevice where the floor meets the wall, and between tiles where necessary.

8 With a wet finger or damp rag, smooth out the caulking. This step is mainly cosmetic. A putty knife can help cut away accidental globs.

9 Let the tub dry for 24 hours. Pat yourself on the back and enjoy a relaxing, leak-free shower!

Don't know what kind of caulking you need? Just go to the hardware store and say, "I want to caulk___," and the employee will give you the appropriate kind of caulking. Take advantage of store expertise and ask for an explanation of how to do the repair. Caulk away!

SHOWERHEADS

Showerheads rarely cause leaks, because water pressure is quite low by the time it makes it to the shower. Instead, the two most common showerhead repairs are installing a new showerhead—usually a vanity repair—or cleaning an existing showerhead for mineral buildups. Both repairs require removing the existing showerhead, which means removing the bulbous part that the water comes out of but leaving behind the shower arm. This is a two-step process. *Before you begin, shut off the water supply to the shower or entire living space.*

REMOVING A SHOWERHEAD

YOU NEED

× 2 pipe wrenches
× Cloth or masking tape

1 Wrap the top and bottom of the showerhead arm with masking tape or a spare cloth to protect the finish. Place one pipe wrench on top of each wrapping.

2 Hold the top wrench steady, while turning the lower wrench to loosen the showerhead. Once it loosens, continue with your hands until you are holding the showerhead.

INSTALLING A NEW SHOWERHEAD

Once you have picked out your desired Massage 3000 showerhead, the package will come with complete installation instructions. The installation itself is quite simple, just a matter of attaching the existing shower arm to the new showerhead and washer (small metal doughnut) and tightening it with an adjustable wrench

or pipe wrench. Wrap the wrench in tape or cloth to prevent damaging the shower arm.

SHOPPING FOR SHOWERHEADS

Man has invented a full variety of heavenly showerhead options, including these:

× Built-in antiscalding features.
× Showerhead turn-off buttons, which allow you to temporarily turn off the water while sudsing up without changing the temperature.
× Pulsating options galore.
× Showerhead height-changing rods, allowing those who live with small children or short loved ones to shower comfortably.
× Handheld shower units, which bring the water closer to what you need to wash and are ideal for elderly or disabled who might use shower seats. Handheld units are also useful for washing wiggling children who object to sitting under a full-force tub spigot.
× Low-volume showerheads, which use a washer to reduce the amount of water coming out of the showerhead. These are environmentally friendly. Be aware that many states require low-water-use showers—sadly, those fire hydrant–like showers at the public pool are a thing of the past. Double-check at the store before you buy.

CLEANING AN EXISTING SHOWERHEAD

You want to clean your showerhead if mineral deposits, soap scum, or other debris are visible; if you notice a low or lopsided water flow; or if your showerhead hasn't been cleaned in a half decade or longer. To clean, lay the showerhead on a flat surface and disassemble it, making sure to *keep track of the order of the parts* and to lay them out in that order. As recommended earlier, if you are afraid you'll forget how to put it back together, take a digital picture for reference.

When you reach the piece with the little water holes, unplug the holes with a toothpick. For a particularly grimy showerhead, soaking all parts in white vinegar can dispel a variety of mineral deposits.

PIPES

Leaky pipes are common after freezing weather, which causes pipes to expand and burst, and in older plumbing systems. Most pipes are behind walls, so you'll be informed of your pipe leak by a growing puddle through a wall or ceiling. If you're lucky, the pipe will happen to be visible, either under your sink or in your basement.

UH-OH, I HAVE A MAJOR PIPE LEAK

If you have a major leak, immediately turn off the water shutoff that controls the pipe and call a plumber, or if you're not sure which shutoff to use, turn off the main water shutoff. Turn on the faucet nearest to the pipe to empty the pipe, temporarily stopping the leak.

If you don't have access to the main water shutoff—a likely situation if you live in an apartment building—try a temporary solution while you wait for the landlord. Dry the pipe as best you can, then wrap the leaky spot with electrical or duct tape. Stick a bucket under the pipe to catch any still-leaking water. Usually a plumber will come and simply replace the misbehaving pipe or set of pipes.

FIXING MINOR PIPE LEAKS

If the leak is coming from a minor pipe slit (read: not an exploded main water supply pipe with severe flooding), and you've located both the leak and the water shutoff, you can try saving some money and fixing it yourself. You have two options:

Hardware stores sell "pipe repair clamp kits," also sometimes called "repair couplings." The kits consist of a rubber sleeve underneath a hinged piece of metal that wraps around your pipe and closes with screws or bolts. While often used as a temporary fix, a pipe clamp kit can serve as a permanent repair for more minor pipe splits.

Your other option is to use plumber's epoxy, the equivalent of cement for pipes. Also seen as a more temporary solution, it can permanently fix minor pipe splits. Epoxy comes in two sticks of putty that you press together with your fingers to activate.

LEAKS BETWEEN PIPES

Leaking pipes are often like a watery game of Telephone: the loss happens at the interchange. Many water leaks happen at the joints (meeting places) between pipes, meaning that the pipes are not actually broken, but just leaking at junctions. After turning off the water supply, there are a couple of ways to fix this.

1   Using two pipe wrenches, place one securely on the upper part of the joint and one on the bottom part of the joint. Gently press the wrenches in opposite directions to tighten the joint. Be *gentle*, as old pipes can respond to pressure by exploding.
2   Go to the hardware store and purchase plumber's epoxy. It's a mix between clay and Silly Putty that is particularly effective at sealing leaky pipe joints. Follow the instructions for Repairing Minor Pipe Leaks, page 142.

IT'S FREEZING COLD . . . AND I HAVE NO WATER: FROZEN PIPES

You know you've been blessed with a frozen pipe when a faucet won't work in cold weather. Frozen pipes begin when a small chunk of ice forms inside a pipe, and then expands to cut off the water supply. If you suspect a frozen pipe, act immediately, because frozen pipes usually burst. The pipes at risk for freezing are located along outside walls, in attics, in basements, and in other areas without full temperature control.

To locate the freeze, feel along the pipe with your hand for the really cold spot. Please don't burn yourself on hot pipes. If the pipe has not yet burst, you're in luck: find a portable hair dryer and aim it at the frozen area, starting in front of the freeze and working backward until it defrosts and water flows again. If the pipe bursts, follow the instructions under Uh-oh, I Have a Major Pipe Leak, left.

REPAIRING A MINOR PIPE LEAK WITH A CLAMP KIT

YOU NEED

- × Old towels
- × Tape measure
- × Pipe repair clamp kit
- × Sandpaper
- × Screwdriver or wrench
- × Bucket

STEPS

1 Turn off the water supply to the pipe.

2 Drain the pipe by turning on the nearest faucet.

3 Thoroughly dry the area, both the pipe and the floor below.

4 Measure the pipe and go to the plumbing supply or hardware store. Ask for a "repair coupling" or "pipe repair clamp kit." They come in a variety of standard pipe sizes.

5 Follow the directions, which will often suggest cleaning the pipe with sandpaper or another abrasive before applying the coupling.

6 Place the coupling over the pipe, and depending on the model, tighten the screws with a screwdriver or the bolts with an adjustable wrench.

7 Turn the water back on and check for leaks.

8 Leave a bucket under the pipe, and check back frequently over the next few weeks to make sure that the leak is properly sealed.

REPAIRING A MINOR PIPE LEAK WITH PLUMBER'S EPOXY

YOU NEED

- × Old towels
- × Plumber's epoxy
- × Rubber or latex gloves
- × Bucket

STEPS

1 Turn off the water supply to the pipe, and drain the pipe by turning on the nearest faucet.

2 Thoroughly dry the area.

3 Go to the hardware or plumbing supply store and purchase plumber's epoxy, or plumber's seal, or pipe epoxy.

4 Put on gloves and, following the directions on the package, remove chunks of seal from each stick; press them together with your fingers.

5 Press the putty around the pipe, both covering the split and extending the full circumference of the pipe. It should look like a hunk of bubble gum wrapped around a pipe.

6 Let the putty dry for 24 hours. If you must use the pipe, wait a few hours and gently turn on the water supply, so you have a light water flow. Keep a bucket under the pipe and check back frequently.

INSULATING PIPES

Preventing future frozen pipes works along the same strategy as keeping humans warm: if you don't want to freeze, put some clothes on. It's the same with pipes. Hardware stores sell cheap insulation sleeves, which are hollow foam tubes that wrap around exposed pipes. Insulation is a wonderful investment if you:

× Are concerned about colder sections of your living space
× Are going on a winter vacation and turning down the heat
× Have frequent frozen pipes

Insulating all hot water lines will also save you ample money on future gas or electricity bills. Hot water loses heat from the moment it escapes your water heater. Every time you turn on a faucet, the pipe must first provide water that has been sitting in the pipe, which is often cold in uninsulated pipes.

Insulating pipes is an easy matter of cutting the foam to the size of the pipe—eyeballing is fine—and wrapping the foam around the pipe. *Note: Hot water pipes are hot. Don't burn yourself while applying the insulation.* In many cases, you don't need to touch the actual pipe while wrapping the insulation around the pipe, but gloves are suggested.

HOT WATER HEATERS

There is nothing sexy to say about a hot water heater. It is just what it sounds like: a metal or plastic water storage tank that uses gas or electricity power to heat water. Most water heaters store a full tank of hot water at all times, though for double the price, newer tankless models only heat water only as needed—or, in the case of Rolls Royce models, keep a half gallon heated, so that you never endure those difficult, naked 21 seconds of awaiting hot shower water. The tank is fed by a branch of the main cold water supply pipe and releases heated water into a main hot water pipe for your home or building. Modern water heaters include various safety elements, such as an over-heating shutoff and a pressure relief valve, which make overheating disasters a problem of the past.

TEMPERATURE: FEVER IN THE MORNING, FEVER ALL THROUGH THE NIGHT. . .

Water heaters allow you to set the maximum temp-erature of your water, allowing you to save on gas or electricity bills. Homes with young children often set the temperature low, making scalding impossible and lukewarm showers a way of life. To see if yours is set too high, do a quick test:

× Turn on your sink faucet at maximum heat.
× Ask yourself: Do I ever use water this hot? Why would one need water this hot? If your hot water is seemingly near boiling, that means that you're paying to heat water that you always cool with cold water. Turn down the temperature on the water heater's little thermostat. Conversely, if your hot water isn't hot at all, slightly raise the temperature.

WHY DO WE ALWAYS RUN OUT OF HOT WATER?

Tank water heaters come with a variety of different tank sizes. In homes with a lot of people—or with one person who takes long hot showers while running the washing machine and dishwasher—you may occasionally run out of hot water, that horrible event

DRAINING A HOT WATER HEATER TANK

YOU NEED

× One water hose
× A nearby drain or outside lawn

STEPS

1 Locate the water heater's incoming cold water pipe (a cool pipe next to the tank with a handle attached) and turn off the water flow by turning the handle.

2 Turn on a hot water faucet anywhere in your home, and let it run at medium pressure, making sure you don't inadvertently flood the sink.

3 Locate the water heater's "draincock," a spigot on the bottom of the water heater.

4 Attach a hose to the spigot and run the hose to a nearby drain or outside lawn.

5 Turn on the spigot. Expect dirty water out of the hose.

6 Once the tank has emptied, turn on the cold water valve and continue letting the hose run until the water runs clean.

7 When clean, turn off the hot water faucet and the water heater spigot, remove the hose, and you're done—the tank will refill itself through its cold water valve.

where the shower water goes cold while you're applying shampoo. Installing a newer, tankless water heater might break your wallet (including installation, $2,000-$3,500), so instead, try better planning your hot water use.

DRAINING TANKED HOT WATER HEATERS

Hot water heaters with tanks should be drained every six to twelve months, an easy process that cleans out the tank and prevents sediment from building up.

The telltale sign that yours needs immediate draining is dirty or cloudy hot water coming from faucets, while cold water remains clean. If this is the case, either tell your landlord to drain the water heater or do it yourself.

UM, WHY IS THE SHOWER COLD?

Cold showers are the soggy icing on the moldy old cake of dreary, running-late mornings, and they happen somewhat frequently. If you don't have any hot water, there are a number of possible causes, all of which surround your hot water heater. Most often, the power or gas to the heater has switched off. Go through the following steps in order:

× Check for a blown fuse or tripped breaker in your main circuit or fuse box and replace the fuse or reset the breaker. The water heater should go back on.
× Make sure that the water heater is not lop sided—unlike your slanted kitchen table, it cannot function properly on an angle.
× If your water heater is gas heated, make sure that the flame didn't blow out. If it's off, relight it following the instructions printed on the heater or call the gas company for help. If it goes off again, clean out the flame area with a thin copper wire (other metals will damage the flame opening) and try again. If it goes out repeatedly, call a professional.
× If you have an electric heater, its thermostat should have a red "Reset" button. Push it once. If it cuts off again, something is wrong with the thermostat or heating element and you need to call a professional.

× If you see water leaking anywhere around the water heater, turn off the power and tighten (or get someone else to tighten) every pipe connection and bolt in sight. If you still have a water leak, you need to get the water heater replaced immediately, before your living space becomes Lake Water Heater.

In the meantime stop further leakage by turning off the cold water pipe (turn the water shutoff near the tank) and draining the tank through its spigot—attach a hose, run the hose outside, and turn on the spigot.

TIP

Many tanked water heaters have an "anode," a magnesium tube that collects impurities so that the anode gets rusty and disgusting instead of the tank itself. The anode needs to be replaced every five years if you're on the cautious side, every ten years definitely.

OTHER WATER HEATER REPAIRS

While water heaters are easy to understand, it is tricky to diagnose specific problems because defects to approximately thirty mechanisms present with the same two symptoms: cold water or a puddle next to the tank. If the above repairs don't work, you will need to call a plumber or heating and cooling guy and have your tank repaired. If the contractor suggests a new tank, always ask if it is possible to make the repair with a new part instead.

CHAPTER 6

HELP, IT'S FREEZING IN HERE! HEATING AND VENTILATION

You probably don't know how to fix many things that break in your living space, particularly those that change from residence to residence. What differentiates that wider category from those listed below is that you will know how to fix these. Home repair is not an innate skill: you have to learn how to do it. Here we are going to talk about heating and ventilation systems.

"Um, I'm cold." Either you ate too much ice cream or there is a problem with your heating system. Heating systems are complex, involving all the major players—electricity, water, and air—and are not for every adventurous person with a toolbox. As a general rule, if you are at all unclear about what you are doing, call a skilled friend or professional, because heating systems make a very poor training ground. Here we will cover only the very basics.

HEATING SYSTEMS

There are five common kinds of heating systems: *warm* or *forced-air* systems, *hot water* systems, *steam* systems, *radiant heat* systems, and *electrical heat* systems. These categories are not mutually exclusive: many refurbished residences have combination systems, so ask the landlord, former owner, or a knowledgeable friend what kind of system you have. You need to know in order to perform the regular maintenance routine that your system requires. "Central heat" is the modern norm, which means that one main furnace controlled by a central thermostat supplies heat to the entire living space. As you can imagine, this is much easier than running around to individual heaters in every room.

The general gist of any heating system is this: a central oil-, gas-, or electricity-powered furnace heats up water or air. Either hot air is circulated through your living space via vents and ducts, or hot water is circulated through radiators and convectors, which heat up rooms. Heating systems usually require a professional because you need to know the intricacies of your particular system.

FORCED-AIR SYSTEMS Identifiable by small vents, these systems have some vents that release warm

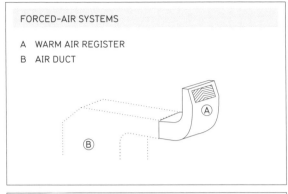

FORCED-AIR SYSTEMS

A   WARM AIR REGISTER
B   AIR DUCT

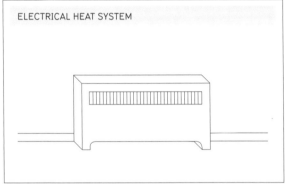

ELECTRICAL HEAT SYSTEM

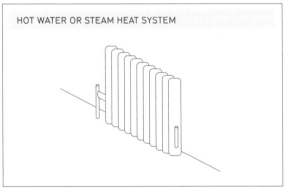

HOT WATER OR STEAM HEAT SYSTEM

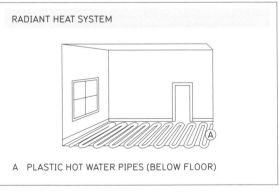

RADIANT HEAT SYSTEM

A   PLASTIC HOT WATER PIPES (BELOW FLOOR)

air while other vents at floor level collect cool air. The furnace fan is attached to one main duct that branches off into smaller ducts. If you have central air conditioning, it most likely shares the same system of ducts and the same thermostat. To even out temperatures between rooms, see Why Is the Kitchen 10 Degrees Cooler Than My Bedroom?, page 158.

HOT WATER SYSTEMS These work by heating water in a boiler inside the furnace. A big pump forces the hot water through the pipes of the house, and directly into radiators in each room. Depending on the system, either the same pipes or a second set of pipes bring the cool water back to the furnace to be reheated. Hot water systems must be regularly "bled" to work properly (see Bloody Radiator, page 150).

STEAM SYSTEMS Common in older buildings, steam systems use water that is heated in a boiler inside the furnace until it creates steam. The steam rises naturally and travels upward through the pipes into radiators in each room. The whole system is built on gravity. When the steam cools and turns into water, it flows back down the pipes to the furnace.

RADIANT HEAT SYSTEMS These use plastic hot water pipes snaked just below the floor to heat up rooms. The system is essentially a hot water system, without the radiators. You know you have radiant heat by elimination: your rooms are clearly heated, and yet there's no sign of a heating element around, and the floors are warm. The system is divided into sections, with each room or two controlled by one thermostat. Radiant heat systems are most commonly added onto existing hot water systems and are more energy efficient by using cooler water temperatures.

ELECTRICAL HEAT A baseboard in each room has a long horizontal heating element inside that uses electric power to heat up. These systems were installed frequently during the Hippie Era, when electricity was comparatively inexpensive. Now they're pricey compared to other systems, but they are also very straightforward and heat up rooms quickly.

ALL ABOUT THERMOSTATS

Thermostats measure air temperature and automatically turn the furnace (or central air conditioner)

on and off to meet a specified temperature. Most are located in one room and work on the assumption that all rooms are about the same temperature.

Most people underappreciate thermostat timer programs. You can save 15 percent on your heating bill every time you drop the temperature 10 degrees for six hours. This means that someone in the know would set his or her thermostat to drop a few degrees during the night, and drop again during the workday; those with an older manual thermostat should manually turn it down before going to work or sleep. Timer programs range from the very simple—two daily temperature switches—to programs with all the bells and whistles, allowing a new schedule for every day of the week. If your thermostat timer says something about "zones," you are even luckier, because you can control your heat by room. Program your timer to heat only rooms that you might use—the TV room, for example, during evenings. Remember that all rooms should be kept at a minimum of 55 degrees Fahrenheit during winter to prevent frozen pipes.

HEATING SYSTEM TROUBLESHOOTING

Here are the solutions to the most frequent, simple heating system problems:

MY FURNACE IS CATATONIC

If you are getting no heat and your furnace appears to be nonresponsive, you may have blown the fuse or breaker that supplies electrical power to the furnace. Open your circuit or fuse box, search for a flipped breaker or blown fuse, and flip the breaker or replace the fuse.

Occasionally the emergency safety switch of a furnace switches off for no apparent reason. If this is the case, switch it back on—it's usually red and about an inch long on the side of the furnace, often labeled.

PILOT LIGHT WOES

If your furnace usually has a little flame (the "pilot light," a standby in all but the newest gas-fueled furnaces, which are now electronically moderated) and you aren't getting any heat, check to make sure the flame is still on—sometimes they go out. To relight the pilot, follow the directions clearly printed on your furnace, or hire a professional or ask a friend to relight the pilot for you. If you smell gas, *do not* try to light the pilot. Open nearby windows, leave the premises, and call your gas company or fire department immediately.

A pilot light that immediately goes out again is probably not getting any fuel. Either there is trouble with the gas supply line or your "thermocouple" could be faulty. The thermocouple is a safety sensor right above the pilot that turns off the gas flow if it doesn't sense heat. If it's broken, the pilot can't get any fuel. In either case, you need a professional.

BLOWING HOT AIR

Vents blowing a limited flow of hot air suggest a clogged furnace filter. Hot-air system furnaces have filters to keep the air clean, and if the filter hasn't been changed in a while, the filter might be so disgusting that no warm air can get through. If you have a landlord, tell him or her to deal with it.

Otherwise, filters are easy to buy; you can get them at supermarkets, hardware stores—just about anywhere—and some are specially made for people with allergies. To replace a filter, you simply swing down the front of the furnace (usually there's an arrow), pop out the dirty filter, and stick in the new one. Problem solved.

TIP

Keep in Mind *How often you need to change the filter is usually dependent on filter quality. Buying a cheap filter means you're going to have to buy another one sooner, so read the package and do the math. Changes vary from every 30 to 120 days. If you've lived in your home for five years and have never done this, the time has come.*

BLOODY RADIATOR

If the top of your radiator or heater is cold but the bottom is warm, you probably have a hot water heating system with air trapped inside the system. This means that instead of warm water circulating to heat your apartment, the tops of your radiators are filled with useless air. To fix this, you need to "bleed" your radiator, letting out the trapped air.

You need a "radiator bleeding key," which can be purchased at any supply store. Take a digital picture of the valve at the top corner of your radiator and bring it to the store. Back home, just open the valve by turning the key until a bit of water comes out, which you will catch with a rag or cup. Don't open it too far, or you will let out a heavy stream of water—you want only the air. You are finished when you have a thin stream of water. You should bleed all your radiators once a year, preferably in the fall.

MY RADIATOR'S REALLY LOUD

Your radiator could wake the dead every time it kicks on. First try bleeding the radiator (above). If that fails, chances are that you have a steam-heat system, and when the steam rushes into the radiator, it's being blocked by old steam that has turned into water. To fix this, you need to slightly tilt the radiator so that the water drains rather than sits in your radiator.

Turn off the radiator and wait for it to cool completely. Get a piece of scrap wood that's an inch or two thick, with a top surface of at least 2 square inches. Look for the entrance/exit pipe on one side of the radiator. Lift up the other side of the radiator *gently*, in the direction of that pipe, and slide the piece of wood under the foot, so that the radiator leans slightly toward the exit pipe. You don't want to wrench the radiator out of its seat; you just want to lift it enough to slide the piece of wood under one side. Problem solved.

MY RADIATOR IS WARM BUT I'M STILL COLD

Radiators unfortunately waste about a quarter of their heat on warming the wall behind them. Luckily, there is an easy way to retain some of that heat: by placing aluminum foil or a foil-covered plastic panel behind the radiator. Professional standards require wallpaper glue and foil-covered panel (usually polystyrene, a kind of plastic), which you can find at your hardware store, though realistically speaking, aluminum foil and flue tape work just as well. If you choose tape, test the tape on a hidden wall spot to make sure the tape doesn't remove the wall paint.

OTHER REPAIRS AND MAINTENANCE

We have exhausted the depths of safe, beginner

INSULATING A RADIATOR WALL

YOU NEED

- × Aluminum foil or foil-covered polystyrene
- × Scissors
- × Flue tape (optional/withstands heat)
- × Wallpaper glue or heavy-duty double-sided tape

STEPS

1 Turn off the radiator and wait until it's cool.

2 Cut a piece of panel or aluminum foil that is slightly smaller than the radiator. You may need 2 sheets of aluminum foil glued or taped together.

3 Cut holes in the foil or panel to go around any radiator wall attachments, so that you can slide the foil or panel right in behind the radiator. Test to make sure that your piece fits in correctly.

4 Slather the back of the foil or panel with wall wallpaper glue or attach flue tape or double-sided tape.

5 Carefully slide the foil or panel into place and adhere it to the wall behind the radiator. If you're using glue, let it dry before you turn the radiator back on.

heating fixes, so for additional repairs, you want to call a professional. If you are in charge of your heating system, particularly a gas-powered system, consider setting up a contract maintenance person to come annually and check the furnace and system. Call up the local gas company and ask if they offer maintenance services or who they might recommend.

CHIMNEYS AND FIREPLACES

Fireplaces are dependent on a steady supply of oxygen and an adequate escape route for smoke. As a fire burns, it sucks oxygen toward it from the room, and expels smoke and fumes upward into the chimney. Modern fireplaces have a metal grate at the bottom, through which ash falls and oxygen flows into the fire. The airflow into the fire and the updraft into the chimney create a little air vacuum, strengthening the cycle.

CHIMNEY CLEANING

Chimneys need to be cleaned thoroughly at least annually, usually in autumn. The smoke and fumes that fires give off naturally adhere to chimney walls and congeal into creosote, which sticks to the walls. Creosote can eventually catch fire and is a major safety hazard.

Professional chimney cleaners are more than happy to visit your abode and clean the whole chimney in an hour. Some landlords will take responsibility for this and some will not, so ask. To save money, you can rent fire brushes. Before you go to the store, carefully stick your head up your chimney and measure the walls where the chimney becomes thinner, so you can rent a size that will fit tightly into the chimney.

TO CLEAN

1 Find an old sheet and cover the mantelpiece and floor with it, holding it in place with heavy bricks.

2   Take any remaining logs or a removable grate out of the fireplace.

3   Expect a big mess of blackness to form under the sheet, so move valuables out of the way and pull back carpeting.

4   Lift the sheet to make a small opening and stick the brush up the chimney, brushing vigorously for 10 to 15 minutes, until it feels smooth and clean. Feel free to take a rest in the middle. When you are done, leave the sheet in place for a couple of hours and let the ash, dust, and grime settle in the fireplace.

5   Rental centers offer heavy-duty vacuum cleaners for fireplace cleaning, but if you're low on cash, donate a thick broom and dust pan to the cause and repeatedly sweep the piles of ash into a big garbage pail until the area is clean.

It is always preferable to also clean from the roof, placing the brush down from the top and brushing vigorously, but this is not possible if your chimney has a cap on it, or if climbing up there would be the slightest bit dangerous. You may want to hire a professional cleaner on alternate years to clean from on high, and do it yourself in the interim.

CHIMNEY TROUBLES

MY ROOM ALWAYS FILLS UP WITH SMOKE

A smoky room means that the smoke is not escaping through the chimney, signaling a blockage. When the fireplace is cool, stick your head up toward the chimney. Look for a big metal arm hanging down over the fire or sticking out from a chimney wall. This is the arm of the "damper," a metal flap that opens and closes the chimney. Make sure that it is open. You can adjust the arm during a fire with a metal poker, simply jabbing at the arm to allow more smoke to escape. Keeping the damper closed when the fireplace is not in use is a good idea.

If the damper is clearly open, stop using the fireplace and have it cleaned. Also take a walk outside and check that the chimney is at least 3 feet taller than anything within 3 yards of the chimney. A tree that has grown taller and wider, or an addition to an adjacent building may be blocking off the smoke flow of the chimney. If no culprit is found, talk to a professional about having a chimney fan installed on the top of the chimney, which will help suck out smoke.

FIRES DON'T BURN WELL IN MY FIREPLACE

Chances are, the fire is simply not getting enough fresh air. Fires breathe oxygen, so a poorly oxygenated fire will barely flame, let alone fill a room with toasty heat. This is frequently the case in older homes, which have been refurbished with modern doors, windows, and ventilation systems. Try opening a nearby window and door. You can also buy "fire bricks" at the store, and prop your grate up on them, so that the fire sits higher and can pull more oxygen from underneath.

SOMETHING IS ALIVE IN MY CHIMNEY

I will always fondly remember the morning I was awoken by an oversized bird that fell down my chimney and was flying around my room in a freaked-out panic, pooping on everything in sight.

To prevent this scenario, all chimneys should have a thin metal netting toward the top. If it sounds like something's alive inside your chimney, it probably is, and you need to call a professional to get it out. An angry baby raccoon who falls while trolling your roof, for example, is not to be dealt with alone. Waiting it out won't help, because fried, dead baby animal is even less fun than angry, alive baby animal.

VENTILATION

In the old days, ventilation was easy: the whole house was heated by a fireplace that circulated fresh air through the space, and during the summer, doors and windows stayed open (and people got mauled by local insects). With the advent of insulation and "closed" homes, not only do homes get stuffy, but they can also easily become humid with central heating, causing potential long-term structural damage from condensation.

The same structures that keep you warm and dry often trap the same trillions of air molecules for weeks on end, making your living space stuffy and naturally warmer. To fix this, the key is not only to move the air around, but to get it *out*, and exchanged with fresh air. A well-ventilated home should be able to avoid air conditioning in all but the hottest weather, while efficiently moving winter heat around to keep heating bills low.

THE NATURAL AIR CONDITIONER

The easiest trick for simple ventilation is to utilize your double-hung window (see Windows, page 67). Most people, when overheated, simply lift up the lower sash. This inefficiently provides only one entrance and exit for all the air in the room. A much better tactic is to *open the bottom window halfway, and pull down the top window a third of the way.* This provides a natural airflow, as hot air escapes out the top and cooler air comes in the bottom.

Also, create a "cross breeze," which is when air flows in one window and out another. You're aiming to create a little wind tunnel, where air rips through one side of a room or space and exits through the other. If there are walls between the two windows you currently have open, you're not creating a cross breeze and you're not helping. Before you flip on your air conditioner, instead try these two tricks together.

FANS

Fans work by moving air around a room, using angled blades to draw the air through one side of the fan and out the other side. The fan blades are attached directly to the shaft of a motor, which spins.

The most common mistake is turning on a fan in a room with no other source of ventilation. This only speeds the movement of the air molecules, thereby heating up the room. Fans work best *in combination* with other forms of ventilation, such as an open door or window, so the air that the fan moves can be replaced with new fresh air.

All fans should be periodically vacuumed to remove dust and grime, because dirty blades spinning dust into the air are gross and wear out the fan. Turn off the fan and hold a vacuum tube near the grille of a standing fan or the blades of a ceiling fan. Periodic vacuuming will make your annual Blade Cleaning Fiesta much easier.

BOX FANS

Box fans should be used to move large amounts of air out of a room. Box fan motors are quite strong and can move an incredible amount of air, but are rather useless in an enclosed space. To position a fan to move the stuffy air *out*, turn the fan on high and put a damp hand along either side of the fan. The side that is "pulling" the air toward the fan should face the stuffy space, while the blowing side should face a window or doorway. Reverse the position to pull fresh air in, though oscillating fans are more adept at this.

CLEANING AND ALIGNING BOX FANS

Noisy fans are a common problem, particularly after years of use. Your box fan is also probably covered with dust and grime. Cleaning and aligning is simple.

OSCILLATING FANS

Oscillating fans are ideal for moving air within a room, as the swiveling head catches air in corners and sweeps it up. Some modern oscillating fans have an "exhaust" setting, meant to move air out of the room, but box fans are much more adept at this.

NOISY FANS: ALIGNING, LUBRICATING, AND CLEANING

To fix a loud oscillating fan, you need to determine what's making the racket. If placing your hand on the grille seems to stop the noise, then a bit of duct tape or well-wound picture hanging wire, holding the two sides of the grille together, or a bit of putty or crumpled paper wedged between two grilles, can fix the problem. If pressing down on the fan helps, check out what is happening under the base of the fan. Sometimes fans lose their base padding or vibrate against the surface they're on. A strategically placed rag can fix this.

Otherwise, the fan blades are either out of alignment or not tightly secured to the shaft, or the shaft hasn't been lubricated since the Eisenhower administration. To fix, you are going to open up the fan, clean off the blades, lubricate the shaft, realign the blades, and tighten their attachment to the shaft.

EXTRACTOR FANS

Extractor fans are the fan boxes that people install in their exterior walls or windows. They work by creating a centrifugal force that pulls air through the fan and out of the room. Kitchens and bathrooms are the most common locations for extractor fans, where moisture, odors, and smoke are most likely. Extractor fans are quite effective at ventilation, changing the air in the room anywhere from four to fifteen times an hour, and are known for "freshening" a room without creating the Wind Tunnel Effect.

The best location for an extractor fan is across the room from a door, as high up as possible, so that the fan extracts hot air, which is naturally replaced by air through the door. The exception to this rule is in kitchens, where the fan should be as near a stove as possible, to prevent dragging odors across an entire room. Most extractor fans need to be installed either directly through a window pane or wall, both of which will require professional installation. However, portable units that fit into windows are increasingly popular and are recommended. Be aware of safety: a portable extractor fan is usually easy for a burglar to pop out of the window, so install a window guard. (For more on window guards and how to install them, see page 175.) Also double-check that the fan is facing the correct direction, pulling air out. Most fans are marked. When in doubt, a wet hand makes it easy to feel the fan's airflow.

When buying an extractor fan, know the volume of the room (length x width x height) before you go to the store. Fans are labeled in cubic feet, which is determined by multiplying room volume x air changes per hour. On average, a kitchen fan should be able to change the air in the room a minimum of ten times an hour, a bathroom fan six times an hour, and a living room fan four times an hour. If you are a smoker, lean toward a stronger fan. Also look at low-voltage options, which will be cheaper in the long run.

CEILING FANS

Ceiling fans are usually of much higher quality than box or oscillating fans, with a correlating higher price tag. Many have warranties that can extend into decades, so if troubles arise, call the manufacturer.

CHANGING THE DIRECTION OF CEILING FANS

Most people assume that fans are only for cooling, but in reality, they are equally adept at warming by drawing hot air downward. Look at your ceiling fan, and note that its blades are at an angle. This means that when the fan spins in a counterclockwise direction, the air is drawn upward; when the rotation is clockwise, the air is forced downward.

During summer heat, the blades should rotate in a *counterclockwise* direction, drawing hot air up and away from you. During winter coolness, the blades should rotate in a *clockwise* direction, pulling down the hot air along the ceiling. To change the rotation of your ceiling fan, turn off power to the fan, and find the little switch on the side of the fan, below the blades. Flip it.

BALANCING CEILING FANS

Your ceiling fan is really loud. Or, when you look up, it's clear that your fan spins on an angle. This means that your blades are far out of balance, which can happen naturally, or when you don't clean your fan for a couple of years, or when you accidentally slam into it while changing a lightbulb. To fix a wobbly fan, you can always try swapping around fan blades so that a heavy one replaces a lighter one. Turn off power to the fan, loosen the screws attaching the blades to the blade iron with a screwdriver, swap a blade with its neighbor, and test the fan.

A faster and more accurate option is to use the Fan Balance Kit that came with your fan, which is a set of weighted strips that you attach to the top of your blades. If the kit is long gone, weight the lighter blades yourself with washers and some tape. (Washers, for those who have forgotten, are flat little metal doughnuts that cost pennies each at the hardware store.)

CLEANING, ALIGNING, AND LUBRICATING A BOX FAN

YOU NEED

× Flathead screwdriver
× Lint-free rag
× Cleaning agent
× Ruler or piece of cardboard
× Lubricant spray such as WD-40 (optional)

STEPS

1 Unplug the fan. Lay it flat, so that the fan motor is downward, below the blades.

2 With a flathead screwdriver, remove the 4 to 8 screws attaching the plastic grille to the frame of the fan.

3 Here you have full access to the blades and can clean them with a lint-free rag and the cleaning supply of your choice. If you're allergic to dust, wear a doctor's mask. Be careful to not knock the blades out of further alignment. While water is not suggested in cleaning electrical appliances, if your blades are a mess, you'll need a moist rag.

4 Noisy fans mean the blades are probably no longer at the same angles. On a newer plastic fan, remove the blades by gripping the center of the blades and pulling upward. Older fan blades may be attached with a screw, which you can unscrew before pulling off the blades.

5 Lay the blades flat on a table or floor. Use your judgement to choose which blade looks properly angled, and mark the highest point of its blade curve on a ruler or piece of cardboard. Gently bend the blades until all match the cardboard height.

6 While you have the blades off, it is worthwhile to lightly spray the center shaft on the fan body with a lubricant. Reassemble the fan.

CLEANING, ALIGNING, AND LUBRICATING AN OSCILLATING FAN

YOU NEED

× Flathead screwdriver
× Ruler
× Lint-free rag
× Lubricant spray

STEPS

1 Unplug the fan. Remove the front grille of the fan by detaching the clips around the edges. Usually there are 3 to 5 clips that you pull or bend off. (Note: Cheap plastic fans are often sealed shut by the manufacturer, so you can't fix them.)

2 In the center of the fan blades there will be either a screw or a big piece of plastic that you can turn to the right. Loosen and remove it.

3 Look at the blades. If they are damaged, call the manufacturer to order new blades. If the material is slightly flexible—old metal blades are easily malleable—place the blades flat on a table. Take a ruler, measure the blade height, and gently bend the misbehaving blades to their proper height.

4 While you are here, clean off both sides of the blades with a lint-free rag. Spray a bit of lubricant on the fan body shaft.

5 Return the blades to their shaft, and tighten the screw or plastic nut holding them in place. A loose screw can cause a noisy fan. Reassemble the fan.

THE WELL-VENTILATED LIVING SPACE

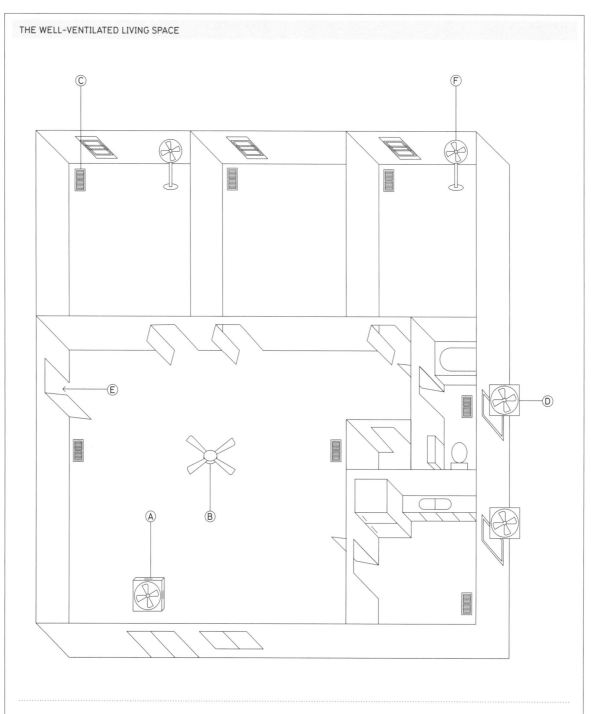

A BOX FAN

B CEILING FAN

C CLEAR, OPEN VENT

D EXTRACTOR FAN

E OPEN DOOR

F OSCILLATING FAN

NOISY CEILING FANS

If the fan appears balanced but is noticeably noisy, one of the many screws attaching the light, motor, or switches may have come loose. Turn off power, climb on a chair, and gently explore the fan, tightening every screw in sight (righty tighty, lefty loosey). You will usually locate the problem this way.

BROKEN BLADES

A problematic blade can be replaced by calling the manufacturer and ordering a new one. Examples include cracked or chipped blades and heavily warped blades. A good way to determine damage is to remove two blades at once, and compare them to each other. Look up at the two to four screws attaching the blade to the blade iron, remove the screws with a screwdriver, and detach the blades. Sometimes a friend is helpful to hold onto the blade while you unscrew. Repeat with a second blade. The blades should lie flat against each other and have the same shape. If this is not the case, replace one.

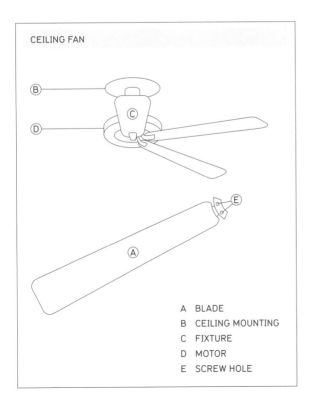

CEILING FAN

A BLADE
B CEILING MOUNTING
C FIXTURE
D MOTOR
E SCREW HOLE

BALANCING A CEILING FAN

YOU NEED

× Lint-free rag
× Flathead screwdriver
× Washers of different sizes
× Scotch tape
× Or, if you're lazy, duct tape, dimes, and pennies

STEPS

1 Before unscrewing anything, clean off the tops of the blades: turn off the fan's power, stand on a chair, and gently wipe off the tops with a lint-free cloth. A vacuum hose may be useful. Sometimes this alone will rebalance a fan—monster dust bunnies are heavy.

2 If a good cleaning doesn't help, find the blade that is most clearly higher than the rest. With Scotch tape, attach a dime or medium-size washer to the top of the blade. Test.

3 Repeat this process with various-size washers on different blades until the fan is balanced.

4 Professional standards require that once you've found the appropriate washer sizes, you permanently attach them by unscrewing a center blade screw, placing the washer under it, and rescrewing it. To do this, look up at the blades and find the 2 to 4 screws attaching each blade to the "blade iron." Loosen and remove a center screw with a flathead screwdriver, place the washer on the top side of the blade, and tighten the screw over the washer. I, however, have had 2 dimes attached to the top of my fan blade with duct tape for years, and this solution has worked well.

CENTRAL AIR SYSTEMS

Central air conditioners work just like regular-size air conditioners (see Air Conditioners, page 114), but bigger. The huge gray units can usually be found either in the basement or outside your home or apartment on a roof or lawn. If it's near your window, you will know about it.

Central air conditioners are attached to a set of large ducts throughout your home, which end at the small vents you see in your room. Sometimes central air conditioners share the duct system with the furnace, and use the furnace's "blower" (a big fan) to spread the air throughout the home. In these cases, one thermostat controls both the furnace and the air conditioner. Usually, the air conditioning unit attaches to a large central duct that climbs through the center of your home or building and branches off to individual rooms.

WHY AM I HOT?

Yes, you're attractive, but that's not what we're talking about. When people complain that they are too hot, usually the central air system works just fine but furniture is blocking the vents. If you think that some of your vents aren't working, remember that half the vents are "collector" vents, collecting warm air from the room, creating a closed ventilation system. If a collector vent is blocked, there is no way for old air to exit the system and your room will get stuffy. If a supply vent is blocked, the cool air supply will automatically shift to another duct and another room, leaving your room hot. Walk around your living space and locate all the air vents. The vent not only needs to be completely clear, but there should be a path for the air to travel out of the vent and into a room, not blocked by beds, furniture, or piles of laundry. As always, if the air conditioning is on, windows should be closed. Make sure all the vents are open by adjusting grates with the small lever on the vent.

NOTE

If you prefer one room cooler than another—say, a cool bedroom for burrowing under covers but a warm bathroom for morning showers—you can also adjust accordingly, using the above directions.

WHY IS THE KITCHEN 10 DEGREES COOLER THAN MY BEDROOM?

Despite the best duct-installation efforts of whoever built your living space, there are sometimes great temperature variations from room to room. If the vents in both rooms are open and there is no other obvious temperature changer, such as sun streaming into one room for six hours a day, then you can balance the temperatures between your rooms by blocking off some ducts more than others. This repair works for heating as well as air-conditioning systems with vents in each room.

× Locate all the vents in your living space and open them, making sure the air has a clear path to travel into the room.
× Set your thermostat to a comfortable room temperature, between 65 and 70 degrees Fahrenheit. Wait an hour.
× Place a thermometer at waist level in the center of one room and wait 2 minutes for the thermometer reading to stabilize. Write down the temperature.
× Repeat in every room of your living space.
× If you have basement access, find where the main air ducts leave the air conditioner, or in a shared heat/air system, the furnace. Follow the duct to where it branches off into smaller ducts toward room vents, and look for the handles on the side of the ducts. These handles are "dampers," rectangular doors inside the ducts that open and close the duct. Turn the handles in the rooms that are too hot to "open." In rooms that are too cool, turn the dampers part way "closed." Do the opposite to adjust the heat flow.
× If you have no access to the basement air ducts, or no idea what dampers are or where to find them, you can balance your ducts by opening and closing the air vents in your rooms. This is more wasteful because your central air conditioner will expend energy cooling the ducts all the way up to the closed vents, but it works. Open the vents fully in warmer rooms, and partially shut them in cooler rooms.
× Wait a half hour, and repeat Steps 3 and 4, again checking the temperature in each room. Adjust dampers or vent openings appropriately until all rooms are approximately the same temperature.

POOR VENTILATION SCENARIOS AND SUGGESTIONS

PROBLEM There are too many people in my apartment, and it gets really stuffy.

SOLUTION Short of knocking off some roommates, walk through the apartment and identify particularly stuffy areas. Increase vent airflow to those rooms. Make sure all the air vents are open and unblocked. Sacrifice some privacy and keep doors open; buy some portable extractor fans for the windows. Encourage roommates to put cedar bags in their closets and shoes, and wash laundry regularly. If your front door is on a hallway, during the winter periodically open the front door and stand there for a while with a box fan on high.

PROBLEM I have many pets, and everyone knows it.

SOLUTION Rather than tackling ventilation for your whole living space, try relegating the pets to one area, leaving you with only two or three rooms to vacuum and ventilate regularly. Walk through and create entrances and exits for the airflow, and install an air cleaner. Litter boxes are best placed in corners. When balancing your vents, increase airflow to the pet rooms.

PROBLEM I smoke like a chimney, and my house smells like it.

SOLUTION Consider buying an air cleaner and place it in the room in which you smoke most. Increase ventilation by opening doors and windows to create a cross breeze. Vacuum and dust regularly.

PROBLEM My room has one tiny window and is smelly.

SOLUTION Place a portable extractor fan in the window or a box fan in the doorway.

PROBLEM My room gets super dusty.

SOLUTION An air cleaner will fix this. Otherwise, dust and vacuum regularly. Clean the blades of all your fans. Keep pets away and don't wear shoes in the room.

PROBLEM In the summer, I'm really hot without the air conditioner on high.

SOLUTION Give the air conditioner a break by opening all your double-hung windows at both top and bottom. Pull down shades in direct sunlight. Buy "sunlight control" film, a clear sheet that you stick to your windows to reduce summertime heat and sunlight. Place oscillating fans inside rooms, and box fans at doorways. Make sure ceiling fans rotate counterclockwise. If your walls are dark colored, consider painting with a pale shade—dark walls absorb around 80% of the radiant heat that hits them.

AIR CLEANERS

Air cleaners are right up there with personal masseuses on the Necessity Scale. However, they can be useful in well-insulated living spaces that feature smokers or a number of pets.

Air cleaners use a fan with angled blades to suck air into the unit, then through a series of filters. Each filter is aimed at a different size and type of pollutant: the first filter catches larger-size pollutants, and is followed, depending on the model, by filters made of charcoal or carbon to catch medium-sized pollutants, and then a high-tech filter for tiny pollutants. The newest air cleaners electrically charge particles to adhere to filters, or finish with an electrical charger causing any remaining pollutants to stick to parts of the room, to be easily wiped or vacuumed up.

As you might imagine, air cleaners are wholly dependent on having clean filters. You need to follow the directions and either clean or replace filters regularly, and wipe down any visible dirty grilles or grime attached to inner parts of the unit. Air cleaners work best when left on all the time, placed in central locations. Electronic air cleaners, which depend on ionizers to charge dirty particles, are much more costly than mechanical air cleaners, which are fans with filters. Before purchasing one, do some quick math with the wattage of the unit to see how much it will cost you to run it for a month and add in the cost of any disposable filters.

CHAPTER 7

HELP, SOMETHING IN MY WALL IS ALIVE! PESTS

Man invented homes for people, and people alone. At first, he also provided for his furry neighbors: mud huts, tepees, stilt homes, et cetera all presented a warm place with food and good company for local wildlife. But over a few thousand years, man got feedback from woman ("Honey, I'm freakin' freezing") and improved upon the concept, adding windows, doors, and walls to effectively shut out the weather gods and the animal kingdom altogether. But the critters had other ideas. Rodents found these so-called homes veritable gold mines of food storage, particularly their "pantries," while termites found that newly popular wood was a termite's best friend. Mold, mildew, and fungus found friends in the drips and leaks of water bowls and pipes, while cockroaches basked in the shadows of walls and floorboards. And thus, the greatest battle in the history of humanity continues. So far, the score is People 2, Critters 1.

Here's a rundown of the popular invaders, and how to kick them out while preventing further troubles.

TERMITES

The major insect threat, at least structurally speaking, is termites. Termites will eat through wood you didn't know existed, including your ceiling beams, your bed frame, the foundation of your home, and your prize sixteenth-century North African wooden flute. Because they eat from the inside out, you need to know how to spot a problem before your chair collapses with you in it. Warning signs include:

- × Peeling paint near ground level that appears different from elsewhere on the structure.
- × A hollow sound when you tap on wood beams or poles.
- × An unusual quantity of flying insects, which look like flying ants, but have four wings of equal size and a thick waist section (no antlike body segments). Termites come in different colors, depending on the locale.
- × An unusual quantity of small shed insect wings.
- × Quarter-inch tunnels that look like beads of cement on top of surfaces (these are the superhighways of light-sensitive termites).
- × Signs of tunneling, especially in cracks, where floor meets wall or where foundation meets house.

Much like humans, once insects find food, they colonize, reproduce, and chow down with speed. Try placing a screwdriver or small knife into a suspicious wood beam. If the knife slides in with no resistance, you have probable termite damage. Pull off a small piece of wood and look for signs of tunnels. If the entire piece of wood is soft, it is probably rotting wood, not termites.

If you suspect termites, with a bit of inspection you should be able to see them and tell your landlord or hire a professional exterminator. Termites are usually controlled by surrounding the home with the termite poison chlordane, not a job for novices.

COCKROACHES

Cockroaches are the most obnoxiously overconfident critters in the animal kingdom. As one of the most successful creatures on the planet—they have a lineage that dates back millions of years—they have the right to be. Their adaptability is infuriatingly impressive: the modern species can live off garbage, food, glue, or anything made of starch—which is mostly everything.

Cockroaches are nocturnal, and they like to hang out under major appliances like refrigerators and stoves, behind walls and pantries, and near warm pipes. To get rid of them, buy a roach spray and spray it in all the cracks you can find that aren't near your food. You might need to try several different sprays. If that doesn't work, brush boric acid powder over creases and cracks, particularly between where roaches hang out and where they eat. Bait traps are also available at local grocery stores. Try multiple strategies at once; if none of these options work, you need to hire a professional.

Be forewarned that some landlords will go out of their way to hide roach problems until you move in, at which point they will insist that you brought the roaches with you. By the same token, it is quite easy to take roaches with you, so if you have a roach problem, empty, wash, and repack everything you own before moving. All you need is one tiny egg in the corner of a box, and you'll have just transported roaches into your new digs.

INSECT	HOW YOU KNOW YOU HAVE THEM	HOW TO GET RID OF THEM
ANTS	You'll see them marchin' around. Black ants come in for food during the winter.	Once ants find food, they return by the same paths. Follow the ant trail back to the nest, which can be as far as 8 or 9 yards from your home. Dump boiling water on the entrance holes of the nest.
CARPENTER ANTS	Often assumed to be termites, carpenter ants can be differentiated by their nests: they live inside wood and they get rid of all the excess wood by dumping it outside in little piles.	Follow the carpenter ants to their nest, which will be inside a wood structure. Place insecticide powder into the entrance holes and plug the holes.
CENTIPEDES AND MILLIPEDES	Centipedes sometimes wander inside through window holes or doors.	Place insecticide powder on windowsills and other possible entrances. Before you kill them, show them to the neighborhood kids who can't get enough of all the little legs.
CRICKETS	Sometimes a boy cricket will follow a girl cricket inside a house during mating season and sing for her at full volume.	Though the love story is touching, the singing will drive you nuts. Turn on lights and follow the song until you find the offender, who might be moving while singing. Spare your reflexes and just throw a towel over the cricket. Then either stomp on the towel or strategically flip it over to take the cricket outside.
FLIES	The annoying buzzing is the fly roaming around, in between dropping disease-laden drops of vomit and excretion on uncovered food.	Keep your food covered. A flyswatter or fly spray will get rid of one or two. Flies are also surprisingly vacuumable: aim the vacuum at them and empty the bag outside. If you find an infestation behind a wall, go rent an insecticide "smoke generator."
MOSQUITOES	Mosquitoes are generally harmless in nontropical regions, though West Nile virus and other mosquito-borne illnesses are on the rise. Mosquitoes are attracted to warm bodies.	The best way to kill a mosquito is to smash it against your wall with a book. If you have a lot of mosquitoes, they're breeding nearby. Mosquitoes will lay eggs in stale water, so look for stagnant water, like a never-used toilet or a dehumidifier.
SILVERFISH	Silverfish are the tiny ½-inch gray bugs that look like centipedes without all the legs. They make frequent appearances in bathrooms. Though completely harmless to you, if you have a lot of them, you should respond.	Follow your silverfish to see where it's hanging out, usually behind wallpaper or between tiles in crevices. Put insecticide powder in there.
SPIDERS	Spiders like darkness and dust, so keep things clean and bright. Clean out fireplaces, because some spiders will hang out around old wood. You will probably eat 8 spiders in your life while asleep.	To get rid of a spider and its web, spray the web with insecticide spray and the spider will die. Remove the web. If you have lots of baby spiders crawling across your ceiling, a bit of insecticide spray will do the job.
WASPS	A little known wasp fact: wasps will kill bees and then raid their hives for honey. They truly are the brutes of the insect world.	In your house, open a jam or jelly jar and the wasp will fly right in; close the jar. Spraying fly spray at the wasp also works, but it is suspiciously poisonous. If you suddenly have many wasps, follow the wasps to their nest, keeping a safe distance. With a plastic spoon taped to a yardstick, dump some insecticid powder at all the entrance holes of the nest.

TIP

The food storage habits (or lack thereof) of the guy next door can leave nearby apartment dwellers with an infestation problem, making you want to poison the neighbor more than the insects. Most insects will disappear with a bit of well-placed insecticide, but if you have children or pets, you need to reconsider your options: surprisingly small doses of insecticide can prove fatal to smaller mammals.

MAMMALIA: MICE, RATS, AND BATS

MOOCHING MIGHTY MICE

Mice are much like grown children who haven't quite seemed to leave home yet. They share your residence because it's warm and has good food. If the food were cut off and living arrangements were made less comfortable, both the mice and children would leave. With mice, you can get right to the point and use poison.

You will know you have mice because you will either see them, hear them rustling, or find their tracks: gnawed holes in the corners of cupboards and food packages, holes behind major appliances such as refrigerators, and droppings that look like little piles of thick black rice. Rodents are active at night, like the edges of rooms, and try to avoid light. They thrive in rooms that people don't use, so try to make a racket in all of your rooms.

Rodents eat most anything, and are notoriously bananas for peanut butter and peanut products. They can eat through cardboard, wood, and thin plastic. To get rid of them, you need to cut off their food supply.

The importance of cutting off *all* food supply is lost on most people: it means no food left out ever; all food in metal, glass, or thick Tupperware containers; garbage inside metal lidded pails; and everything else stored in the refrigerator. Mice will find any available food—they don't have anything better to do—so when in doubt, keep your food in the fridge.

POISONS

PROS You never have to see or touch the rodent.

CONS Can be deadly to pets and children and must be handled with gloves. If the mouse dies between your walls, your apartment will smell like decaying mouse. The smell is significantly worse if the mouse brings the poison back to its nest and kills its entire family. However, this is rare—for the vast majority of poison users, the mice just disappear.

WHAT YOU DO Each poison wrapper has its own instructions, but the best method is to build or buy a shin-height wooden box, and cut two 2½-inch floor entrances on opposite sides. Put the box against the wall, place poison and bait—cheese, peanut butter, or bacon will usually work—in the box, and leave the room. The easier option is to buy blocks of poison, and drop them behind appliances and in dark corners. Check back for signs of little teeth.

SNAP TRAPS

PROS The rodent dies, and you'll feel glory in seeing it dead. Clearly, the death deters other rodents.

CONS You have a rodent corpse.

WHAT YOU DO Traps can vary a bit in shape in size, and each will come with specific directions. Set the traps 5 to 8 feet apart along a wall where mice run back and forth, with the bait—peanut butter, chocolate, or cheese—facing the wall. Your best strategy is to leave the bait on the traps for a few days *without setting the traps.* This will get the rodents used to a food source. Then you set 'em. To get rid of a dead mouse, either use gloves to throw the whole snap trap into double-bagged garbage or bury it outside.

HUMANE TRAPS

PROS Mousey gets to live on, after a brief traumatic experience of being suddenly trapped in a plastic or wooden box.

CONS Humane traps rarely actually work

WHAT YOU DO Follow the directions. and set up the little box with bait (see Poisons, above). The trouble is that affordable humane traps seem to have great difficulty in catching their intended prey. The expensive traps work well; you simply leave the traps out overnight, then in the morning take the traps outside and release the mice. To increase your luck, try leaving bait in the trap for a few nights without setting the door to swing shut, so that Mousey gets used to it.

GLUE TRAPS

PROS You don't directly hurt the cute little innocent mousey.

CONS You have a live rodent to deal with. Frequently the rodent will freak out and pull its feet off while trying to escape. If the rodent does this, you might have to kill it, in which case "humane" is not an appropriate adjective.

WHAT YOU DO Set up the glue trap according to instructions and place it along a wall. Leave the room. Come back in the morningand throw out the whole trap

---

You can always call an exterminator, but if you want to try to deal with the problem cheaply, you have a few options available at local grocery stores.

THE TOWEL-WITH-A-POT PLAN

This may be more interactive than you want to be, but if you are unafraid of Mousey and need to catch him, chuck a huge towel or blanket on top of him as he darts across your room. This will create a slow-moving bulge that you can easily put a pot on top of. Now Mousey is trapped, and all you need to do is scrunch up the towel so that you can flip the pot and Mousey will be trapped inside. Dump Mousey outside, far away from your home. Wash everything a lot.

PLUGGING HOLES

You want to also cut off the entrances mice are using into your kitchen and other rooms. Look for holes in the walls and floors behind your cupboards, pantry, stove, and refrigerator. When you find them, plug them up amply with steel wool from the grocery store. You might want to do this during the day, lest you accidentally trap a nocturnal mouse in your kitchen for the near future. Know that mice are determined little creatures, and will spend two years eating through your steel wool solution. Periodically replug the holes, even if you're mouse free.

OH, RATS

Rats pose a serious health threat that cannot be ignored. In addition to carrying a variety of diseases, they are much more aggressive than mice, and

they damage homes at a faster rate. Rats are larger than mice, and are much less scared of people. They can also perform major feats of strength, including running for hours straight, surviving falls from great heights, and swimming.

If you have rats, you'll see them, hear them in your walls, or see obvious chewing damage. Before you spend money on an exterminator, call your local Health Department immediately. Rats are considered a public health hazard and are attended to with particular speed in some urban areas. Animal control may also come to your rescue. Call around.

BATTY BATS

Bats are nocturnal animals that set up colonies in uninhabited places, such as abandoned country homes. Bats can carry rabies, among other diseases, and are therefore considered a public health hazard. They rarely, however, show any interest in people, and can be useful in eating other pests.

If a bat flies into your room by accident, feel free to call animal control if you're scared. Otherwise, open all the windows and close the door, and the bat will eventually leave. They are nocturnal, so if a bat gets caught inside during the night, you may find it sleeping on your wall during the day. You can capture it with a container against the wall, slide a piece of cardboard underneath, then dump the bat outside. If you're afraid of the bat, leave it on the wall for the day, open the windows to the room, and turn all the lights on. Shut the door and the bat will fly out at night.

If you are one of those unlucky people who has bats colonize in your attic space, you or a calm person you know can shine a bright light on the bats during the daytime. They won't like this, and will leave however they came in as soon as it gets dark. Hire someone to seal off any obvious bat holes.

WATER DAMAGE: CREEPING SPORES

Water damage is usually signaled by bulges, cracks, or sagging along walls, or an obvious puddle where water should not be. Before most water damage problems, there are obvious warning signals that are ignored. The repairperson will say:

"Well, did you see the crack in the wall?"
"Yes."
"About how long has it been there?"
"Um, maybe three months."
"Was it getting worse?"
"Yup, it just kept getting longer. And then a stain started around it."
"When did the water start dripping?"
"Yesterday."

So the signs of your water leak were in front of your eyes for a full 120 days, but you didn't recognize the crack and accompanying stain as problematic until you had a puddle. Water damage and its signs are not to be ignored!

WHAT IS ROT?

When people talk about "rot," they are talking about fungus, which grows when wood is exposed to moisture. It also happens to grow on old food, dead animals, and a variety of other tasty locations, but that's another book. The wood wetness creates a happy home for fungus spores, which multiply with aplomb, living off the wood and severely damaging it. There are two types, wet rot and dry rot.

WET ROT

No, this isn't what happens to your brother's socks. Wet rot happens when wood is quite wet, and it is common around old or poorly installed windows and doors. You know those old wooden windowsills with pieces of wood that chip off? That's wet rot. Once the cause of the moisture is stopped, the fungus will die. Inside and outside your house, you usually first see wet rot in the form of peeling paint. Place a finger underneath the peeling paint, and if you feel spongy wood, you have wet rot. If the wet rot is caused by weather, the wood might be dry the day you find it. Wait until it rains, and check for spongy wood again.

To fix wet rot, you have to cut off any damaged wood, replace it with new wood, and then cover it with two or three coats of fungicidal wood sealant. For wet rot on structural parts of the house, you need a professional. If it's just a 2-inch span on your windowsill, feel free to cut out the old wood, hammer in a new piece of wood, and cover it with fungicide yourself.

DRY ROT

Dry rot is a much bigger problem than wet rot, because there's no good way to stop the damage. Dry rot grows where there is very little moisture, usually in unventilated spaces like old basements. You will see whitish gray threads of fungus in new dry rot; in bad dry rot, pieces of wood will come off in balls and the area can be a reddish color, surrounded by white fungus.

Dry rot spreads quickly, even into bricks and cement, so if you see some, you need a professional. The obviously affected area needs to be removed, as well as a 3-foot surrounding radius. Ventilate the area as best you can and get rid of any obvious causes of moisture.

MOLD

Mold growing on bathroom walls is usually a minor problem, created by mold spores that have taken advantage of condensation from your shower. If every time you shower, your bathroom mirror fogs up until you can't see yourself and takes 10 minutes to defog, this is a sign that there is not enough warm air to absorb the moisture your shower expels into the air. You need to increase the available air by showering with a window or door open, or a dehumidifier in the bathroom. Gray, white, and black spots on walls are usually signs of mold, and can be scraped off and forgotten about. Any mold problem that doesn't wash off needs a professional immediately. For removal instructions, see Why Are My Walls Growing Mold? (page 51).

WEATHER LEAKS

Water leaks caused by outside rain or snow are easy to locate. Signs include streams of water running down the inside of a window, puddles inside doorways, and water dripping from a roof or ceiling. These usually dry up as soon as the weather changes. For a major leak, call a professional; for a minor problem, such as a small window drip, apply caulking over the hole (see Caulking Other Places, page 138) or apply weather stripping (see My Window Lets in More Cold Air Than an Air Conditioner, page 67).

WHY IS WATER DRIPPING THROUGH MY CEILING?

A soft, sagging ceiling with a huge puddle in it needs to be dealt with immediately. Quickly turn off the main water shutoff and go find a few big buckets. Move anything that's not waterproof out of the area. You want to carefully release the water from the ceiling so that the ceiling doesn't collapse. (A small hole in the ceiling is easy to fix; a collapsed ceiling is not.) With a utility knife, awl, or sharp kitchen knife, poke a small hole into the center of the saggy ceiling. The water will drip down into your buckets, relieving the ceiling of pressure and preventing further damage. Call a professional. If your floor or ceiling is unstable, leave the premises and call for help. For pipe-leak solutions, see Pipes (page 141).

CHAPTER 8

HELP, THERE'S AN EMERGENCY! HOW TO BE ALARMINGLY SECURE

The phrase "Be safe!" is popular. It's called out during good-byes, and it means to not be an idiot and walk home alone at 3 AM by way of a deserted park. Or to drive the speed limit in a conscientious, sober manner.

But what about once you're home? How do you make the place where you spend a third to half of your life safe from intruders or potential disasters? You've probably never heard of many of the safety mechanisms mentioned in this chapter. This is not good. The chapter is geared toward women—whether living alone or with friends—who might not be home-repair savvy, but should be safety savvy.

ALL ABOUT BREAK-INS

The average break-in takes a few minutes: a burglar pops his hand through some glass, opens a door or window, takes whatever valuables are in sight, and leaves. This simple crime often happens during daylight or while others are home.

For women living alone, the stakes are higher. While the majority of attacks against women happen outside the home, your neighbors know if you are often or always alone, and you want to make sure that your living space poses as many entrance challenges as possible. Every neighborhood has a few creeps, and no, you don't want to meet them.

However, logic is on your side: most trespassers are not pros in the techniques of breaking in and will therefore be stumped by some very basic locks and safety systems. Intruders are known to take the path of least resistance, so your job is to not only make breaking in difficult, but also to make your living space *look* more difficult for a criminal than nearby options. Choose any combination of options on the next few pages that best fits your living space and lifestyle.

TIP

Stand outside and look at your living space. If you were very agile, where might you let yourself in? Is there an adjacent building that offers easy access to your living space? Make sure that this cannot happen. Look around: Can you see your valuables through windows? Where could a lurker easily hide? Fix the problems you see

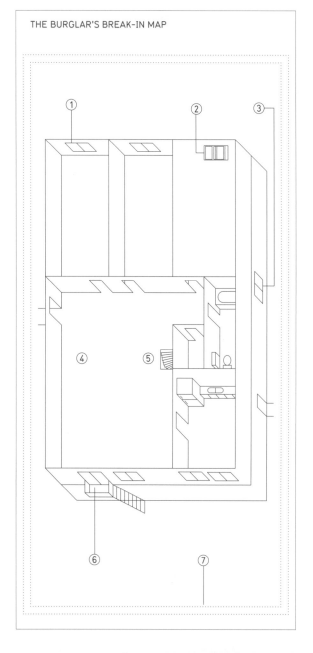

THE BURGLAR'S BREAK-IN MAP

MR. BURGLAR HAS ARRIVED: MAIN ENTRY RISKS

This list highlights the most frequent points of apartment or household entry.

× **FIRST-FLOOR WINDOWS** Always a major safety concern. Make sure that all windows are adequately locked. See Window Safety, page 174.

× **WEAK WINDOWS** Windows with glass that is installed with putty can be easily removed. Cutting the putty with a knife removes the entire pane silently. Check to see that your glass is firmly attached to the window sash.

× **SECOND-FLOOR WINDOWS** Many women leave these windows open, assuming no one can get up there. Getting up there is quite easy. Keep them locked or install window guards.

× **SKYLIGHTS** Skylights often offer an easy way for burglars to see where you are and break in. Make sure there is a very good lock on your skylight.

× **SLIDING DOORS AND WINDOWS** These are a burglar's best friend. If you have them, install key locks on the top and bottom and a wooden bar in the track.

× **FRONT DOOR** You need a peephole and a strong dead bolt lock. A security chain will make late-night food deliveries safe, so no one can force the door. A light outside your front door will not only ensure that you can see who is there, but highlight any suspicious front-door activity to your neighbors.

× **BASEMENT AND ATTIC DOORS** If you have any kind of basement or attic door, stick a combination lock on it from inside the house. This way, any burglars who enter from the top or bottom levels can't enter your living space.

× **BACK DOORS** Many back or side doors offer a hidden space where a burglar can take his time breaking in. Install motion-activated lights and very strong lock systems.

× **GATES** Keep gates locked, making both entry and exit harder. Gates that can be opened by reaching over an arm provide excellent privacy for a burglar breaking into a side door, and then an easy exit for him to walk through with your television. Get a real lock.

SECURITY MECHANISMS

DOOR SAFETY

Doors are the most common entrances for intruders. An ideally safe door should have:

× a main doorknob and lock
× at least one dead bolt lock, in addition to the main lock
× a security chain
× a peephole
× a bright light or motion-detector light outside the door
× a metal-coated top layer

With this system, breaking in would require forcing or jimmying two locks and a security chain under a bright light. The peephole ensures that you know who is on the other side of your door.

Wooden doors are easily cut through. While few intruders actually take the time to cut through a door, a small saw can cut a hand-size hole through a soft-wood door in thirty seconds, while hand tools can cut a lock out of a wooden door in three minutes. Many urban doors are metal coated for a reason.

 TIP

When you move, it is a great idea to add a new lock to the door, because you have no idea who else has keys. Particularly if you live in an apartment building with frequent turnover, a host of people probably have access to your apartment. The easiest option is to have your landlord or a locksmith change the lock cylinder, a repair that replaces the center of your old lock, giving you new keys. At the very least, put a security chain on the door.

SHOPPING FOR DOOR LOCKS

There are many types of locks, each with its own self-explanatory installation instructions. You can make adequate safety locks a contingency of signing a new lease, but buy the locks yourself so that only you have keys. Here I will tell you what to look for when shopping for locks. There are four main overlapping categories:

BOLT LOCKS Considered a necessity on any door, a metal bolt lock slides into the faceplate on the door frame. Well-made bolt locks are nearly impossible to force open, and can't be opened with creative credit card maneuvers. They can, however, be tampered with by pros from the outside.

TWO-SIDED KEY LOCKS Doors frequently serve as both the entrance and exit for a burglar. These locks (usually bolt locks) require a key to exit from the inside, thereby preventing intruders from escaping with loot through a main exit. They are also handy for those responsible for young children or senile adults who have a habit of wandering out, and for this reason are common in family homes. Keep in mind that these locks can present a safety hazard if during a fire emergency you're fumbling through your purse looking for a key rather than exiting immediately. They are also useless if you find yourself leaving the key in the lock permanently.

MORTISE LOCKS Mortise locks are installed inside the door, behind a thick plate of metal, with only a keyhole and metal plate visible from the outside— no screws, bolts, or knobs. You have probably seen these in the city. Mortise locks are considered the safest type of lock, because tampering with them is difficult. The more external parts a lock has, the easier it is to tamper with.

MULTIBOLT LOCKS Multibolt locks are ideal for apartments with one- or two-door entrances in a neighborhood where security is a problem. These locks have one key lock that controls four bolts, one on each edge of the door, making a break-in through the door virtually impossible. You will need someone to install the system for you, but once installed, your doors are safe.

HOW TO INSTALL A SECURITY CHAIN

Security chains are much easier to install than locks, so if you are low on door security, add a chain or two. Chains that are opened or closed with a key are ideal, but if you are more worried about locking yourself in during a fire than locking intruders out, skip the key. Install the 3- to 6-inch chain *below* your primary handle or dead-bolt lock.

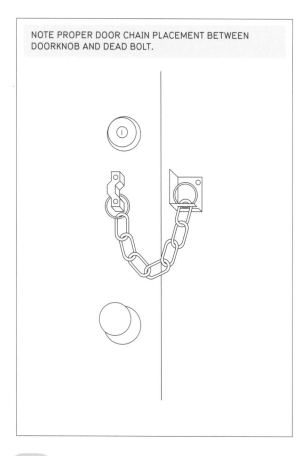

NOTE PROPER DOOR CHAIN PLACEMENT BETWEEN DOORKNOB AND DEAD BOLT.

 NOTE

A key that suddenly won't fit in a lock means that your lock was probably tampered with while you were away. Replace the lock and reevaluate your home security.

NOTE

If your door is metal-coated, you should ask a handy friend to gauge whether it's possible to drill through the surface. You will need a powerful drill and special drill bit.

I SEE YOUUU . . . HOW TO INSTALL A PEEPHOLE

Peepholes, in addition to allowing you to spy on people across the hallway or street or highway, are pivotal for door safety. You can see who wants to come in and ask for identification to be shown, a

INSTALLING A DOOR SECURITY CHAIN

YOU NEED

- × New security chain
- × Carpenter's level or yardstick
- × Pencil
- × Safety goggles
- × Power drill (see Going Hardcore: How to Use a Power Drill, page 27)
- × Screws (should come with package)
- × Flathead screwdriver

STEPS

1 Hold up the 2 plates of the security chain and and mark where on the door and door frame you would like to attach them. Some packages provide a paper template for this purpose. Use a carpenter's level or yardstick to make sure the 2 plates will be level, and have a friend hold up both plates with the chain attached while you open the door. It should open only a couple of inches.

2 Hold each plate in place and draw dots with a pencil through the screw holes.

3 Using the drill bit size suggested in the security chain instructions and wearing safety goggles, drill a hole into each pencil dot.

4 Hold each plate in place and insert the mounting screws into the holes with a flathead screwdriver.

INSTALLING A PEEPHOLE

YOU NEED

- × New peephole
- × Tape measure or yardstick
- × Pencil
- × Power drill (see Going Hardcore: How to Use a Power Drill, page 27)
- × Safety goggles
- × Flathead screwdriver

STEPS

1 Go to the hardware store and purchase a peephole that can be adjusted for any door width. Purchase the widest view that you can find.

2 Shut the door and use a tape measure to find the center vertical line of the door. Mark with a pencil where on the door you want the peephole. If you live alone, your eye level is fine. If you live with children or short people, be nice and move it lower.

3 Using the drill bit suggested in the instructions and wearing safety goggles, drill a hole directly through your mark on the door, until the bit comes out the other side of the door.

4 Open the door and insert the outside lens of the peephole into the hole.

5 From the inside of the door, screw the eyepiece into the hole.

request that qualified workmen will be prepared for. Peepholes come in two tubular parts, an outside lens and an inside eyepiece. Installation is easy: you drill a hole in the door, slide the lens into the outside of the door, and screw the eyepiece into the hole from the other side.

INSTALLING BRIGHT DOOR LIGHTS

The easiest way to install a bright porch light or motion detector light is to forgo electricity altogether and purchase a battery-powered motion-activated light. A low-wattage floodlight will also work, though you will have to turn it on and off each night and morning.

The point here is not to blind your visitors—the light should not shine directly at visitor eye level; nor should it blind you as you look into your peephole, or blur the visitor's face into a peephole shadow. An overhead light that will detect any movement in the door area is perfect. If that is not possible, try a light off to the side. Before you install, have a friend hold the light up in a variety of positions at night, and see if you can identify her through your peephole.

To install, find a wood surface to the side or above your door, and attach the light by drilling holes for each screw hole, and then inserting the screws through the light base into the wall or ceiling with a drill or screwdriver.

WINDOW SAFETY
See Windows, page 67, for more window information.

The safest doors in the neighborhood will not help you if your windows are wide open, leaving the screen as the main safety mechanism. Screens are as recommended against intruders as the prayer method against pregnancy.

Contrary to popular opinion, the crescent latch between double-hung windows is also not a safety device, and neither are window locks controlled by little handles or levers. These are all something of a joke to burglars, because they can simply break the glass, turn the lever, and jump into your living space. Look around at your windows and realize how unsafe you are! For a variety of safer window-locking options, see following.

TIP

Plexiglas is much more difficult to break through than glass. If you have a door or first-floor window with glass panes, have the glass replaced by Plexiglas.

SHOPPING FOR WINDOW LOCKS

There are as many different kinds of locking mechanisms as there are windows. Here are your options.

KEY LOCKS Any lock that is key operated increases security by making it impossible for an intruder to break the windowpane and reach in to unlock the lock. But these locks also come with the risk that you will lose the keys or be unable to escape in a fire. Weigh the risk carefully, depending on your environment. To narrow down the confusion, you can always purchase a bunch of locks that use the same key.

WINDOW PINS A window pin is a metal pin that goes through the center of both window rails (the body of the window around the panes), so that neither can be moved. Inexpensive and easy to install (much easier than locks), they can be used on any wooden double-hung window and are highly recommended.

MORTISE LOCKS Much like mortise door locks, mortise window locks are dead bolt locks built into the window, so there is nothing to tamper with on the surface. However, they can be used only on sturdy, thicker windows and are difficult to install. They also are not a visual deterrent to burglars. Unless a friend will install them for free, sticking with other locks might be a better bet.

SURFACE HANDLE AND KNOB LOCKS Windows come with a variety of handle- or knob-controlled locks with visible parts that hold windows closed with latch and bolting mechanisms. While these locks are quite strong and visible as a deterrent, the trouble is that an intruder can break a glass pane and reach the knob or handle. Make sure that you have enough locks for your window size: larger windows definitely need two locks.

SASH STOPS Sash stops, much like they sound, block the sash from moving past a set point. There are a few varieties, some of which are screwed into the window frame and permanently block the window track, and others that have a turnable bolt that shoots out from the window frame to block the track. Sash stops are useful in homes with children, preventing windows from opening to toddler-head size. It is virtually impossible to break into a window with key-lock sash stops; knob- or lever-controlled sash stops can be overcome.

WINDOW GUARDS Window guards are more effective at keeping children and pets inside than keeping intruders out, though they certainly serve as a visual deterrent. Many people are unaware that window guards have an emergency release in case of a fire.

SLIDING DOOR AND WINDOW LOCKS Sliding doors and windows are an intruder's best friend. Install key locks, one at the bottom that bolts into the frame, and one at the top. For doors, get a foot lock, which is easily opened and locked with the touch of a toe. In the meantime, place a beam of wood along the bottom track, making break-ins more difficult.

HEAVY-DUTY WINDOW GRATES You'll notice window grates blocking the first-floor windows of nice apartments in urban areas. Made of heavy iron and painted black, these grates make it impossible for someone to get to the window, but also make it impossible for you to get out in the event of a fire. (Pricey fire escape versions, with an inside release latch, are available.) To avoid the jailhouse look, models are molded with visually appealing patterns. Grates need to be installed professionally and may be the only option in high-crime areas.

INSTALLING WINDOW PINS

Window pins make it impossible to lift a double-hung window at all, preventing unwanted entry. To install, you drill a hole through both window rails (the center overlapping part when both windows are closed), insert the two hollow pieces of metal into each hole, and insert the bolt through both holes.

INSTALLING WINDOW GUARDS

Installing a window guard is a simple matter of installing the guard into two sides of the window frame with screws and a screwdriver.

INSTALLING WINDOW GUARDS

YOU NEED

× Tape measure
× New window guard (includes screws)
× Pencil
× Power drill (depending on model)
× Flathead screwdriver (depending on model)

STEPS

1 Measure the size of your window frame and sash and go to the store. Window guards come in a few standard sizes; if you have an oddly shaped window, order a customized guard from a manufacturer.

2 Stand in front of the window and adjust the window guard to the proper size: the edges should fit snugly inside the tracks that the outside window uses. Place the guard as you want to install it, making sure that it is out far enough not to interfere with opening and closing the inside window.

3 Some models are simply wedged in place, and your work is done. Other models need to be screwed into the right and left window tracks, usually with 2 screws in each track. To do this, you mark the location of the screw holes with a pencil, and then drill holes on top of the pencil marks, using the drill bit size suggested in the instructions. On higher floors be *very careful*, keeping the inner window sash low and your head on the inside of the window. Use a drill or flathead screwdriver to insert the screws through the window guard into the holes. Tighten the screws, and you're done.

YOU NEED

- × Tape measure
- × Pencil
- × New window pins
- × Power drill (see Going Hardcore: How to Use a Power Drill, page 27)

- × Safety goggles
- × Wite-out (optional)
- × Hammer (sometimes)
- × Soap or Vaseline (sometimes)

STEPS

1 Move any nearby objects that you don't want to be covered in sawdust.

2 Shut the window and use a tape measure to find the center of the window where both rails are in line with each other. Use a pencil to mark the center of the rails, where you want to install the window pin.

3 Read the directions on the window pin package and find the correct-sized drill bit for your power drill. Usually it is around ½ inch.

4 The biggest hazard of this installation is drilling all the way through both window rails. You don't want to do that. To prevent this, open the bottom window, and line up the drill bit against the width of the 2 window rails, so that it is inserted 80 percent of the way through both. Mark this place on the bit with dark pencil marks or a spot of Wite-out.

5 Close the window fully and place the drill bit into the drill. Wearing your safety goggles, with your power drill, drill a hole straight through the dot you have marked, stopping at the point you marked on your drill bit. You will probably have to apply pressure onto the drill. Be careful to not drill all the way through both window rails.

6 Open both windows, pulling the top window down and the bottom window up, so that you have full access to both holes.

7 Insert the metal tube part of the window pin into each hole. Sometimes, this requires a bit of tapping with a hammer, or a bit of lubrication with Vaseline or soap.

8 Shut the windows. Depending on the model that you bought, you need to slide the main pin through both holes. Some models use a key to do this: you attach the key to the main pin, stick the pin into the hole, and then remove the key.

9 Admire your newly safe window!

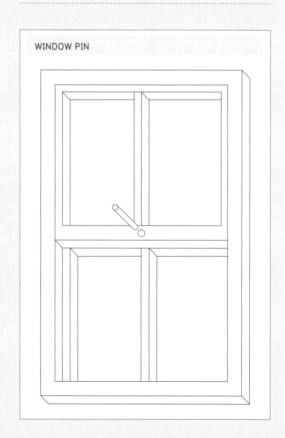

WINDOW PIN

HOME ALARM SYSTEMS

Having a good system of locks throughout your living space is more imperative. However, alarm systems are important in the feeling of safety and security that they provide. A good dog might sense an intruder before the system does, but the system can instill a feeling of protection for women living alone, women often alone with children, or women who have experienced trauma. People living in large spaces, where they could not hear a basement burglar while watching television upstairs, are the best candidates for alarm systems.

Alarm systems often require a good dose of discipline to run correctly: you will need to turn on and deactivate the system regularly, and on more complicated systems, remember to monitor some zones of the house but not others. If you can afford to subscribe to a service, many alarms contact emergency authorities immediately; other systems deter would-be intruders with internal alarms and motion-detector lights.

ALARM SYSTEM OPTIONS

There are two categories of home alarm systems: those designed to detect movement at entrances and those designed to detect an intruder inside. Which type and specific sensors you choose depend on your lifestyle. If you live alone and want to make sure no one breaks in while you are home alone, a system that guards the entrances of your home makes sense; a bunch of children would set off the same system constantly. While you're on vacation, systems that sense intruders inside are more useful, saving the mailman unnecessary trauma. Professional systems contain a few key parts:

MAIN CONTROL PANEL Controls the entire alarm system through detectors attached directly to the panel. You activate and deactivate the system using a pin code, and can set the system to monitor certain regions. If you subscribe to a security service, the company headquarters can read your panel, see which detectors are going off, and call

emergency services. Most panels have a silent alarm to be used in the case of a personal attack.

SENSORS Alarm systems use a variety of sensors. *Infrared beams* can be set across areas such as a garage door or part of a backyard, and will trigger the alarm when the beam is broken. *Magnetic sensors* can be placed on a door and door frame (or window and window frame), setting off an alarm when the door is opened. *Low-frequency sound alarms* detect breaking glass, while *pressure-sensitive mats* detect people walking over rugs. Infrared sensors can detect intruder body heat, while special screens *woven with wires* will set off alarms when cut. Other *vibration detectors* in doors and windows sense movement consistent with jimmying or forced entry. Last, most systems are set off by attempts to cut alarm or phone wires. Choose sensors to match your lifestyle, pets, living space, and budget.

ALARM STYLES Alarm styles range from school-bell alarms to flashing lights to silent authority alerting. Some security services automatically call your land-line phone. Your alarm preference depends on your setup and safety concerns. More visible and audible exterior alarms can help authorities identify your house.

SMOKE AND CARBON MONOXIDE DETECTORS These detectors can be automatically attached to the system. In addition to protecting you, if you subscribe to a security company, the fire department is automatically called when a smoke detector goes off, thereby protecting your home whether you are inside or not.

REMOTE CONTROLS Some systems include remote control options. A key chain control can be ideal if a contractor needs to visit midday or if a special friend offers to make you dinner before you get home— simply deactivate from where you are. Depending on the model, distances can range from a few hundred feet to neighboring states.

TIP

Budget-Safe Alarms Alarms can be surprisingly cheap. Individual alarms, such as an individual magnetic sensor for a window, can cost as little as a few dollars, while basic movement-sensing alarms for a door can cost $5. The local electronics store can equip you with five or six alarms for around $30.

DO-IT-YOURSELF ALARM SYSTEMS

If you are low on both cash and household wiring skills, you want to install a wireless battery system, where sensors communicate with a control panel via radio signals. You will regularly need to make rounds with batteries. To install, choose the system and sensors that you want, and attach them to windows and doors according to the instructions. In some cases, such as a glass-vibration detector on a window pane, you simply remove a safety strip and adhere the detector directly onto the pane. This installation is fast in smaller living spaces, where only a few windows and doors need sensors.

TESTING NEW AND OLD SYSTEMS

Set the control panel to a silent alarm that does not alert authorities and go around your living space to test all the sensors. Feel free to employ a friend in everyone's favorite game of Pretend You're an Intruder. Have him or her run around and try to break in to see which alarms go off. Adjust and add sensors appropriately. You will need to do this periodically, to make sure that all sensors still work. On a new system, you want to leave the silent, nonemergency alarm on for a few days, until you have figured out your schedule, learned how to trim the tree branch so it won't set off the window alarm, and set sensors so that Fluffy doesn't end up with a criminal record.

FIDO, THE OTHER ALARM SYSTEM

Before you consider an expensive system, consider a dog. Dogs sense the presence of others long before people and alarms do, and they will bark to alert you, happily freaking out your friends. Some breeds are much better guard dogs than others, so do your research. A dog will present no challenge to a violent intruder, but petty criminals will often run.

OTHER ROBBERY PREVENTION STRATEGIES

If you are robbed, it will probably happen while you're not home, so it's not likely to pose a threat to your personal safety; you just won't own anything nice anymore. Aside from not drawing attention to yourself, your valuables, or your relative wealth, here are easy suggestions:

BE LESS ORGANIZED A family friend was once robbed. She lived comfortably in a state of disarray and had her good jewelry spread out over a few drawers, mixed in at random with clothes, socks, and papers. As a result, the robber didn't get anything of value. It is much easier for a burglar to grab a fancy jewelry box than sift through the explosion area that is your room.

INVEST IN HOMEOWNERS' OR RENTERS' INSURANCE Homeowners' insurance is insurance on your home and anything in it, for as little as a few dollars per month. Renters' insurance is ideal for apartment dwellers who feel safer knowing that their belongings are protected. For both, the insurance frequently extends to objects stolen outside the home, such as a laptop taken at a café, as well as items damaged during a disaster such as a fire or flood. Make sure to purchase insurance that includes "replacement costs," as opposed to the estimated value at the time of damage. Call up insurance brokers for quotes and specific coverage included. Take pictures of your valuables and store the photos outside your home, so you can prove what was stolen.

STORE VALUABLES IN A HOME OR BANK SAFE Many stores sell home safes, small to large metal boxes with combination locks. Most are fireproof, and too heavy and awkward for a burglar to carry out. It's better if they're placed in an unusual location, such as in a drawer of paper supplies. Jewelry or financial notes are better stored in a bank safe. Bank safes are rented out for a few dollars a year and need two keys: your key and the banker's key.

USE LIGHT TIMERS Lights on timers are the easiest way to pretend you're home when you're not. It's worthwhile to buy the more expensive timers that let you set different programs for different days. Some models are made for radios, creating household noise when no one is home, or keeping Fido company.

PUT UP SECURITY SYSTEM STICKERS You're too poor for a security system, but this doesn't mean you can't hang a motion-detector light and find a friend to give you a few security system stickers to place on your doors. ("This home is protected by ABC Security Company.")

SMOKE ALARMS, CARBON MONOXIDE ALARMS, AND GAS ALARMS

SMOKE ALARMS

Smoke alarms should be on the ceilings of your main hallway and your bedroom (smoke rises, you may recall), with at least one on every floor. Many people forget about fire hot spots like attics, garages, and basements, so don't forget. If you rent, you can require your landlord to install them.

Most smoke alarms are battery operated and need to be tested regularly. Newer, pricier models can be installed directly into your electrical system or security system, along with a battery backup in case of power outages.

If you, like the author of this book, regularly set off your alarm with accidental gourmet burn-fests, purchase an alarm with a temporary shutoff button that will reset the alarm while you air out your kitchen—unless, of course, you take pleasure in loud, screeching noises for an extended period of time.

Vacuum off the alarm regularly—it can't detect smoke if it's completely covered in dust—and test it every time you think of it.

CARBON MONOXIDE (CO) ALARMS

CO alarms protect you from death via the CO fumes of malfunctioning appliances such as furnaces, clothes dryers, stoves, fireplaces, and water heaters. CO is the invisible, odorless result of unfinished fuel combustion, and it kills in minutes. If you have only one alarm, place it outside of your bedroom, between 14 inches and 5 feet off the floor.

CO alarms have digital displays and will record CO readings that are too small to trigger the alarm. If you have a CO reading higher than zero, whether it's 3.6 or .0004, vacate the premises and call your local fire department nonemergency number.

GAS ALARMS

You only need a gas alarm if you have an appliance that runs on gas—mainly, a gas-powered furnace or a gas oven. Gas alarms should be placed on the wall right above the appliance, such as on the kitchen stove wall. If the alarm goes off, quickly put out any cigarettes or candles and turn off the main gas line to the living space. Don't touch any light switches, even if they're on. Leave the premises and call the gas company's emergency line; if you don't have that number on hand, call 911 and they will connect you. Gas alarms need the same maintenance as smoke alarms.

FIRE HAZARDS

Even if you're not in a major emergency, there are still a number of hazards holding court around your residence that could quickly turn into emergencies. Escaping through thick smoke is the equivalent of being blind and lost in a volcano, so know your escape plan well. Fire departments will send a free expert over to help you plan a route, especially for children.

COMMON FIRE HAZARDS

This is all common sense, and yet every year lots of people manage to set their living spaces on fire. To avoid this fate, keep an eye out for:

× **APPLIANCES LEFT ON** Short of lighting a match, the easiest way to start a blaze is to leave on an electrical appliance and walk away, only to have it overheat and spark—think stoves, fans, lights, space heaters, anything that plugs in.
× **CANDLES** Obvious, yet frequently fire starters. Burn candles only when you are watching. If you like smelly candles, use aroma pots instead—they're tea lights that burn under yummy-smelling oils, but are much safer because of limited heat and burning time.
× **CIGARETTES** Abstinence works. If abstinence isn't your style, use protection—never smoke where you might fall asleep, and put out cigarettes in ashtrays only.

- × LIQUID SUPPLIES Most cleaning supplies are extremely combustible. Any solvents, cleaners, or fuel should be carefully arranged in a cool, low cabinet, locked tight if you have children and checked on regularly. The Pine-Sol you have upstairs sitting in the sun is a fire hazard, and the lawn mower gas in your garage near your furnace is just asking for a spark. If possible, store chemicals in a shed away from your living space.
- × KITCHEN FIRES The most common kitchen fires are are started by forgotten cooking. Frying-pan oil will start on fire if left alone, so never leave while cooking.
- × OLD PAPERS AND RAGS Spontaneous combustion is that cool thing you learned about in middle school, when piles of old papers or rags suddenly start flaming. (Humans occasionally spontaneously combust as well, but addressing that would require an entirely different book.) That box of old notebooks in your attic, the crate of oily rags in your basement, and the stack of saved newspapers and magazines in your closet are all fire hazards. Keep them cool and well ventilated in plastic crates.

SHOULD I OWN A FIRE EXTINGUISHER?

Experts recommend them, but due to their cost, bulkiness, and care needs, extinguishers are not popular among the Young-and-Relocate-Frequently set. If money is not an issue, you should have one located in the center of an emergency escape route, so you could use it to get out if needed. Purchase one rated "A-B-C," which means it is effective against all kinds of fires. Twice a year, look at its gauges to make sure there is still pressure inside the tank.

Also purchase a fire blanket and keep one on every floor. This is not the item for bargain shopping— buy a good one. In case of a fire, throw the blanket over the flames to cut off oxygen to the fire, and turn off any obvious fire causes. Fire blankets do work on kitchen fires and should be stored above the stove. A variety of household supplies will put out different kinds of fires—baking soda, for example, will put out a grease fire. However, if you come running into a room and see flames, you're not going to have time to analyze the cause, so use a blanket.

NATURAL DISASTERS

Natural disasters are usually much more disastrous because people are unprepared. No matter where you live, you should have some weather concerns. Newcomers are particularly prone to being caught off guard, such as East Coasters who conveniently forget about earthquakes when moving to California, and senior citizens who swear by optimism when moving to hurricaney Florida.

You need to have a battery-powered radio available for all bad weather, so you can hear local advisories. (If the storm is bad, your TV isn't going to work, and you're not supposed to be hanging out in your living room, anyway.) Flashlights and batteries are also important. A few two-liter soda bottles filled with tap water and ample room-temperature-safe food (think powdered milk and energy bars) are also essential.

While you can't predict the weather, you can learn some simple steps to avoid catastrophe:

TORNADO If you receive a tornado warning, turn off the electricity to your home and the main gas line before the storm strikes. You should have a low place with no windows in which to hide during a tornado, such as a basement. After the storm, first carefully look for wall cracks and moving foundation to check the stability of the structure, then turn on the electricity if it's off and check for short circuits.

HURRICANE Take inside any loose items from the porch, balcony, or backyard, such as lawn chairs or garbage pails. Tie down anything that might move and get rid of any dead branches on nearby trees. Lock all doors and windows, pull all shades, and if you are expecting a severe storm, nail boards over the windows. You should also have a stash of flashlights and batteries.

FLOOD Take all valued items to the highest available point in your home, or to a higher location such as a friend's apartment, and place all heavy furniture and appliances on blocks. After the flood, once you are sure your residence is structurally safe, vacuum up mud and water before they dry. You'll need to wait for everything to dry (weeks or months) before most repairs. Strangely enough, it is recommended that during severe floods, you open basement windows to let water in to avoid a cave-in from outside pressure.

WINTER STORMS Wrap the water pipes with blankets or insulated jackets, and leave faucets trickling to prevent frozen pipes. Make sure windows and doors are closed and locked, and plug all drafts. Have enough food, water, and flashlights on hand for a few days.

EARTHQUAKE If you are in a quake zone, before you move in, make sure your residence has extra bracing and foundation bolts. (Make sure your super or landlord installs these.) The chimney and hot water tank should be physically strapped into place. During the quake, stay under strong furniture or a doorway. If you are in a low-lying area near a body of water, after the quake move to high ground as quickly as possible to avoid flooding or tidal waves.

THE KIT OF PERSONAL WELL-BEING

One cannot have a safety chapter without mentioning first aid kits. Here is a list of recommended items for your safety kit, according to the people who know best, the American Red Cross. Not all items are directly relevant to home repair, but they are good to have around anyway:

- × safety pins, big and small
- × latex gloves
- × sunscreen
- × Band-Aids
- × 2- and 4-inch sterile gauze pads
- × triangular bandages
- × Ace bandage
- × scissors
- × tweezers
- × needle
- × antiseptic
- × thermometer
- × aspirin or nonaspirin pain reliever
- × syrup of Ipecac (for accidental poisoning)

Keep your kit easily accessible and make sure to replace what you use and regularly throw out expired products.

CHAPTER 9

HELP, I'M BROKE! FRUGAL FIXES

Repairs should never take up a significant portion of your budget, regardless of how small that budget may be. This chapter is focused on keeping your repair costs minimal. Ranging from commonsense suggestions to directions on how to scrape by, the following pages are overflowing with ideas to keep your greenbacks where they belong—in *your* wallet, not the repairperson's.

Most important, remember, *if you don't have the skill or funding to repair your living space, don't break it in the first place.* Most repairs can be prevented by gentle use, maintenance, and not breaking your belongings. If you can't fix it, *tread lightly.*

ON NOT FIXING IT

"Fixing" and "fixing well" are two very different things. Door knockers and sinks exist for a reason. Who needs a doorbell, anyway? And who *really* needs a dishwasher? Not fixing it is always an option. If something that you never use breaks, leaving it broken is a completely valid option.

THE DUCT TAPE CORPS

A very classy person once said that you need only two things in life: duct tape and WD-40. If it doesn't move and it should, use the oil. If it's moving and it shouldn't, use the tape.

Within reason, they're right. There are safety concerns with the introduction of duct tape and grease to mechanical and electrical items (*do not* dump grease into your broken ventilation system), but if you are satisfied with a propped table leg or a taped door handle, go for it. It only needs to be usable, not sophisticated. Functionality is everything.

DON'T FIX IT, HIDE IT

You might consider closing off broken sections of your living area to others. For example, if you currently cannot afford to nicely furnish your whole home or need to hide a noticeable break, there is no reason that you can't set up a living room area

and close a few doors. Guests do not need to see every inch of your living space, and they don't need to know that all you have in your bedroom is a mattress, an alarm clock, and a large water stain. When in doubt, decorate with books: used books are cheap, as are garage-sale bookcases. You can stylishly line your walls and seem educated at the same time, while hiding a lot of damage. And you might even learn something.

SUGGESTIONS FOR CHEAP NONFIXES AND CONCEALMENTS

- × Hide water stains with paintings, photographs, or wall hangings.
- × Conceal damaged tables or propped-up legs with tablecloths.
- × Use the broken sink for storage (you don't need three sinks).
- × Remove your doorbell altogether.
- × Cover wall damage with a bookcase.
- × Utilize hardcover books as props of any kind throughout the living space.
- × Use the trash, as opposed to the garbage disposal that seems confused by fruit.
- × Dry and store your dishes in the dishwasher that is too expensive to fix (wash them in the sink that's not storing anything).

QUESTIONS TO ASK BEFORE NOT-FIXING

- × Is not fixing this item a safety risk?
  - If a potentially dangerous item stops functioning such as a gas stove, you need to take care of the problem regardless of how often you use it.
  - Smoke detectors, carbon monoxide detectors and fire alarms also need to be working at all times.
  - Just because it's functional doesn't mean it's usable. A clothes dryer with a leaky dryer hose, for example, will still dry your clothes, but it will also burn your house down.

- × Will fixing this cost more than I originally paid? Will it cost me two-thirds as much as I originally paid, and do I want a new one anyway?

- Many household items, such as vacuums, equal their original cost in repair fees.

× Is there an easy fix that I would be satisfied with?
  - If you would be happy sticking a book under the leg of the table you bought at a garage sale, do it. You can always use a floor-length table cover, and no one will know the difference. The items you use daily need to be functional, not flauntable.

× Is it worth the hassle?
  - If you would have to miss work to hire a repairman to fix your showerhead, it might be worth it to you to pay the few extra dollars in monthly water bills until you get around to fixing it. (To gauge this, leave a bowl by the drain to see how much water drips in twelve hours. If it's only a couple of ounces and you don't mind wasting water, you could ignore it until a friend can fix it next month.)

× Will I need to get this item fixed when I want to sell my living space?
  - A broken doorbell and a broken entryway light will not impress anyone. If you are planning to sell, sublet, or rent your living space in the future, you might as well do it now.

With these questions in mind, not-fix away. Three cheers for duct tape.

CHEAP FIXIN'S

DON'T BUY NEW, REPLACE OLD

Fixing breaks yourself is a guaranteed way to save money on home repair. Many breaks, particularly in older appliances, are due to individual small parts that have worn out over time. These parts can be as cheap as a few dollars and rather straightforward to replace. If you hire a professional or buy a new appliance, you will end up paying thirty to forty times the cost of the parts.

For example, take the belt that turns your clothes dryer drum. If the belt snaps, your dryer will no longer work, and it will cost around $100 for a professional to come fix it. If you were to replace the belt yourself, it would cost around $6 and take a half hour to repair.

For this reason, if your goal is to save money, you should (a) understand what broke and what needs to be fixed, and (b) learn the basics of home repair so that you can perform minor repairs yourself. It's that simple. Fixing it yourself is always free.

SPARE PARTS

Many people end up calling repairpeople because they don't know where to purchase replacement parts for older appliances. Luckily, there are special dealers who buy large quantities of older parts, and your replacement piece is only a phone call away. Try looking in your local phone book under "Appliances—Supplies & Parts" (or a similar heading) to locate the nearest dealers, then simply call up and ask. You will also save money buying directly from these dealers as opposed to your repairperson, because in most cases professionals know that you have no clue how much a part costs and will triple the price on their estimates and bills. If you can't find a dealer, try calling the original company's customer service line—they will be able to tell you where to find spare parts.

BROKEN ITEMS ARE CHEAP

While much of this book is centered around either performing or avoiding home repair, with your newfound home repair savvy from reading this book, you can now take advantage of the ignorance of others. Broken items are cheap—tables, reclining chairs, vacuum cleaners, toasters, air conditioners, anything—so acquiring broken items on purpose can be an efficient way to save money. Most people simply trash household appliances the minute they break, so if you have a good eye for easy fixes or a friend with a good eye for easy fixes, you can acquire what you want for little to no cost, and then repair it.

PLACES TO FIND FIXABLE ITEMS FOR FREE OR CHEAP

× Garage sales
× Thrift stores
× Your block on garbage day
× City streets on any day
× Flea markets
× Your friends' houses
× Local classified ads, online and in papers
× Used-merchandise magazines
× The office garbage pile

These are all also great places to acquire tools—the same wrench that is $10 at the hardware store will be $.50 at a garage sale.

Once you have purchased the item you want, a simple paint job or part replacement can have your purchase back in tip-top shape. Covering items that are less than fashionable is easy with pretty fabrics, which can be purchased for a couple of dollars at a fabric store. For those on very tight budgets, remember that "retro" looks are always in, so that ancient toaster at a garage sale could not only be functional but also the pièce de résistance in your kitchen.

If you are looking for a specific item, such as a cheap air conditioner, feel free to place an advertisement in your local community Web site or message board. "Got a broken air conditioner? I'll take it," should get you an air conditioner from someone who doesn't know about filter changes.

BIG SECRET STASHES OF FREENESS

Another little-known secret is the extreme value of apartment building basements. Superintendents often have a basement storage room filled with the furniture and equipment that former tenants have left behind, all of which they are happy to get rid of. Feel free to call local apartment complexes in search of cheap items—not only are the goods often very affordable, but they are generally in good condition. The posher the building, the posher the goods.

PAINTING CHEAP FURNITURE

A good coat of paint is often the difference between a piece of junk and perfectly good furniture. Painting is always easier than refinishing wood. Paint covers the furniture in color; finishing allows a clear view of the wood below, but highlights imperfections and requires a much more thorough job of stripping previous work. In summary, painting is a project of a few hours, while quality finishing can take a weekend of ample scraping. So, we will talk about painting.

For rough wood, sand it down with 120-grit sandpaper before you paint and wipe off all the dust. Fill holes with "wood filler," a pasty goo that smoothes out imperfections. Painting furniture is just like painting walls, so see Painting (page 46) for details on brushes and paints.

CHEAP GROUPS THAT FIX THINGS

Most communities offer a number of local repair groups—volunteer groups or budget-minded non-profit organizations that will come to your home and perform repairs for little or no cost. While the details of these groups vary from place to place, they are worth checking out. Variations include a club of retirees that performs basic home repairs inexpensively, as well as a group aimed toward aiding lower-income residents in need of repair aid. (In my town, the organizations are called Umbrella and House Medics.) I also know of more than a couple of recent retirees who perform cheap repairs on the side.

These groups are sometimes hard to locate given the wide range of titles and affiliations, but flip through your phone book or call the local hardware store. "Hi, I'm on a budget and I was wondering if you could tell me what organizations in the area provide low-cost home repairs?" should do the trick.

RIVETING RETIREES

The elderly are a great untapped gold mine of fix-it help, and they appreciate feeling needed. Older retired men have a lot of free time on their hands, and many are handy from the days of shop classes in high school and repairing tanks in the First World War.

Unlike the techno-oriented and college-educated (read: useless) men of recent generations, older men spent many years dependent on their ability to use their hands and often went to vocational schools that furthered these skills. Judgment is key here—if he needs a cane, ladders are probably out. When in doubt, ask the wife if he's handy.

BAKING SODA TO THE RESCUE

If there were an award for the cheapest and most useful product ever, baking soda would win. It's even edible—what more could you ask for? As a general rule, anything that smells should be soaked in or washed with a baking soda and water mixture. Here's a small list of its many uses:

- × **CARPET CLEANING** Sprinkle the contents of your box over the rug, let it sit for an hour, then vacuum.
- × **REFRIGERATOR FRESHENING** An open box in your refrigerator will absorb the noxious odors of nasty food. Baking soda companies suggest changing the box every three months; you can get by with annually.
- × **TOOTHPASTE** A water and baking soda combination will keep your pearly whites gleaming. Baking soda admittedly doesn't contain fluoride, but it will work for the morning you wake up and realize Fido ate your Crest.
- × **DEITCHING** A pasty mix of water and baking soda can calm itchy skin, rashes, and insect bites.
- × **SCUFF MARK REMOVER** Sneaker stains on tile or linoleum can easily disappear with a wet sponge and baking soda. Crayon stains can also disappear.
- × **SHOWER CURTAIN CLEANING** If you're too lazy to lug your shower curtain to the nearest washing machine, a wet sponge covered in baking soda will clean it up.
- × **DISH CLEANING** Some water, baking soda, a scouring pad, and scrubbing can remove the toughest stains. Unlike liquid dish soap, which works by greasing up the stain molecules until they slide off, baking soda scours off stains.
- × **DESMELLING** Smelly sponges, clothes, and fabrics lose their odors after a few hours in a tub with some water and baking soda. This practice is particularly useful for cloth diapers.

- × **HARDCORE HANDCLEANING** Baking soda can safely scour off mud, grease, and dyes in hand creases. Before your resign yourself to blue hands, try some soda.
- × **ANTACID** Sodium bicarbonate (aka baking soda) is a prime ingredient in most antacids. A half teaspoon in a half glass of water won't be as yummy as the cherry antacid pills you chew by the handful, but it will probably work.
- × **MICROWAVE CLEANING** Put water and baking soda in a microwave-safe bowl and turn it on for a minute. Microwave smells will dissolve.
- × **LAUNDRY SANITATION** Sprinkle some in your laundry bin to get through another week.
- × **DRAIN CLEANER** Pouring baking soda down the drain while running warm water can freshen up a drain.
- × **FIREFIGHTING** Baking soda puts out grease fires, electrical fires, and fabric and furniture fires. Keep a box above the stove for this reason. Just dump it on the flames.
- × **GRILL POLISHING** Baking soda can remove the blackened goo that attaches to barbecue grills. Sprinkle baking soda over the cool bars, wipe down with a sponge, and let the mixture soak.
- × **FRUIT CLEANING** Sprinkle some baking soda over fruits and vegetables in the sink for a good clean.
- × **HAIR DEGREASER** When showering's not an option, sprinkle a bit (a bit) of baking soda along your part line. It will soak up grease, giving you an extra ten shower-free hours. But be careful: Too much sprinkling will create the Blotchy Premature Graying Look.
- × **LAUNDRY IMPROVER** Many swear by adding a bit of baking soda into the washing machine to improve stain removal.
- × **KITTY LITTER CLEANING** The deodorizing powers of baking soda are particularly useful where fresh feces are involved. Coat the bottom of a kitty box with a layer of baking soda.
- × **COUNTER CLEANING** Formica and marble countertops can be cleaned to a shine with baking soda and a sponge. Note that baking soda doesn't contain antibacterial properties and won't kill the bacteria left by raw meat, but it will remove residue and stains.
- × **BATHROOM CLEANING** Baking soda is great for cleaning bathroom surfaces. It's essentially a scouring powder and mild abrasive that will wipe up sink gunk, toothpaste gobs, and mold with aplomb.

- × COFFEE CLEANER SALVATION If your coffee-maker gets as nasty as most, make "coffee" with baking soda and water. (Skip the filter and java.)
- × SILVER POLISH Silverware can be polished with a damp rag and baking soda. Be careful with fine sets, because some can get scratched. For your everyday ware, it's fine.
- × BURNED-PAN SALVATION Undo your latest gourmet disaster by soaking the pot or pan in the sink with baking soda and warm water for fifteen minutes. Then wash with baking soda and a sponge. The burned food should come right off.
- × ASHTRAY DEODORIZER Still smoke? Periodically soak ashtrays in baking soda and water.
- × SMELLY-SHOE PREVENTION Sprinkle baking soda in your shoes. I don't need to explain why.
- × BATHROOM CLEANING Baking soda is great for cleaning bathroom surfaces. It's essentially a scouring powder and mild abrasive that will wipe up sink gunk, toothpaste gobs, and mold with aplomb.
- × BAKING SODA BATHS Motherly wisdom recommends warm baths with baking soda for skin maladies ranging from chicken pox to eczema. Double-check with your doctor, because my mother is not a doctor.
- × EDIBLE CLAY If you're turned off by the chemicals in children's clay, try adding 2 parts water, 2 parts baking soda, and 1 part cornstarch. Adjust for proper consistency. When your nieces say it doesn't look like clay, add food coloring.
- × EMERGENCY DEODORANT Dry powder dusted into armpits will pass for emergency deodorant.
- × PANTY PRETTY If *au natural* isn't your style, sprinkle a bit onto white panties.
- × GARGLING RESCUE You just ate a garlicky meal with your hot date, and during your two-minute bathroom reprieve, noted that you're out of mouthwash. Dump a teaspoon of your bathroom baking soda into a cup of water and gargle away.

FREE FIXIN'S

LEARNING FOR FREE

You should never have to pay a dime to learn how to fix something. There are a myriad of beginners courses offered locally on every conceivable kind of repair. Local businesses will often offer free courses to encourage business at their stores. This could not be a better deal: if you want to learn to fix something, all you have to do is *show up*. Look through your phone book in search of free classes, and within a call or two you'll find what you are looking for through word of mouth.

PLACES TO FIND FREE COURSES

- × Any hardware store, particularly big chains
- × Community centers
- × Fire and police departments (usually safety-related classes)
- × Auto repair shops
- × Electronic equipment stores

ATTENTION, BLEEDING HEARTS

Local volunteer programs that build homes for the underprivileged, such as Habitat for Humanity, will not only teach you how to build and install various items but will also allow you to do the work yourself. In this case, you'll learn how to use various tools and see how homes are built, wired, and insulated, while gaining a very clear understanding of home repair. In this case, you are learning everything you wanted to learn, while doing good for the community. If you are low on funding but have some time to offer, this may be the choice for you. After a few months of Saturday mornings on the job, you'll be able to remodel your own apartment on the cheap. Check the phone book.

FREE FIXES FROM THE SMALL SCREEN

There is one sneaky but very cool way to get major repair and renovation work done on your living space for *free*.

FREE FIXES *(fr¯e fik·sès) n. pl.: Zero down payment, zero ever payment. New bedroom.*

Take a chance and volunteer your living space for a television program. Public television features a variety of programs dedicated to everything from basic home repair to decorating; cable stations have a wider range, including ever-popular shows where home repair novices get a budget to redo their living space with a professional. Most shows give contact info in the credits. Some shows are based on surprising your roommate, so you might have to write an application about how much your roommate really wants a new kitchen.

The show's general audience, your living arrangements, and the kind of work you want done should decide the programs. If you want an all-American, white-picket-fence-type place, then maybe the music station geared toward eternal trendiness is not for you.

A LIVE-IN REPAIRPERSON

A less glamorous but equally functional option to free repair work is to make an agreement with a subletter or renter for rooming space in exchange for chores. (Married women should roll their eyes and say, "He's called my husband.") If you are in a position to sublet or rent a room or section of your living space, as little as a couch or a small room, this may be an option for you. You can either allow the person to live there for free for an agreed-upon amount of work per week, or you can offer a significantly reduced rent. Recent immigrants, handy college students, or recent graduates will jump at this kind of offer. We all know the person who lived in a walk-in closet for a year because it seemed like a good idea. Put up some ads and find that person.

STAINLESS STUFF

People throw out all sorts of items just because they're stained. This is enormously wasteful, particularly when a few stain-removal tricks can clean up the item completely. When you spill, no matter the fabric or the stain, *immediately* blot up as much as you can with a paper towel or light-colored rag. This often removes enough of the stain that laundering can remove the rest.

The reason that many stains are labeled "stubborn" is because people aren't using the proper chemical to fight the stain. For example, all the protein-based stain removers in the world won't be helpful on the oil stain on your favorite pants; nor will all the oil solvents in the world help a milk stain.

The stain-fighting rules are the same for any stain: immediately run the stain under cool water *before* it has set. If you're out on a hot date, if you ever want to wear the outfit again, excuse yourself to freshen up or suggest that your guest freshen up while you save your couch. A number of companies sell pocket-sized combination cleaners that can be immediately put on a stain, even while you're wearing it. As always, test the stain fighter on a hidden edge to make sure it won't damage the fabric or color.

THE FOUR MAIN STAIN FIGHTERS

From now on, there are three main categories of stains: "inky," "protein," and "oily." The category of stain dictates the stain treatment. You should keep a small supply of each of these in your bathroom.

GLYCERINE Glycerine is ideal for "inky" stains, such as pen stains, dark wine stains, or fruit juice stains. Let the glycerine sit on the stain before using your super-secret weapon, liquid dish detergent, which is made to remove food dyes.

DETERGENTS These are the laundry detergents, officially called enzyme detergents, that you find in the laundry aisle—Wisk, Tide, et cetera. They work best on protein-based stains, such as milk or blood. Protein stains are anything that comes from a person or animal, including sweat, feces, blood, and milk.

(Yum.) For a bad stain, first run the stain under cool water, before applying detergent directly onto the damp stain, and letting it sit for twenty minutes.

OIL REMOVERS Oil removers, officially called oil solvents ("solvent" = dissolver), remove "oily" stains such as lotion, butter, or accidental sprays of cooking grease. Oil removers should be applied to the stain and left to sit for at least fifteen minutes. The big name brand is Carbona.

COMBINATION SOLVENTS A number of stain removal sticks and sprays have begun to include both enzyme and oil removers. Name brands include Shout and Stain Stick.

OTHER STAIN FIGHTERS

VINEGAR A 1:1 mix of white vinegar and water is ideal for loosening dyes from fabrics, particularly non-washable materials such as your couch upholstery. First soak the stain in vinegar and water, and then apply the appropriate oil solvent or detergent. Vinegar is also an excellent odor remover for everything from the exercise shirt that you really want to continue using to your carpet, which can handle a 1:5 vinegar-to-water rinse. The vinegar odor disappears surprisingly quickly.

BLEACH Bleach will get rid of most stains, with the caveat that it will turn the stain and the surrounding area bright white. Bleach essentially eats right through both stains and the fabrics below, so the idea is to use a 1:6 part mixture on a stain just until the stain disappears, and then thoroughly rinse off any remaining bleach.

CONFUSING STAINS

The stains that you're probably not quite sure how to classify:

× **COFFEE AND TEA** Immediately run cold water over the stain, then use a combination solvent. Wash normally.

× **GUM** Hold an ice cube onto the gum and crack

off what you can. The remaining stain is an oil stain, so use an oil solvent.

× **URINE** This will begin coming up around child-bearing age. Soak in a 1:1 mix of vinegar and water. Then wash with detergent.

× **MUSTARD, GRASS, FINGER PAINT,** and **COLA** All will leave behind a dye stain on your white shirt. First soak in a 1:1 mix of vinegar and water, then use the secret weapon, liquid dish detergent.

× **ANTIPERSPIRANT, DEODORANT, CHOCOLATE MAKEUP, CANDLES, CRAYON,** and **TOMATO SAUCE** When in doubt, you're probably dealing with a protein/oil mix and need to use a combination solvent.

> **NOTE**
>
> *For removing carpet stains, please see page 77.*

THE FUNKY SHOWER CURTAIN THAT COULD

"How do I clean my shower curtain?" is one of the ageless questions of our time. The stains you see are a combination of soap scum, body oils, and mold.

If you have a vinyl or plastic shower curtain, you can take it off its rings and dump it into a washing machine gentle cycle along with ½ cup of baking soda. In a pinch, regular detergent will work as well. Take it out of the machine before the spin cycle and hang it back up to get the wrinkles out. (People at the laundromat will learn from you.) If you have a cloth curtain, you can usually wash it alone, but read the tag instructions.

To prevent curtain mold and stains in the first place, periodically wipe down vinyl and plastic curtains with a bathtub cleaning spray or water. Always leave the curtain fully spread after showering so mold can't grow in the creases.

And remember, while showering, the curtain should be inside the tub, with you, so water can't get out. (People seem to have issues with this concept.)

PREVENTING FUTURE BREAKS

While most preventative maintenance sections are a yawn, this one is both entertaining and incredibly informative—and it will make the difference between someone who piddles in repair and an independent, self-sufficient person who knows his or her stuff. If it's gonna break, it's gonna break. However, with a bit of awareness and occasional maintenance, you can at least recognize breaks before they happen and prevent a major crisis—a water leak is a much cheaper problem if you catch it when it's a drip, not a flood.

YICK, THAT DOESN'T LOOK SO GOOD

As a person with nonadvanced repair skills, you need to be able to spot basic damage early. So look. Periodically walk around and glance at things. Though it seems obvious, the easiest way to wipe out your bank account is to ignore damage and wait until it's too severe to ignore. If something doesn't look right, trust your instincts—it's probably not right. Things to look for:

SIX SIGNS THAT SOMETHING IS SCREWY

- × Missing or damaged exterior **SHINGLES** or **FLASHING** Damaged areas will be obviously nonsymmetrical with the rest of the wall or roof, unless the whole thing's a big mess.
- × Things that should be flat and smooth, but aren't. **SAGS**, **CRACKS**, and **BULGES** in walls or ceilings, interior or exterior, are big warning signs of foundational damage.
- × **SOFT SPOTS** in walls or a foundation. Anything that should be hard but isn't, such as a hardwood floor with a weak spot or a beam that feels frail, needs help.
- × **CABLES** or **WIRES** that seem messy, such as cabling that hangs from the ceiling. This is a fire waiting to happen.
- × **HOLES**, always bad, are more than a cosmetic issue. Holes caused by rodents or insects are notable in their nonsmooth edges; water holes are soft.

- × **DROPPINGS**, usually in corners, are also an indicator of an infestation problem, as are freaked out house pets.

Looking around your apartment or house should be a matter of general awareness, not an all-day project. On your way out shopping, glance around the exterior of your living space. While you're cleaning up, peek at the walls and ceiling of the room. If something doesn't look right, you will know it, particularly after walking around a few times. If you're not sure, compare it to another section of your house. For example, if you notice a window that doesn't seem to hold 90-degree corners, go look at another window just to make sure you're not imagining things. Being generally awake and aware is the key here.

MUST-DO MAINTENANCE

Living somewhere involves a small amount of that scary thing, responsibility. There is a descending scale of regular apartment and house maintenance. The really important tasks for basic safety and functioning are listed below under Really Must Do's. Tasks that will save you a lot of money in later repair bills are listed under Really Should Do's. The Falling with Grace section explains your annual autumn checkups, and the Nice Touches section explains the tasks that will keep your living space Mom approved. At the end of the book is a calendar that conveniently organizes all these tasks into an annual schedule for you.

REALLY MUST DO'S

- × Test your smoke and carbon monoxide alarms *every two months*. It's easiest to do this at the same time every year—try holidays. For those who prefer the secular, the longest and shortest days of the year, the first and last days of school, and the semiannual changing of the clocks work as well, unless you live in time-warped Arizona. Change batteries *biannually*.
- × Clean or change air conditioner and furnace filters *every four months*, depending on the filter

quality, if you would like to continue to be comfortably temperatured. The first day of every season will work.

× Flush out the water heater *two times a year*. (See Hot Water Heaters, page 143.) Otherwise, lots of sludge builds up inside. It's kind of cool to watch all the junky stuff flow out.

× If you have outdoor shrubs around your exterior walls, trim them back from the house or apartment windows as needed, at least *every three months*. Shrubs are invitations to pests, rodents, and animals and can damage the living space by decreasing air circulation and allowing moisture buildup. Even if you're not in charge of them, you should keep them away from your exterior walls.

× If you have a fireplace, clean the chimney or hire a professional chimney cleaner *once a year*, or *twice a year* if you use it a few times a week. It's no fun holding your honey in a room filled with smoke.

× Get your heating system checked and serviced by a plumber *each fall*. Heating systems are not to be toyed with by inexperienced-but-optimistic women, so enlist the Repair Powers That Be—i.e., the guys with the trucks.

× Test everything. If it has a test button, press it *whenever you think of it*. Alarms, water heaters, garage door openers, temperature relief valves, etc.

REALLY SHOULD DO'S

× Clean out the clothes dryer lint trap *after every load*. Letting a lint trap fill up is a wonderful way to start a nice big laundry-room bonfire.

× Perform regular heating system maintenance. What you do depends on your system (see Heating Systems, page 148).

× Clean your stove as often as seems necessary for your use. Most have a "clean" function. If you're microwave dependent, clean it at least *four times a year*.

× Dust or wipe off appliances, pipes, and alarms *three times a year*. Dust buildup can break everything from water heaters to computers. Keep any dust, dirt, or grime off smoke and carbon monoxide alarms, always.

× Test fire extinguisher gauges *twice a year*. A depressurized fire extinguisher in a fire is about as helpful as a pile of paper.

× Have your septic system professionally looked at *annually*. You'll thank me. Septic leaks are a nightmare.

× If you have them, inspect your washer and dryer hoses *annually*. At the slightest sign of cracking or aging, replace them. The whistling wind tunnel noise is also the preinferno noise.

× Check all gas lines for signs of aging and wear *annually*.

× Test any appliance lights *annually*. For example, the red light that tells you your dishes are clean is useless if the bulb is out.

× Have either a professional or someone who knows knows what he's doing check for termites and other pests *annually*. Good places to look are where wood meets residence, such as where a balcony attaches to siding.

FALLING WITH GRACE

The season is called fall for a reason—if you're not careful, you could easily tumble into the icy, wet bowels of winter hell. To prevent this, it is best to perform most annual maintenances each autumn, to make sure that your living space is in tip-top shape for winter weather.

× Check *outdoor waterproofing* each fall—gutters, downspouts, roof health, everything. Even if you're a renter, it's a good policy to point out future disasters to the landlord. The entire exterior of your living space needs to be in good condition for pounds and pounds of snow. (Remember, it even snows in Florida.) If you live on the top floor of an apartment building, be especially aware of potential roof leaks.

× *Install storm windows*. Don't be optimistic and keep your screens in because you like 40-degree air at night—you're going to end up with a screen that's frozen in place for three months and window rot.

× Patch up any *exterior openings*. The cracked window that is not a problem in autumn weather will be a disaster in winter weather. Not only will the insects and vermin come inside because they're cold, so will a steady flow of water of varying temperatures.

× *Change your outdoor lightbulbs* every autumn. Even if the bulb's not dead yet, it is much easier to switch a lightbulb in fall weather than in the dead of winter with frozen hands on a 10-foot ladder over ice.

× *Trim any shrubs or trees* in front of your windows to allow maximum sunlight in during the winter, in the name of having cheaper heat bills, preventing opportunistic wildlife from crawling in, and limiting deep dark winter depression. Carefully hanging out an upper window with a branch cutter is acceptable, as long as you can't fall out and you own the tree you're cutting.

NICE TOUCHES

× Clean your drains *monthly*. Plug the drain, partially fill the sink or tub with hot water, and let it flow down. If you are a perfectionist, boil a kettle of water, add 2 teaspoons of baking soda, and dump the concoction down your drain without giving yourself a steam burn.

× *Periodically* lubricate your locks by rubbing the tip of a pencil against your key and putting the key in the lock. (The graphite lubricates the lock.) In humid regions, use lock lubricant spray instead.

× Defrost and clean your refrigerator regularly. If your fridge is eight to ten years old, do this every *two months*. If it's a newer fridge, use your best judgment.

× Clean removable gas stove burners *weekly*. Even gross rice kernels can start a fire if they're old enough.

× If you don't use your dishwasher regularly, make sure to run it at least *once a week* to keep its seals moist and the surrounding area dry.

× Reverse the motor of any ceiling fans *twice a year*. (See Ceiling Fans, page 154.)

× *Periodically* test and adjust the oven heat with a thermometer. If you regularly manage to burn everything despite following the recipe to a T, your stove could be off by forty degrees. Or you could just be a bad cook.

TOTO, YOU'RE NOT IN COLLEGE ANYMORE

Cleaning is a key part of general maintenance. Much like with humans, cleaning prolongs the life of anything. For example:

× Cleaning your stove, inside and out, makes it work better and last longer.

× Cleaning your bathtub reduces the chance of a caulking leak.

× Cleaning your floors will keep them attractive and abrasion free.

× Cleaning your kitchen will discourage insects and rodents from running you out.

× Cleaning your body will improve your private life.

Clean everything at least *monthly* (though you should probably clean your body more often).

A CLOSING THOUGHT ON REPAIRS

Regardless of the budget repair strategy you choose, there is one overriding piece of advice: *Always think simple.* Take for example the story of Busy Brenda:

BUSY BRENDA, A STORY OF HOPE

One day in April, Busy Brenda picked up her car from the repair shop in exchange for an uncomfortably large bill. That day after work, Brenda noticed that her car radio didn't work. Aside from being upset that she could no longer sing along with Carly Simon, Busy Brenda was distraught—she had just spent thousands of dollars on her car, and she didn't want to spend any more money. But she also didn't know how to fix her radio. In her head, she started running through a list of potential contractors—her auto repair shop versus the local electronics company versus her brother-in-law—and grew increasingly agitated at the thought of more work being done on her vehicle. In reality, Brenda's radio ailment was a simple blown fuse, which was quickly reconnected by her neighbor that evening. Brenda was so excited that she changed her car oil.

THE MORAL:
Always think simple. If it doesn't work at all, chances are that a wire came loose or a small part needs to be replaced. When things are well taken care of, complicated and expensive repairs are the exception, not the rule.

10

CHAPTER 10

GETTING SOMEONE ELSE'S HELP TO FIX IT

Oh no, it broke! Now I'm going to miss a whole day of work while I wait for the repairperson to show up, and then there's gonna be the hefty repair bill that I can't afford, not to mention cleaning up this mess, and, oh God, my floor is covered with water... Ah! My rug! It was new...

This is not a good way to start your day. Why bother waking up? You don't know how to fix your break, so you automatically envision hiring someone and paying large bills, and then you get upset. In order to avoid this early-morning (or late-night—these things are never convenient) scenario, this chapter explains how to be prepared for potential fixes *before* something breaks. The same break that can cause total chaos in your life—losing a day's income, changing your schedule, emotional distress—can be a calm exercise in common sense if you have next to your telephone a list of friends and professionals to call. This chapter will teach you how to compile that list, and it will save you a lot of damage. From now on, you never need to know specifically how to fix a major problem; you only need to know how to respond and who to call.

THE ART OF NETWORKING: FREE HELP

If you avoid home repair and keep expenses minimal, your best strategy is to create a system of friends and acquaintances who will *repair your living space for you*. Instead of panicking, you can simply pick up your phone, call your neighbor, your friend's boyfriend, or your coworker, and arrange for him or her to come help you. The complicated world of pipes, wrenches, and vents is now a social exercise.

THE HANDY NEIGHBORHOOD

Every time you call a repairperson, there is probably someone within a block of you who could have done it for free. The signs of who is useful are often obvious:

you will see your neighbor balancing on a ladder, hear the chainsaw through the wall, or see the guy always working on his car. You'll also see repairpeople regularly knocking on the doors of those who don't do their own work. So *look*. Visualize the dad next door bending over your water heater with a wrench. Your building or neighborhood is your proverbial toolbox.

Once you have decided who does what, you need to actually talk to your neighbors so that they might help you before the cow jumps the moon. (If you live in New York City, skip to the next section.)

FIVE CONVERSATION STARTERS

× THE COMPLIMENT ANYTHING PLOY "Wow, that plastic snowman is stunning!"
× THE BANANA BREAD SCHEME "Hi, I just wanted to welcome you to the neighborhood with some banana bread." It will help if you have banana bread.
× THE PARTY INVITATION TEMPTATION "Hi, I live across across the hall and I'm throwing a little gathering tonight. I was wondering if you might like to stop by?"
× THE NEW CAR EXCUSE "Wow, I was just admiring your new car. What a beaut!" Men eat up car compliments. It's like food for them.
× SHAMELESS FLIRTING "I find there's nothing sexier than a man who can repair a doorbell."

As a general rule, what one neighbor doesn't know, the other one will. One might be good with pipes, another with electrical wiring. You don't need one neighbor who does everything; you need a few who cover most bases.

EXPLOITING FRIENDS AND COWORKERS

Friends and coworkers make up another battalion of potential networking options. Your friends should like you enough to do favors around the house. (Offer to feed the difficult ones.) Even if your friends and acquaintances themselves are useless with a hammer, chances are that they know someone who isn't. Examples of this phenomenon:

× The woman who walks her dog in the dog park next to you every morning might have put herself through school doing repair work, or be married to a repairperson, but you won't know if you don't talk to her.

× The guy whose cubicle is next to yours might spend his free time renovating his second garage into an extra bedroom, but you won't know if you don't ask him how his weekend was.

HANDY COMPANIONS

In the words of my mother, "Never underestimate the importance of handyman boyfriends." Or girl-friends. When you see one—either your own, or one of your friends' or coworkers'—bells and whistles should go off in your head. Fix-it mates will be at your beck and call, and all your problems (at least the repair ones) will be solved. If this opportunity does not present itself, you can also scope out the useful significant others of your acquaintances. Take the example of Arlene and Brick the Carpenter:

ARLENE AND BRICK THE CARPENTER: A LOVE STORY (SORT OF)

Arlene has maintained her own apartments for two decades, despite being fundamentally helpless with a toolbox. However, she once had a coworker whose longtime boyfriend, Brick, is a carpenter. In a pinch, Arlene contacted Brick to fix a doorway problem. Brick has now fixed Arlene's apartment for fifteen years. Brick keeps his prices down because Arlene is a friend of his girlfriend. Arlene has since recommended Brick to a number of her friends, which keeps Brick happy because he enjoys the extra business. Everyone wins with handy companions.

YOU'RE OUTTA HERE!

This seems obvious, but repairpeople have a habit of being obnoxious to those they perceive as dense, so: *Anyone who makes you feel stupid or incompetent is banned from your networking list.*

It takes an IQ of around 50 to unclog a drain—though it can require some muscle—so anyone who makes you feel slow or unintelligent should not be doing your repair work. This is pivotal, particularly if you ever want to learn how to repair things yourself, because you want someone who will amicably explain what he's doing while he's doing it. Talking down is un-acceptable. And rather than seeing you as a threat to their business, most repairpeople are more than happy to teach, with some hoping for a nice tip.

FINDING A PROFESSIONAL BEFORE IT BREAKS

You suddenly have a spewing toilet, a major termite infestation problem, or water dripping through your walls. Your friends don't have the expertise to help, so you hastily flip open your phone book and call a random repair company. Ack!

Not all repair companies are created equal. If teen-agers Josh and Billy McDonough decide that they need some extra gas and pizza money, they can list themselves in the phone book as McDonough Bros. Home Repair. Enough said. You need a list of trusted professionals at your fingertips. And to make them "trusted" professionals, you need some references, which are referrals or recommendations from others who have hired repair professionals.

TIP

It's usually a good idea to wait a week or two after work is done to ask about satisfaction, because if it breaks again, it will usually take more than a few hours to do so. Wait until time has passed, and all bills are received and paid.

THREE CHEERS FOR DIFFICULT PEOPLE

To get references, you could just ask a friend what company fixes her pipes. But that wouldn't be very much fun. Instead, you know that woman who complains about *everything*—she can't eat a meal without sending it back and writes letters of grievance on a regular basis? That difficult, picky, hard-to-deal-with woman whom you and your friends can't fathom being married to? (A good place to look for such a woman might be your mother-in-law, if you have one.) This is your new Reference Woman.

Call her up, pretend you like her, and ask who does her home-maintenance work. If Reference Woman says that someone does a quality, affordable job, you are thereby assured that the company or contractor she recommends is the best one around. Difficult people are great.

CRUISING THE NEIGHBORHOOD

Another way to find reliable home repair professionals is to look around your neighborhood. If you see a truck parked in front of a neighbor's house, jot down the company name and number. Then go back and ask your neighbor if he or she was satisfied with the work.

ARE YOU FLEXIBLE?

Handy people tend to fix everything, and good repair help is like gold. If you find a professional that you like, ask them what else they do. For example, take the story of Reliant Rita and Deck the Pool Cleaner:

RELIANT RITA AND DECK THE POOL CLEANER,
A LOVE STORY (SORT OF)

Reliant Rita inherited an old country farmhouse having no former home repair experience. After a number of general upkeep catastrophes, she decided that she really liked her pool cleaner, Deck. ("He was really nice, respectful, and reliable, and always explained what he was doing.") While many people would just be grateful to have a clean pool, or to
own a pool in the first place, Reliant Rita one day decided to ask her pool cleaner, "What else do you do?" It turns out that Rita's pool cleaner is also very good at general home repairs. Thus, everyone is happy: Reliant Rita has someone she can rely on, and Deck has extra evening and weekend income that he appreciates.

YOUR RESOURCE LIST

Once you have compiled a collection of friends and professionals, make a list. Keep it on the wall next to your kitchen phone or load it into your phone's memory.

Depending on your living arrangements, you need to have a list of professionals who do the following work. Prepare for the worst—if you have only one tree in sight, it could fall on you, so list a tree guy as well as people who do the following:

× electrical maintenance
× plumbing
× extermination and pest control
× heating and cooling
× window, door, and lock repair and installation
× appliance installation and repair
× painting and wallpapering
× carpeting and floor work
× tiling (floor and bath, including walls)

If you live in a traditional house, you also need people in these areas:

× sewer maintenance
× tree removal
× masonry
× sheetrocking (aka putting up walls)
× carpentry
× landscaping
× driveway repair

Never fear, this is a list of the kind of work that needs to be done ("plumbing"), not the worker who does the repair ("plumber"). General contractors usually do several kinds of work, so you will probably need only seven or eight professionals, not sixteen. It's also a good idea to jot down who recommended a company. Companies love references. Here is an example of a resource list.

IT BROKE: WHAT DO I DO?

It broke. Finally. You knew it was only a matter of time, and yet you continued to ignore your destiny until it started spewing in your face. Don't worry, we understand. Before you reach for that phone book in a dripping panic, take a deep breath—you have some options. (Please note that this section is geared toward nonemergency repairs. If your break involves smoke, leaking gas, water near electrical outlets, or any other sign of physical danger, please see the chapter on dangerous breaks, Help, There's an Emergency! Being Alarmingly Secure, page 168.)

THE OPTIONS

a Get one of your friends or acquaintances to fix it
b Hire a professional to fix it.
c Fix it yourself.
d Don't fix it: The following pages explain how to smartly hook friends or professionals.

SUSAN'S RESOURCE LIST

CARPENTRY
- Neal Collins (Eszter's husbnd)—734-9838
- Linda Masters—563-9058 (work), built own porch, not sure would help?
- Contact Carpentry—734-5849 (recommended by John)

PLUMBING AND HEAT
- Joe Conley—734-4859 (Deb's boyfriend, #34, apt.2), good plumbing, some electrical
- Kinder Plumbing Company—483-3940 (recommended by Mrs. Donley; does heat too)

ELECTRICAL AND TILING
- Don Watson—485-3211 (Sara's husbnd, tiled bathroom last year, watched kids in April)
- Joe's Electrical Company—734-9748 (recommended by Jane)

TREE WORK
- Rooterrific, Inc.—734-1134 (recommended by Jane)

POOL WORK, PAINTING, LANDSCAPING
- John Hastings—734-7761 (from work; painted Jane's house; landscapes on side)

PAVING
- Pandora Pavers—734-0033 (paved last year; cheap)

EXTERMINATOR
- Dan (Sue's boyfriend)—485-2004 works at Bonwin Pest Control

SEWER/SEPTIC
- Steve's Sewer Co.—734-5918 (recommended by Mrs. Donley)

MASONRY/SHEETROCK/GENERAL CONTRACTOR
- Black Contracting Company—734-2567 (did Afra's addition; great!)

CARPETS
- Continental Carpets—485-CARP (recommended by Jane; clean and install)

USING FRIENDS AND ACQUAINTANCES

You are now equipped with a list of potential contacts, so you can simply scan the list and make a phone call. But unless your neighbor is also your significant other, "Come fix this" is not going to work. People need some form of incentive for helping others. This said, your job is to give the person on the other end of the phone a reason for why repairing your break is worthwhile to them. Herein lies the *Art of Bartering*.

THE ART OF BARTERING

The Art of Bartering: The skill of using your non–home-repair skills and talents in return for others fixing your things for free.

Everyone has his or her own talents, and now you are going to exploit yours to absolve yourself of home repair fees. Just because you are helpless with a wrench does not mean that you don't cook a mean manicotti and swing a powerful shovel. So pick up the phone and explain what you need and what you can offer.

SIX POTENTIAL BARTERS

PET-SITTING

"I know you usually pay a pet-sitter when you travel, but I would be happy to watch your cats."

SELLING POINTS Works best on neighbors who are passionate about their pets. Try dog-walking as an alternative.

FREE MEALS

"Would you like a free meal? I cook an impressive lasagna. I'm cooking it tonight anyway, and I would love company."

SELLING POINTS If you have a crush on your neighbor, you could be doubly successful tonight. Great on men who don't cook.

YARD WORK

"I really need some help with this, but in return I would be happy to save you some time this weekend by mowing your lawn/raking your yard/trimming your hedges."

SELLING POINTS Anyone who is busy or hates yard work will take you up on this instantly.alternative.

SHOVELING

"I'd gladly come over and shovel your sidewalks; I was doing mine anyway."

SELLING POINTS Aim for retirees. If you have a snowblower, twenty minutes of walking back and forth will save you a couple hundred dollars.

BABYSITTING

"I would be happy to watch your kids this weekend so you and Jan can enjoy a nice night on the town."

SELLING POINTS A major winner with strung-out parents.

CHILD TUTORING OR LESSONS

"I used to teach high school, and I would enjoy helping Monique prepare for her SATs," or "I played Division I basketball in college, so I would be happy to shoot some hoops with Danny."

SELLING POINTS Tutors and lessons are expensive, so offering skills to a family that couldn't afford them otherwise is a great help. Lessons are particularly useful in long-term bartering arrangements.

HIRING PROFESSIONALS: ESTIMATES, BILLS, AND NOT GETTING RIPPED OFF

You think you need a professional. Though much of this book is focused on methods of avoiding professionals and their costs, there are a myriad of home repairs for which a professional is necessary, either due to the severity of the break or because no one you know is qualified (hint: expand friend group soon).

DO I REALLY NEED A PROFESSIONAL?

If you are not sure whether you need a professional, ask yourself a few questions:

× Are their any potentially unsafe elements in the repair, such as gas lines, poorly maintained electrical lines, or water mains? Would I know how to respond if a problem developed with one of these?
× Do I understand what is broken, why it is broken, and how it should be fixed?
× Do I know someone who I am confident would be able to fix this for me?
× Are there any heavy lifting or complicated maneuvers that I would not feel comfortable performing myself?

WHEN IN DOUBT, ASK

If you are not sure of the severity of a break or whether you do need professional help, ask someone. Try: *"Hi, I don't have electricity in part of my apartment, and I'm not sure if I have an easy fuse problem or a larger electrical wiring problem. I can't even tell if the problem is inside my house or if the wires outside are damaged. Would you mind coming over and glancing around to help me figure out who I need to call? I would really appreciate it."*

ON NOT GETTING RIPPED OFF

Before you call a contractor, you need to have a general picture of what broke and why. You can find information on the Internet, in a home repair reference guide, or by having a friend give you a quick summary.

Prepared (pri-'perd). adj.:
1. *Informed enough to know what needs to be done.*
2. *The ancient art of not getting taken for a ride.*

For example, if you call the electrician and say, "Um, the lights won't work in half of my apartment," the electrician will immediately smell money. He or she can easily make up a story and overcharge you from Pluto and back for a simple repair. Even if you are not completely clear on what is broken, appear competent. You will often speak to a receptionist or operator. Though they are not repair personnel, they talk to people like you for a living, and can sense a paycheck through the phone line.

MAKING THE CALL

On the phone, you need to explain:

× What is broken
× Why it is broken ("I stepped on it," "I fell on it," etc.)
× What repair you think needs to be performed
× What you would like the repairperson to do—fix it, give an estimate, etc.
× Any history of breaks involving the same appliance

This last point gives relevant information and is code for "I've been through this before, I understand what's going on, and I will know it if you scam me." If you are genuinely not sure of any of these, don't make anything up—professionals are trained to assess what repair is needed.

PHONE TIPS

Mention who referred you—a contractor will often give better treatment to friends of old customers than to random people who call in a panic out of

WHAT TO SAY ON THE PHONE	WHAT NOT TO SAY
"Good morning, how are you? . . . I have some old broken shingles, and I need to get them replaced."	"Something's wrong with my roof thingies."
"Hi, my hot water heater is leaking and I need someone to come over and patch it for me—I had a similar problem last year. I've turned off the hot water to the house for the meantime, but I would like it fixed as soon as possible."	"Everything's ruined! There's water all over my basement and I don't know what to do and everything is ruined, ah! Get here fast; I'll pay anything!"
"My kitchen drain is clogged and I can't seem to unclog it due to years of deposits—it's stuck, and I'm not strong enough. Do you think you could send somebody over? It should be a simple job."	"Help, it's broken!" Or, "I can't use my sink. Fix it."
"Good afternoon. I need to get a hole patched in the cement brick wall of my basement. I would like to get an estimate sometime this week."	"KILL! Kill the animal that's eating holes in my house! KILLL IIIIIIIITT!!"

the blue. Try starting with "Hello, my name is Alicia Dorr, and I was referred to you by your longtime client Mrs. Donley."

You also want to make sure that the repairperson is both insured and bonded, so ask about both.

Insured (in'sured) adj.:
1. *The act of being covered by insurance.*
2. *If he falls off your roof, your bank account is not responsible for his back surgery.*

Bonded (bönd'ed) adj.:
1. *A timeless connection between two people.*
2. *Certification that a repairperson is backed by his company.*
3. *If the repairperson messes up the repair, the company fixes it, not you.*

BEING NICE PAYS

It is much easier for the repairperson to scam Ms. Horrible Annoying Shrill Woman than it is to rip off Sara Pazzini, a friendly accountant who misses her long-distance boyfriend and really wanted to be an astronaut. Names and details turn checkbooks into people, so be as nice as possible, particularly if your funds are limited. Providing a beverage and choice of radio stations helps, too.

ALL ABOUT ESTIMATES

If you suspect that you're in for a major repair, you might want to call multiple contractors and ask each of them to give you an *estimate*. This means that the repairperson will show up, assess the damage, and give you a written approximation of how much it will cost to fix the break—there will be no fixing.

ESTIMATE POINTERS

× Comparison-shopping is expected with major repairs or renovations, so call as many contractors as you like.
× Cheaper is not always better.

× Estimates are usually free; thus the term "free estimates."
× It is normal practice to ask for references from former customers, especially on expensive jobs.
× For common, small jobs, some contractors will give a rough estimate over the phone.

EVIL ESTIMATORS

Repairpeople have been known to cut corners with unsuspecting clients. If you have a hole in your basement wall that you would like patched and the repairperson glances and says, "Well, you need to have your whole wall gutted and reinstalled and that will cost about seventeen hundred dollars," ask for it in writing. If he or she scrawls out "$1,700" on a piece of paper and wants you to sign it, get a new contractor. This is a true story.

BALLPARK FIGURES

You always want an estimate *in writing*, on some form of official company paper. A repairperson will rarely put in writing a cost that would rip you off, because then you could take that estimate to one of those sleazy TV shows or bored news stations that expose fraudulent businesses. As you introduce yourself to the repairperson, say that you want an estimate in writing to compare to another contractor that you had look at the job earlier. (It's okay to make the last part up, just have a company name in mind.)

Your estimate should include:

× What is being fixed
× Hourly labor rate
× Approximate time frame of the repair
× Estimated costs of tools, products, and materials
× Terms of payment

QUESTIONS TO ASK (ESPECIALLY FOR LARGER JOBS THAT WILL TAKE MULTIPLE DAYS)

× "How long does this usually take?"
× "What factors would alter the total bill?"

× "Are there any potential complications I need to worry about?"
× "Will this repair be disruptive?" (Closed-off areas, scaffolding, power or water shutoffs.)
× "Does the weather affect this repair?"
× "How does your company schedule for people with daytime commitments?"
× "Is this a fair price?" (Worker bees might be surprisingly honest.)

You should be given ample time, at least a few business days, to consider an estimate, so if you are skeptical about any costs listed on the estimate, check your suspicions with a friend or on the Internet, and then call the company to inquire. Repair companies are not used to savvy clientele, so if you are right, you will usually walk away with a fair price. Once you are comfortable, call the company for a *contract*, which you should always look over with someone who knows legalese before signing.

Most importantly, *save the estimate*! Estimates are useless if you lose them before you get the final bill to compare them to.

DING-DONG, THE REPAIRPERSON'S HERE

Hallelujah, the repairperson has arrived, and only an hour later than planned. If the repair needs to be done immediately and you arranged this with the contractor on the phone, show the repairperson directly to the break. Feel free to ask for a verbal estimate for a small repair before the repairperson begins working, just to ensure that you will not be upset over the bill an hour later.

A repairperson's presence is your opportunity to learn how to perform repairs yourself, so don't leave the room and make phone calls for an hour. Instead, stay put, watch what the repairperson is doing, and feel free to ask intelligent questions. Most repairpeople will be more than happy to talk with you, and will appreciate the break from silence. By watching carefully, you will not only educate yourself about this repair, but you will be sure that the repairperson is not slacking off or using your toothbrush.

Repairpeople are intimately acquainted with grease, dirt, rust, and the other common repair juices. If you would prefer to keep your living space as clean as possible, place a tarp over the floor in the area of the repair and over any white carpet you would prefer not to rendezvous with the repairperson's shoes. Move anything that you don't want to get dirty from the immediate area, and expect to have dirty fingerprints around the area of the break—this is home repair, after all.

THE BILL

When the repairperson is ready to leave, the repair bill needs to include:

× Hourly labor rate
× Time spent working
× Cost of tools, products, and materials
× Terms of payment

If any of these items are missing, question the repairperson or call the company. If a bill is significantly larger than a given estimate, compare the bill to the original estimate, and if you can't account for the difference, call the company.

PERSONAL SAFETY

While 99 percent of professionals are good people who have no interest in threatening your personal safety or stealing your belongings, you need to keep in mind that you are letting a complete stranger into your house. This is why a reference can be so important—chances are, if your sister has been using a contractor for ten years without problems, you won't have problems, either.

In some cases, contractors perform work on major projects while the owners are not home during the day. Multiple workers may have key access to the house. This said, be smart about it and be creative. For example, if a contractor needs access to a power source, be innovative and thread an extension cord through your mail slot before you leave instead of handing over a key, or plan the work for when you will be home on vacation. Try to limit the number of people in your home. You will have to

allow bathroom use, but you are giving a number of strangers an inside look at your valuables and their layout, so at least shut doors.

SAFETY PRECAUTIONS

× If you are not comfortable with the repairperson—you have a bad vibe, he or she appears intoxicated, anything—do not invite the repairperson inside. Call the company and ask for another employee.
× If possible, invite a friend over for your repair appointment.
× Keep an eye on your repairperson, which you should be doing anyway, since you're learning.
× Remove anything of great monetary or sentimental value from the immediate vicinity. If your checkbook is lying on a table next to your broken vent, move it. If you keep all your savings in unmarked $1 bills on the floor of the bathroom where the repair is being done, move them. (Put them in a bank, for instance.) Why ask for trouble?
× If you do notice something missing, no matter how small, report the theft to both the head contractor and the police as soon as possible.
× If something you consider harmless but inappropriate takes place, report it to the company immediately. This is probably not the first time.

In general, safety and theft issues will not be a problem, but common sense is key.

THE ART OF BUNDLING

The Art of Bundling is your major tool to saving money with professionals. If the repairperson needs to come anyway, you might as well get more than one item repaired. The strategy here is to minimize expenses by having multiple repairs performed at the same time.

Bundling (b'nd-leng) n.:
1. *The act of saving lots of money by having small repairs performed alongside major repairs.*
2. *The fine art of waiting until your toilet explodes to get your doorbell fixed.*

For example, let's pretend that your doorbell breaks in May. If you were to call a company to get it fixed, they might charge you as much as $100 to fix it—a repairperson has to drive to your house, talk with you, fix the repair, write up a bill, and drive back to the company. For repair companies, time is money, and your repair took time.

However, who really needs a doorbell anyway? Your friends could just knock for a few months. Then, in August, your toilet regrettably explodes. You immediately determine that a professional repairman is required to deal with the toilet. If, on his way out the door, you were to say, "Oh, excuse me, I was wondering if you could possibly take a glance at my doorbell? It doesn't seem to be working," the repairperson will probably fix it for you, and either not charge you, or charge you around $15. This is $85 in savings.

The Art of Bundling is an age-old tool of the repair-impaired around the world and is highly recommended for all minor repairs that are not time pegged. If an air conditioner breaks in early September, it might be fine to put off getting it fixed until your friend accidentally drives her car through your garage door in December. When in doubt, wait for a major repair job. Other things will break, I promise.

REPAIR REFERENCES FOR THE REAL WORLD

Though staring at your broken water heater makes you feel helpless and alone, there are actually a wide variety of resources at your disposal. While this is by no means a complete list, below are a variety of free sources of information to help you fix your breaks. Knowing what's out there is the key to empowerment!

PAGE ME YELLOW

Yes, you should own a Yellow Pages. The phone book is your major ally in finding home repair help and resources. The categories are different in each phone book, but look up "Refrigerators and Freezers" or "Appliances" or "Electrical Equipment," depending what supplies or contact information you need.

For smaller jobs, search "Handymen." While most companies in the handyman service category do jobs that you should be able to do yourself, such as cleaning gutters and washing decks, they are worthwhile if you have the funding but not the time. Feel free to ask them for random jobs: "Could you please remove the bird stuck between my walls without hurting the bird?" They love this stuff.

BOOKWORM IN A TOOL BELT

If nothing else, this book has prepared you to avoid emergency and panic-inducing breaks, so you should always have time to do a bit of library research on your way home from work. Your local library contains an entire section filled with home repair books, including books of the easy-to-read, "I'm not stupid but I like big pictures" variety. While it is always a good idea to own at least one good home repair guide, you can usually borrow the specialized information you need.

OTHER STUFF IN THE LIBRARY

Your library branch probably has a number of other resources, including:

× A collection of audiovisual home repair resources, such as movies of someone else using tools to install things. (Yes, it's G-rated.) Helpful stuff.
× Some libraries have online access to millions of magazine articles, all of which are easily searchable in a database. For example, if you're a crunchy-granola type and you want to buy an air conditioner, you could type in "air conditioners" and "environment" and click on "last twelve months" to find articles on new eco-friendly cooling units. Entire magazines exist for every obscure, specialized topic you can imagine, so the repair or women's magazines should hold what you're looking for.
× There are also magazines that rate the performance of a wide variety of products so you can make educated decisions about appliances, and know ahead of time what's probably going to break.
× Librarians themselves. Though many of them couldn't identify a volt ohm meter from a box wrench if you paid them, they still know their library stuff. Explain what you're trying to do, and they can tell you where to look. They have spent their whole lives in the stacks, after all.

BEFORE YOU CRY, CLICK

There are also a vast number of Web sites geared toward all aspects of home repair, such as:

× COMPANY PRODUCT WEB SITES
In an attempt to be seen as user-friendly while avoiding actual human contact, tool companies and appliance manufacturers offer Web sites explaining how their products work. Check out the "Frequently Asked Questions" section, which is code for "Problems People Seem to Have with Our Products."

× DO-IT-YOURSELF AND WOMEN'S WEB SITES
There are a number of online D.I.Y. and women's communities aimed at empowering women, most of which contain substantial sections on home repair. Unfortunately, many of these sites have much more information on decorating than repair, but they are still useful.

× FINANCIAL ADVICE WEB SITES
Tend to perceive home repair as a waste of money, and therefore have useful sections on both avoiding home repair and preparing a rainy-day fund for when home repair can't be avoided.

× REPAIR WEB SITES
There are many sites dedicated solely to home repair directions, differing by target audience.

While some sites are geared towards professional handymen, with tips of the trade, others are aimed at weekend warriors.

× **MAGAZINE WEB SITES**
Almost every magazine there is has its own Web site, and those that have advertisers often post articles for free. Women's magazines oriented toward home life often have a columnist or section on home repair, with frequent fix-it tips and repairs of the month.

TENDER LOVING CARE FROM YOUR NEIGHBORS

Cities and towns tend to be filled with oft-neglected resources. New Neighbors committees, community centers, and town halls are all filled to the brim with people who can help you. (If they can't, they'll play the phone-transfer game until someone useful picks up.) Remember that you are never the first person to have ever experienced your repair problem. The woman who has lived down the street for twenty years has had your problem, so ask around.

FINDING PRODUCT PARTS OR INFORMATION

Contact the manufacturer of a product to acquire new parts. Many instruction manuals list both manufacturer contact information and nearby service centers. The World of Parts still exists primarily as a mail-order universe, so usually you will call up a manufacturer, explain the part you need, and give a credit card number and they'll mail it to you. You can track down new instruction manuals this way, too. If you're having trouble contacting a manufacturer, the library has a selection of books with titles like *Brands and Their Companies*, which will provide a phone number.

HELPFUL PEOPLE IN UNIFORMS

Your local police, fire, and animal control departments are just the tip of the iceberg of home repair aid.

× **POLICE DEPARTMENT** The nonemergency num-number will get you the information you need for potentially harmful breaks. Depending on the situation, a patrol car might stop by, especially if you live in a small town where teenage parties are the primary challenge to local safety.

× **ANIMAL CONTROL** Listed in the phone book, though the police nonemergency number will transfer you over. Depending on who picks up, they can be very helpful with what to do about the big hole the raccoon left in your attic. Smaller units are often open only during business hours, so calling the police department might be your sole option.

× **FIRE DEPARTMENT** Firemen are trained to deal with a wide variety of hazards, including any break that involves heat, smoke, gas, sparks, electricity, and/or water. Unless you want the big red trucks with the lights showing up, use the nonemergency number and sound calm.

× **POISON CONTROL** Poison control is a wonderful resource. The operators are trained to deal with your random questions: "My room smells like sewage mixed with cabbages and cough syrup. Is this poisonous?" They know everything.

× **HEALTH DEPARTMENT** They unfortunately no longer wear uniforms, but you can still talk to them for information and resources on health risks. Infestations and mold problems are considered threats to public health, and are therefore in the arena of the health department; mentioning that you "sometimes" have small children in the house will garner a faster response. Finding the right person in your local health department can involve an endless maze of answering machines and unenthusiastic government employees, but they will eventually help you.

THE CALENDAR

Good stuff is always at the end of books as a reward for diligent readers like you. Here is a summary of your Must-Do and Should-Do maintenance lists, organized into a calendar for your pull-out pleasure.

Maintenance should become automatic for you with each of the seasons. Note that no task should take more than twenty minutes, especially if you've done it before.

JANUARY

01 Test your smoke and carbon monoxide alarms and change their batteries. Hit the oven "Clean" function while making coffee, and flush out your hot water heater. Test the pressure relief valve while you're there.

15 Change your furnace filter or bleed your radiator.

APRIL

01 Schedule a chimney cleaning if applicable. Trim back shrubs from outer walls.

FEBRUARY

X Cabin fever has set in. Take month off.

MAY

01 Change your furnace and air-conditioner filters. Test smoke and carbon monoxide alarms. Flush out your hot water heater and test the pressure relief valve.

15 Clean the stove, test oven temperature.

MARCH

01 Test smoke and carbon monoxide alarms. Test fire extinguisher and locate fire blanket. Clean the stove.

30 SPRING CLEANING DAY
Clean everything—vacuum, clean the stove, dust, scrub, clear out drains, organize.

JUNE

01 SUMMER CLEANING PARTY
Clean everything—stove, floors, walls, surfaces, drains, everything. While you're dusting, reverse your ceiling fan motors.

JULY

04 Test smoke and carbon monoxide alarms
before the barbecue starts. Change alarm
batteries. Trim back shrubs from outer walls.

AUGUST

01 Change your air-conditioner filter. It's hot,
take rest of month off.

SEPTEMBER

01 Test smoke and carbon monoxide alarms.
Bleed your radiators. Schedule a fall heating
system check, and if applicable, a septic
system check. Flush out your hot water
heater and test the pressure relief valve.

15 INSPECTION DAY
Test your fire extinguisher, inspect all gas
lines, and examine washer and dryer hoses.
Test all appliance lights. Schedule a pest
check. Wave at the local kids going back to
school.

OCTOBER

01 Bleed your radiators. Test smoke and carbon
monoxide alarms. Clean your stove and test
your oven temperature.

NOVEMBER

01 Post-Halloween Cleaning Party: Get the
candy in Tupperware before the insects find
it, and clean your drains. Trim back shrubs
from outdoor walls. Change your furnace
filter or bleed your radiators.

15 Fall Maintenance
× Change outdoor lightbulbs.
× Install storm windows.
× Inspect and patch any openings to the
exterior.
× Trim shrubs and trees for the winter.
× Examine exterior for waterproof health.

DECEMBER

01 WINTER CLEANING
Go nuts with cleaning supplies, but remember
to open a window. While you're up high
dusting and changing lightbulbs and such,
reverse your ceiling fan motors. Remember
to clean out the drains and bleed your
radiators.

INDEX